Henry Martyn Boies

Prisoners and paupers

A study of the abnormal increase of criminals and the public burden of pauperism

in the U.S.

Henry Martyn Boies

Prisoners and paupers
A study of the abnormal increase of criminals and the public burden of pauperism in the U.S.

ISBN/EAN: 9783337127312

Printed in Europe, USA, Canada, Australia, Japan

Cover: Foto ©Andreas Hilbeck / pixelio.de

More available books at **www.hansebooks.com**

PRISONERS AND PAUPERS

A STUDY

OF THE ABNORMAL INCREASE OF CRIMINALS, AND THE
PUBLIC BURDEN OF PAUPERISM IN THE UNITED
STATES; THE CAUSES AND REMEDIES

BY

HENRY M. BOIES, M.A.

MEMBER OF THE BOARD OF PUBLIC CHARITIES, AND OF THE COMMITTEE ON LUNACY
OF THE STATE OF PENNSYLVANIA ; OF THE NATIONAL PRISON ASSOCI-
ATION ; OF THE PENNSYLVANIA PRISON SOCIETY, ETC.

G. P. PUTNAM'S SONS

NEW YORK   LONDON
27 WEST TWENTY-THIRD STREET   24 BEDFORD STREET, STRAND
The Knickerbocker Press
1893

" FIND OUT THE CAUSE OF THIS EFFECT :
OR, RATHER SAY, THE CAUSE OF THIS DEFECT ;
FOR THIS EFFECT DEFECTIVE, COMES BY CAUSE."

HAMLET, ACT II., SC. 2

PREFACE.

THERE are four hundred and forty-six charitable, reformatory, and penal institutions in the State of Pennsylvania, inspected at least once each year by its Board of Public Charities. They have a wide variety of objects, methods, management, and inmates. The view which a member of this Board obtains, therefore, and the impressions he receives of pauperism and criminality are of a very general nature, inducing a consideration of the subject as a whole. Most of the literature of these subjects, on the contrary, is confined to particular and distinct phases of them.

I have endeavored in this book to present this general view of the case as it appears in our country; to emphasize the waste of human sympathy and public funds which results from what appears to be inconsiderate and misdirected methods of treatment; to suggest not only possible improvements in these methods, but radical changes in direction; and, finally, I have proposed a positive remedy, which, however people may disagree concerning its practicability, I think no intelligent person will deny to be efficacious.

v

If the time has not yet arrived, it is certainly approaching fast when the public welfare, the progress of civilization, the elevation of humanity, the regeneration of the race, will be recognized and obeyed as the supreme motive in the social organization,—the final purpose of legislation, as well as of religion and philanthropy. The highest happiness, advantage, and prosperity of the individual, indeed, is only to be secured by such a widening of the scope of public care, as will comprehend and benefit the entire social mass.

If the facts and statistics which I have collected in hours snatched from the engrossing cares of widely different pursuits become useful to those interested in philanthropic studies, or tend to give direction to public thought and discussion toward the amelioration of present oppressive conditions, I shall be amply repaid for my labors.

I have introduced some illustrations of symmetrical human development, both ideal and real, as standards to which the abnormal may be compared, and as examples of what is possible in development, " to point a moral or adorn a tale."

I desire to gratefully acknowledge the aid and encouragement rendered me in the preparation and publication of this work by Mr. Cadwalader Biddle, Secretary of the Board of Public Charities of Pennsylvania, Prof. John J. McCook, Hon. Alfred Hand, Rev. S. C. Logan, D.D., Charleton E. Lewis, Esq., Gen. R. Brinckerhoff, Eugene Smith, Esq., Mr. M. J. Cassidy, Mr. Edward H. Hunter, and others ; without which I doubt if I should have had the

courage or ability to print it in this permanent form.
Much of the matter was published in a local newspaper, and the desire expressed by friends that it
should be made available for easy reference has been
chiefly influential in adding another to the innumerable list of books which floods the reading public.

HENRY M. BOIES.

SCRANTON, PA., November, 1892.

CONTENTS.

ix

ILLUSTRATIONS.

VENUS OF MILO.
IDEAL TYPE OF WELL DEVELOPED WOMAN.

PRISONERS AND PAUPERS.

CHAPTER I.

ABNORMAL INCREASE OF CRIMINALITY AND COST OF PAUPERISM IN THE UNITED STATES.

The Growth of the Criminal Class Nearly Three Times Greater than the Growth of Population.—Vicious Immigration, Intemperance, and Unintelligent Laws the Chief Causes.—Our Jails Nurseries of Crime.—Our Court Penalties Often a Disgrace to Civilization.

THE eleventh census of the United States, as it is being published, furnishes statistics of a national growth in numbers, wealth, and general prosperity unparalleled in the history of civilization. Our own people, if not the whole world, seem to have accepted these marvellous records as indicating the existence on the American continent of conditions and environments of a national vitality destined to develop here, in the immediate future, the supreme race and people of the world—the consummate flower of humanity. Some of the disclosures made are, however, shocking, if not appalling, in the highest degree to our confidence in the future. One of these is the abnormal and disproportionate increase in the criminal class in society. That increase is from 1 in 3,500 of our population in 1850 to 1 in 786.5 in 1890, or of 445 per cent. ; while the population has increased but 170 per cent. in the same period.[1]

In the last decade, with an increase of 24.5 per cent. in population, the number of the inmates of our penitentiaries, jails, and reformatories has increased 45.2 per cent., or nearly twice faster than the general population![1] This, too, in spite of the enormous multiplication of churches, Christian efforts of all kinds, schools, educational progress, and various philanthropic agencies of an elevating and conservative nature, attended with a lavish expenditure of money and labor.

Such a disproportion cannot continue indefinitely without a relapse into barbarism and social ruin. It is more startling because such a state of things does not exist in other civilized nations, as public records show.

In England criminal convictions have fallen from 15,033 in 1868 to 9,348 in 1889. In Scotland, from 2,490 to 1,723 for the same years, and in Ireland from 3,084 in 1870 to 1,225 in 1890. During this decade there has been a fair increase in the population of those countries ; also a considerable growth in wealth ; a notable influx of foreigners from the Continent, mostly of the lower orders, into London

[1] *Statistics of the Tenth U. S. Census,* and *Bulletins Nos.* 71, 72, and 95 *of the Eleventh Census.*

particularly, similar in social conditions to the mass of emigrants to the United States. The number of imprisonments in France has increased but threefold in half a century.

Such an exposition of the actual foundations for our boasts of the beneficence of free government and American institutions cannot be permitted to continue. This horrid growth must be stopped. It will be when the people, who are the rulers, understand the causes and learn how to apply the necessary remedies ; as Bishop Gillespie has well said, " Public abuses do not exist where there is public knowledge." Of course it is understood that exceptional and peculiar conditions have contributed somewhat to increase this disappointing disproportion between the worthy and unworthy in our citizenship. In 1850 our colored population was mostly enslaved, and it was the interest and policy of the slave-holder to keep his property out of the public criminal list by the infliction of domestic punishment and by personal management. But now our colored population, emerging from the degradation of slavery and naturally prone to allow the excitement of liberty to run into license, furnishes over one third of our convict class, although it numbers only 7,470,040, about one eighth, or 13.5 per cent., of our total numbers.[1] Doubtless, too, the ignorance and comparative helplessness of the colored race, with the unreasonable prejudice of white officials, the desire of politicians to disfranchise voters, and of others to secure a greater plenty of convict labor, have unduly swelled

[1] *Census Bulletin No.* 199.

the number of arrests and convictions among them out of proportion to the actual criminality of the race.

Another circumstance peculiar to our country is the almost unrestricted immigration of the lower classes of foreigners from all lands. Foreigners of the first and second generations constitute at present about twenty per cent. of our population. But they furnish more than half the inmates of our reformatories, over one third of our convicts, and nearly three fifths of all the paupers supported in almshouses! Our paupers, foreign born, or of foreign parentage, equal in number all the white native paupers of purely native origin with the colored paupers taken together! These figures are derived from Rev. F. H. Wines' report upon the eleventh census, and are believed entirely reliable.[1]

In addition to these extraneous causes may be noted some of a domestic character.

First, an unnatural increase of intemperance, which is the first cause of nearly all crime. Whether this is at all due to peculiarities of climate, the fervid, nervous energy of life here, exciting desire for alcoholic stimulus, and the freedom of indulgence which is everywhere possible, as some think, or not, it is certain that the legal or legislative handling of intemperance has so far been an absolute and complete failure, either in prevention, restriction, or cure. The drink habit is still spreading. Drunkards are increasing in numbers, and no enactments have yet

[1] *Census Bulletin No.* 199.

been framed which provide a rational and scientific force or authority for dealing with the subject either with a view to prevention or cure.

A second cause of the increase of crime and pauperism is found in the crowding of the people to the centres, or the constant increase of the urban population. Twenty-eight of our largest cities have increased 44.86 per cent. in ten years, while the twenty-eight cities of England increased but 11.2 in the same time. Our total urban population has grown from 12.5 per cent. in 1850 to 27.7 per cent. in 1890, there having been in the last ten years an increase of 60.5 per cent. in our urban population in cities of ten thousand and over. The packing of these millions of humanity into blocks and squares in tenements means vastly more than the mere crowding of the depraved and criminal together, where they teach and aid one another in crime. It involves the huddling whole families—father, mother, and children —into one room, in which to live and sleep in the midst of the uncleanness of beastly poverty and the indiscriminate cohabitation of the sexes. It involves not only the greater temptations to intemperance, licentiousness, and crime, with increased facilities and opportunities, but far worse, the universal disgorging of the children indiscriminately into the streets for air, exercise, and play. In these streets the human tide mingles much as, in the sewers beneath, the pure rains and waters of the service pipes are mixed, compounded, and lost in all the waste and filth of the city, and flow away in a conglomerate uniform flood. So the children of the street soon reach a social and moral equilibrium of a complexion and character not far removed from the death-gendering dregs from which the city must be cleansed. Girls and boys crowd the curb-stones and door-steps late into the night, corrupting one another and familiarizing themselves with sin before they reach their teens, so that the very source and springs of social life are poisoned.

A third cause for the increase of criminals is found in the existing laws for their punishment and the unintelligent manner in which they are administered. In their principles and scheme these laws are an inheritance of mere barbarism, with modified penalties. Deprived generally of their chief efficacy by the diminution of the death penalty and continuous durance in their execution, upon the demands of an advancing civilization, they have retained most of the evil effects of false ideas concerning the treatment of criminals and crime. Hence they now contribute to the increase of both, and tend to nullify the very purpose of their existence. Our criminal court and jail system are a reproach upon our intelligence, a disgrace to our civilization, an unnecessary extravagance in our social economy, a curse upon our philanthropy and religion, and an outrage upon humanity.

Our jails are conducted as public schools of crime and nurseries of criminals. Into them our constabulary and courts hustle ravishers, sodomites, corrupters of youth, murderers, burglars, thieves, drunkards, prostitutes, and all the foul members of society they can lay hands upon, with children convicted of petty larcenies or of incorrigibility, with detained witnesses, and people accused of misdemeanors or crimes not tried. Inside the walls, comfortably housed, clothed, and fed, supplied with tobacco and cards, with promiscuous intercourse permitted during a part, if not all, the day, the professional criminal and the hardened sinner recount their adventures to an interested audience, and delight to initiate the more ignorant into all the mysteries of iniquity. Incarceration here has no deterrent dread for the "rounder," while the erring one, confined for a first assault, soon becomes assimilated to his companions, and joins the ranks of crime. Except for the brief period that the victims are restrained of their freedom of action, our jails are a menace rather than protection to society.

These causes sufficiently account for the humiliating and disappointing record of our social development. It is absolutely essential to the arrest of the serious disease that the potency of each should be recognized, carefully and patiently diagnosed in the light of the present science of penology and sociology, if effectual remedies are to be discovered and applied. The subject is one of paramount interest, not only to the sociologist, philanthropist, and Christian, but it reaches and powerfully affects the welfare of every individual member of society, even to those who regard only their own selfish enjoyment, prosperity, and existence. It demands instant and intelligent consideration and immediate action by citizen and legislator alike. Aside from the loss and damage to society entailed by robbery and arson, and the waste of life energy of the criminal, the cost of criminal arrests and maintenance is, next to that for education, the largest item of public expenditure, as it constitutes nearly one tenth of the total burden of taxation in the state.

CHAPTER II.

The Number of Criminals has Increased in a Decade over Fifty per Cent. Faster than Population, the Cost of County Jails More than Four Times as Fast, and the Public Expenditures for State Institutions Five Times as Fast.—Local Causes Examined.—Importance of the Question.—Proper Direction of Reformatory Action.

THE statements which we have made upon the disproportionate increase of the criminal class in the United States cannot be dismissed as only of general or national importance, to be dealt with solely by legislators, boards of charity, and philanthropic societies. Their baneful and terrible influence extends to the home and pocket of every individual member of society.

The official statistics of Pennsylvania speak on this subject in a language which all can understand. Let us examine and consider them, even if they should proclaim unpalatable or humiliating truth. They are of vital and personal interest to us all. A study of the detailed reports of the Board of Public Charities of Pennsylvania for the years, 1880 and 1890 reveals a very alarming and unnatural increase in the number of criminals and of all other wards supported at public expense. The total num-

9

ber of inmates of the various public institutions in the State, on the 30th of September of each of those years, with the percentage of increase in each class, is shown in the following table.

	1880	1890	Per Cent. of Increase
Population of State	4,282,891	5,248,574	22.5
Inmates, Penal Institutions	5,449	7,340	34.7
Defective Classes	6,070	9,712	60.
Sane in Almshouses	6,648	6,905	38.
Totals,	18,167	23,957	31.8
In County Jails, (included above)	1,648	2,195	33.19
Committals during the Year	45,842	54,950	19.8

The aggregate of all classes supported and assisted at the cost of the public, including " out-door relief " and reported vagrants, in 1890 was 61,816; one in 84.9 of our population ; about 1.18 per cent.

The following table also shows the expenditures of the various penal and eleemosynary institutions of the State during the years 1879 and 1889 respective.

Penitentiaries	$536,056	$570,857
Reformatories, Workhouses, and Jails	980,016	1,329,353
State and Private Insane Asylums	527,297	1,222,475
Deaf, Blind, and Imbecile Asylums	262,797	439,477
Almshouses	1,193,512	1,184,495
Totals	$3,499,678	$4,746,657

An increase of 35.3 per cent. in a single decade.

The Huntingdon Reformatory and the Norristown and Warren Insane Hospitals were not in operation in 1879.

The cost of county jails alone, was $372,290 in 1880, and $723,013, in 1890, an increase of 94.2 per cent. There was expended in support of all classes, including hospitals, homes, etc., (some of which items were estimated, as accurate returns could not be secured) in 1880, $4,480,351, and in 1890, $9,511,970, an increase of 110.9 per cent. in a single decade !

It appears, then, from these official tables that the number of criminals has increased in the last decade 54.6 per cent. faster than the population. The cost of county jails has multiplied more than four times as fast, and the public expenditures upon all penal, reformatory, and charitable classes about five times as fast. The cost was equal in 1890 to the burden of a bonded debt, bearing interest at four per cent., of $237,799,250. Such a debt resting upon the Commonwealth would mean ruin and bankruptcy. Capital and manufactures would flee beyond our borders from it as though our soil were smitten with the plague. But the incubus is dragging upon the neck of our prosperity just as heavily as though it were a bonded debt, whether we realize it or not.

Each year the demands of our charitable and penal institutions grow larger, more urgent, and numerous upon the public treasury, as well as upon private benevolence. Our best people seem to devote their chief thought to the relief of present distress, without consideration of the causes which produce the growing requirements; while our lawmakers occupy themselves more with projects for increasing the revenues by taxation, in order to provide larger sums to pour into these public sieves, than with the study of measures for stopping the leaks in our social economy. Already the majority of our people, the tillers of the soil, complain that the burden of taxation is greater than the wide and fruitful acres of their grand domain can bear. Hence they are striving to shift its weight upon the shoulders of commerce and manufactures, which will surely slip from under it far easier than they imagine. If relief is necessary for our farmers, it must come from a wiser economy of expenditure, a diminution of the needs of a philanthropic social organization, by intelligent legislation calculated to remove the causes and cure the diseases which afflict society; rather than by a lavish extravagance of appropriations wrenched from other sources. Indiscriminate public charity nourishes and cultivates public pauperism just as certainly as indiscriminate private charity increases mendicity.

The increase in the number of convicts in Pennsylvania has been quite as great as the general increase in the nation; and this, too, notwithstanding the fact that our foreign-born population is only about 16 per cent. and our colored population only 2.09 per cent. of our total numbers.[1] These two prolific sources of criminals in the country at large must be, therefore, practically eliminated from our consideration of the causes of the increase in our own State. The population of our cities having 10,000 or more inhabitants has increased in the last decade 35.6, which is just .9 per cent. more than the increase of criminals in the State.[2] We are con-

[1] *Census Bulletin No.* 183.   [2] *Census Bulletin No.* 165.

strained, therefore, to the conviction that very grave and serious reasons exist in our domestic administration and our social conditions for this unenviable prominence of criminal growth.

It may be observed that the cost of our county jails has increased over 94 per cent. in ten years. This aggregated in the 69 county jails $723,013 in 1890, an average weekly cost per prisoner of $4.19, with a range for the individuals of from $7.51 to $2.03.

The inspection of the Board of Charities reveals an almost total disregard in all jails—managed, as most are, by county sheriffs—of any consideration for the reformation of the prisoners, or moral preservation of the falsely accused. These jails permit a promiscuous and unrestrained commingling of the most depraved and vilest professional convicts with children, accused persons, and detained witnesses without let or hindrance. In many cases even sexes are not separated. Total idleness of inmates, with double beds, and two inmates of the same cell at night seem to be the rule. There is a general lack of regular chaplains, of religious or moral instruction, or of even philanthropic visitation. Unrestricted visitation by outside friends and companions, and supply of depraving papers, literature, cards, tobacco, and often liquor, are permitted. In short, there is an utter absence of all conservative and reformatory influences, a prevalence and activity of almost every means of corruption; which must inevitably result in the confirming of all inmates in a criminal course of life.

A single case, which is vouched for by the author's personal inspection, is believed to be a fair type of the jails in the State and country.

A recent visit to the jail in Sunbury, which is reckoned one of the best in the State, disclosed the circumstances and privileges of fifty-four inmates of all classes. Among them were two bright, nice-looking boys, one thirteen and the other fourteen years old, who had been incarcerated already two months, and would have to remain two months longer before trial. They were accused of stealing four bottles of ginger-beer !

Another boy of sixteen years was waiting trial for attempted rape — a depraved and vicious-looking wretch.

In the female department, which was merely separated from the male corridor of cells at one end by a wooden partition, through which access was had to it, there were placed six females. Here was a Polish woman with her three children, all under ten years of age, none of whom could speak or understand English, indicted for selling liquor without license ! Probably the poor creature had never so much as heard of a license. Here in one cell, to which all had access, lay a woman apparently dying of syphilis. A good-looking fourteen-year-old girl, confined as an " incorrigible," and three other hard-looking creatures completed the complement.

The two boys and the budding girl had been committed by the same " Justice," whose elevation to office would seem to have added quite an increment to his original want of sense. These may be taken as specimens of the life placed in durance in this public institution.

Now can there be any doubt but that this whole body of fifty-four inmates will be as hopeless criminals as the worst among them before three months shall elapse?

If any are not, they will be miracles of grace, triumphant over a most adverse system. This is not an abnormal or even an unusual condition in Pennsylvania jails, as even a casual visitation will reveal. Nor can the chief blame be laid upon the jailers, many of whom do the best they can with their perplexing charges and inadequate provision and powers.

The fault is in the system which makes possible such a foolish and fatal administration. Judges and justices plunge children into these hot-beds of vice, apparently without thought of consequences, or because no alternative is left them in their clearance of court duty. Those who have fallen under penalty of law for a first or trivial offence are huddled indiscriminately with hardened villains, and left indefinitely often, where scarcely a single hand is stretched out to save or help them. It would seem that philanthropy even exchanged hope for despair at the portal of a county jail.

Another fruitful source of criminality in our State is the growing laxity of parental discipline and care. Children are turned over more and more to secular and Sunday-school teachers for training and religious instruction. Warden Brush, of Sing Sing Prison, who has given much study to penology, and has had long experience with prisoners, in an admirable paper read at the last Prison Congress, gave as the cause which sends most men to prison " the lack of family discipline." Children on the streets, in the saloons, brothels, and places of public amusement, neglected at home, can hardly fail of moral ruin.

It is impossible to say whether unrestricted liquor selling has contributed to any disproportionate increase of intemperance in this State, or whether the utter lack of intelligent legal dealing with drunkards differs with us from that existing elsewhere. Certainly we are no better in that respect than are others, and we may discover in our inadequate statutes concerning drunkards a sufficient reason for their increase in numbers and general failure to reform.

Much too is doubtless due to a very general misconception of duty which prevails among the officers of the law, the constabulary and police, who are apt to regard themselves simply as agents for the apprehension of criminals rather than for the prevention of crime, which is the real and main purpose and . object of their office. Doubtless also our very increase in wealth and material prosperity, making prominent before the eyes of all classes of our people a liberality of expenditure and luxury of living heretofore unknown, has excited cupidity, envy, and desires for indulgence, which cannot be honestly satisfied. In confirmation of this, we find that over 76 per cent. of the crimes punished in our penitentiaries were against property, and only 24 per cent. against the person.

We will consider causes more fully in connection with projects of remedy hereafter. It is desired first to arouse public attention to the fact that our present methods of dealing with crimes and criminals are a monstrous and dangerous failure.

The number of the indigent and defective classes has increased over 30 per cent.—that is, about 8 per cent. more than our population (almost 1 per cent. per annum); and almost the entire increase of the amount expended upon all classes has been in support of charitable institutions of various kinds, making evident as impressive a failure in our management of the dependent classes as appears respecting the criminal classes. The flood of crime must be checked, and the number of criminals diminished; a more intelligent and economical support of dependants inaugurated, or our social and civil organization must of necessity crumble into chaos. It is impossible that this disparity of criminal and pauper increase should continue indefinitely, or even long, without disaster. This is not a figure of speech, but a mathematical verity, as certain as the multiplication table.

Christianity and philanthropy have been anxious, exercised, and diligent in the amelioration of the condition of the poor and the prisoner; but it would appear that the exigencies of this noble work had so completely absorbed attention as to obscure and distract thought from the grander object of reducing their numbers by operating wisely to diminish the causes of poverty and crime, and to restore the pauper and criminal to a self-supporting, honorable,

and productive condition in society. The inspec-
tions of the Board of Public Charities show now,
however, that the indigent of the State are well provided for, and that its prisoners are everywhere
treated with humanity and kindness. Under its
careful supervision there has been a constant improvement and progress toward excellence in the management of public institutions of all kinds, and even
solitary instances of bad or brutal treatment have
become exceedingly rare. The popular tendency
indeed is to coddle the jail-bird, so that in many jails
he fares better than when he is free. The time has
come to govern the methods of treatment by principles which will discourage pauperism and crime
and decrease their burden upon society without
inhumanity.

The facts thus inadequately stated, which are,
with complete details, preserved in official docu-
ments and buried in both annual and special reports
in every State, certainly suggest a subject of national
proportions and of vital concern to every intelligent
citizen. Our issue is not with the Commonwealth of
Pennsylvania alone, for the burden and danger
involves the whole nation. In the following chapter
the facts as they appear in a single county will be
given as an illustration of what may be found by the
earnest inquirer generally. The truth brought to
the light will show that we have pressed upon our
attention questions of the most serious consequence.

CHAPTER III.

THE RECORD OF A SINGLE COUNTY.

Detailed Public Costs of Crime and Pauperism in Lackawanna County, Pennsylvania. — Appalling Increase. — Unnecessary Waste of Half the Money Raised for Jails and Poorhouses.— Costs Compared with Other Counties in Pennsylvania.—Appeal for Local Action.

IF the condition of the nation at large is alarming in respect of the increase of criminals, and of the State quite as disturbing as that of the nation, our interest in the subject may be localized and intensified by a detailed comparative statement of the percentage of increase in one county in the last decade. Many will be shocked to learn that bad as the foregoing tables have appeared for the nation and the State, the showing of Lackawanna County in detail is much worse than that of the State as a whole even, as appears from the following figures taken from the reports of the Board of Public Charities for 1880 and 1890 for Lackawanna County.

It is probable that a similiar examination would disclose similiar conditions existing all through the country.

Inmates of Jail and Almshouses in Lackawanna Co., Pennsylvania	1880	Maintained in Other Institutions.[1]	1890	Maintained in Other Institutions.	Per Cent. Increase.	Cost per Capita per Week.
In County Jail.........	3	20	75	62	495.6	$3.82
In Blakely Poorhouse....	6		11	27		
In Carbondale Poorhouse	4		8	14		
In Hillside Poorhouse..	135		231	11		
In Northern Luzerne Poorhouse.........	18		11	3		
In Ransom Poorhouse..	61		53	31		
Total	224		314	86	78.5	

The increase of the population during this decade has been 59.1 per cent., which is a greater increase than is shown in the number of paupers, but less than one eighth the increase of criminals. The increase of the cost of maintaining the paupers of Lackawanna County has, however, been excessive, like the numerical increase of criminals, and presents a very discomforting comparison for the consideration of the frugal and industrious.

The cost of the support of paupers in Lackawanna County, including "out-door relief," with the average weekly cost in 1890, is shown in the following

[1] The number maintained in other institutions by the different Poor Boards is not given in the report for 1880.

table, together with the percentage of increase in the decade.

POORHOUSE	1880	1890	Per Capita Cost per Week in 1890.	
Blakely................	$4,221	$9,629	$3.04	Per cent. of Increase
Carbondale.............	4,459	4,727	5.54	
Hillside	33,407	74,738	3.62	
Northern Luzerne.......	992	2,450	2.64	
Ransom	10,622	12,609	2.26	
Total for Lack. County..	$53,701	$104,153		93.9
Cost of County Jail	8,307	20,547	$3.82	147.3
Total............	$62,008	$124,700		101.1

The population of Lackawanna County in 1890, according to the census returns, was 142,008, of whom those of foreign parentage numbered 54,760, or 38.6 per cent.[1] The number of taxables recorded in the County Clerk's office for 1889 was 59,373, and the assessed valuation of property in the county in the same year was $23,333,058. The cost of supporting the county poor and prisoners during the year was then a tax of 5.3 mills upon every dollar of valuation, and equal to a per capita tax of 82.8 cents upon each man, woman, and child in the county, or of $2.10 upon every taxable recorded for the preceding year.

The average weekly cost of prisoners per capita in this county jail is $1.79 in excess of the well

[1] *Census Bulletin No.* 183.

managed Allegheny County Prison, where it is but
$2.03 per week. Even in Philadelphia County
Prison the weekly cost is but $2.39. The weekly
cost per capita of the maintenance of paupers in the
State ranges from .78 per week in Centre County,
where it is least, up to $5.54 in Carbondale Poor-
house, one of the most expensive in the State.

The foreign population of this county, which in
1880 was 30.1 per cent. and in 1890 was 38.6 per
cent. of the whole population, furnished over 70 per
cent. of our paupers. If the same proportion exists
as shown in the United States census for the whole
country, they have furnished over one third of our
convicts. No colored convicts or paupers are
reported in this county, although the colored population numbers 357.[1] An examination of these statements certainly discloses both a shocking increase in
criminality, and a wasteful extravagance in the cost
of maintaining our poor, which demand immediate
attention and remedy.

Allegheny is a city of 104,967 people,—a city little greater in numbers and very similar in elements
to Scranton, the county seat of Lackawanna. Its
244 paupers were sustained in the Allegheny City
Home, a well-designed and admirably managed institution, eight miles from the city, during the year
1890 at a weekly cost of $1.45 per capita. A good
farm furnishes employment and much of the provision for its inmates, who also do most of the necessary work of the institution, and make most of their
own bedding and clothes.

[1] *Census Bulletin No.* 183.

The grounds about the City Home are pleasant and tastefully kept. The buildings are always neat, in good repair, and orderly; the inmates well-fed with plain, well-cooked, and neatly served food. They are apparently as contented and satisfied as it is desirable for them to be. Its department for the insane on the female side is as comfortable and home-like as any similar institution need be made. The management of the institution leaves very little to be suggested in the way of improvement; while the condition of the paupers is quite as comfortable and pleasant as it ought to be. The weekly cost is abundantly sufficient to secure the best results.

At Pittsburg City Farm the weekly cost per capita in 1890 was $2.05; at the Luzerne County Home, $2.26; at the Blockley Almshouse, in Philadelphia, but $1.27; at the Schuylkill County Almshouse, $1.92. Indeed in thirty-one, out of the seventy-one poorhouses in the State, the weekly cost was less than $2.00 per capita.

If the weekly cost of the paupers of Lackawanna County had been no greater than that of the Allegheny County Home, the burden of our poor-tax might have been reduced over one half,—that is, instead of $104,153, it might as well have been $52,057. It will be noticed that the highest weekly cost occurs in the Carbondale, Blakely, and Northern Luzerne poorhouses, the last situated near Clark's Green. Yet it is evident that in these the inmates receive far inferior care and live in much less comfort than in the Allegheny City Home. Five institutions, with five farms, five superintendents, all with their hired staffs, are all employed to accomplish what could be done in a much more satisfactory manner in one institution, on a single farm, with one superintendent. The proceeds of the sale of four of these farms and improvements would, probably, be sufficient to provide ample and suitable accommodation for all their paupers in one place. Some wise legislation, with intelligent management, might effect a reduction in our taxation, which would be a sensible relief to the whole people of our county. Wherever in this State all of the paupers are cared for in one institution, the results are the most satisfactory, both in their philanthropic and economic aspects.

At the same time, the same number of criminals in our jails could have been maintained at the average weekly cost of those in the Allegheny County Jail (viz., $2.03), which would have saved $10,054 in the last year. Thus we find through these evident facts an actual and unnecessary waste, in one year, of $62,091 in the maintenance, in one county, of its prisoners and paupers! This inexcusable loss is only emphasized if the results of the system are compared with the administration of other counties in the State. Schuylkill County supported 129 prisoners in 1890 at a weekly cost of $2.43; Dauphin County, 73 at a cost of $2.63 per week; Montgomery County, 66 at a cost of $2.36; Northumberland, 64 at $2.30.[1] Wardens, appointed to serve during good behavior, govern all of these jails, except that of Dauphin, and convicts are made to earn as much as possible of their own subsistence.

[1] *Report of the Board of Public Charities, State of Penna.*, 1890.

Thirteen of the sixty-nine country prisons supported their inmates on less than $3 per week; and twenty-six at less than Lackawanna County in 1890; our 62 convicts in the Eastern Penitentiary cost the county but 66 cents per week.[1]

Ranking as the fifth county in the State in wealth and population, having for a county seat the fourth city in the Commonwealth, our penal and charitable institutions, and their management, fall far below the degree of excellence which we are entitled to expect. Our citizens have earned a reputation for intelligence and progressive public spirit, which is not consistent with their neglect of these important subjects. We have not only been inattentive to the increase of our criminals, but heedless of the unnecessary cost of their maintenance, until the consequences have assumed proportions which would seem to require instant and skilful treatment. There is no imaginable good reason why these expenses should exceed the average of the State. It should be expected rather, that our institutions should be models for the rural sections to imitate, as are those of Philadelphia, Pittsburg, and Allegheny.

[1] *Report of the Board of Public Charities, State of Penn.*, 1890.

CHAPTER IV.

THE NEED OF REFORM BY LEGISLATION.

The Annual Costs of Criminality and Charity—The Evils of General Taxation for Local Purposes—Has the State a Right to Resort to This Policy—Some Figures about the Average Annual Tax and How It may be Reduced—Defective Penal Legislation—Unsystematic and Unconstitutional Methods.

THE Legislature of Pennsylvania has appropriated during the last ten years for the criminal class, together with so-called charitable objects, the following amounts:

For the Insane............................	$2,016,995
For the Deaf and Dumb..................	1,494,447
For the Blind............................	535,000
For Feeble-Minded Children.............	747,500
For Hospitals and Miscellaneous Objects. ...	2,145,280
Poor Boards and Directors have Expended..	16,444,002
This Makes a Total Expenditure for the Defective and Dependent of............	$23,383,224[1]

During the same period the Legislature appropriated:

Upon Penitentiaries, Reformatories, and Houses of Refuge....................	$4,241,878
And Counties Expended upon Jails and Inmates.......	5,849,884
Making a Total for the Criminal Class......	$10,091,762 [1]

[1] *Reports of the Board of Public Charities of Pennsylvania.*

26

Thus we have a grand total of cost to the people of the State, for both classes, of $33,474,986.

The actual cost of the criminal class, however, must include a much larger sum, impossible to be accurately stated ; including that which is expended in the detection, arrest, and trial of prisoners ; with expenses of constables and courts. It ought to include also the loss and damage inflicted upon society by the crime and predatory habits of the criminals. The mere statement of these enormous sums must impress every intelligent observer with the conviction that they are out of all proportion to the benefits derived by society from their expenditure. The public certainly receives no adequate value for its money.

In preceding chapters we have endeavored to indicate how proper legislation may reduce almshouse and criminal costs. Let us now consider the possibility of reduction in these other items of expense by the correction of improper legislation. Much of this is the result of a false popular opinion and understanding as to the proper objects of State appropriations, and much to an unnecessary and wasteful cost of maintaining proper objects.

One might conclude that our people had become confused as to the real idea of government. The object of government is the protection and benefit of the governed in this country. Taxation should be submitted to only for the securing of these objects, promoted with intelligence and executed with true economy. State institutions for criminals under long sentences or confined for reformation

are evidently correct in design. Because in such
institutions only can economical arrangements be
made for proper employment and self-support,
systematic treatment had with a view to reformation,
or a careful determination made as to the proper
time and method of restoration to liberty. So also
are the State institutions for the insane, the deaf
and dumb, the blind and weak-minded, composing
unfortunate classes which can be best cared for in
this way and treated by themselves, with special
adaptations, methods, purposes. For competent
superintendents, medical specialists, and attendants
are not found in sufficient numbers in the general
county institutions to warrant in them the expectation of successful care of these classes.   They have
come to be wisely regarded as the wards of the
State, to be cared for by legislative appropriation.
For them the State must provide. Hence the minimum of cost must be secured by wisdom and economy in the management of all the institutions
designed for their treatment.

In the insane hospitals probably over 75 per cent.
of the 7,649 inmates on the 30th of September, 1891,
could be occupied, advantageously to themselves,
with useful labor, so that they might contribute a
large portion of the cost of their own maintenance.
This has been demonstrated to be the case in many
institutions, both in this country and abroad.

One of the most painful impressions made upon a
visitor to our hospitals for the insane, is the absolute
idleness of the inmates ; who sit and lie about the
corridors and rooms, day after day, week after week,

year after year, with absolutely nothing to do, or to occupy their attention,—nothing to distract their diseased minds from their own misery. This enforced idleness and confinement transforms, for them, what should be a pleasant home and retreat, into a prison ; escape from which becomes their constant longing, and their almost universal appeal to every one from the outside world. Productive labor would be for them as grateful and useful an agency of cure, as it would be a measure of economy to the taxpayer.

The institutions for the deaf and blind are intended and used chiefly for the education of these classes, and their preparation, while young, to sustain themselves independently outside. But they can, and in some cases they do now, largely reduce their expenses by the work done by the pupils or inmates.

To wise management therefore we must look for the economy of maintaining the defective classes. Public attention has apparently been so intently directed toward securing adequate and comfortable care for them, that now, when it appears that this has been secured, it rests satisfied, as though its full duty were discharged by protecting them from want and suffering, whatever it may cost. As a matter of fact, what has been solved is but the primary and simplest part of the problem. How to restore the largest number to independence as members of society, how to restrict with humanity the propagation and natural increase of defectives, so as to keep these classes at their minimum, and how to properly care for those necessarily supported at public cost with the smallest possible burden upon the public, are now the vital questions of government concerning them. These ought now to be the subjects of philanthropic study.

A saving of at least a million dollars a year of the present annual expense in Pennsylvania could certainly be effected, with an increase of comfort to the dependent classes, if the best methods should be employed in their treatment. Legislative appropriations for hospitals and miscellaneous charities have averaged, during the last ten years, $214,528 per annum, increasing in amount at each session, until the session of 1890, which voted the princely sum of $690,745 a year for 1891 and 1892 for these purposes!

The pernicious practice termed "log-rolling," which has prevailed so pertinaciously in Congress in regard to public buildings and improvements, seems to have crept into our State Legislature. Every Assemblyman and Senator appears to have been emulous to carry back to his constituents as large an appropriation as possible, in evidence of his ability, and even to have been willing to vote for any member's "little bill" who would vote for his. Philadelphia and Allegheny, having the most numerous representation, of course got the largest slice of this luscious legislative melon ; but most of the important delegations secured at least a bite. Many of the institutions aided have had cunningly coupled to their names the worthy title "of the State of Pennsylvania," to give color to their claims, although their sphere of operations is manifestly local

It must be evident to all that unless this leak can

be stopped decisively and speedily the limit of supportable taxation must soon be reached.

But the imminence and magnitude of this danger are not the only or even the most important reasons for checking it. Appropriations to hospitals and local charities of actual, real, unsectarian, and undenominational organization, if made by a two-thirds' vote of the Legislature, may not be contrary to the letter of the constitution, but they are certainly contrary to the spirit of that constitution, and in violation of sound, fundamental principles of popular government. As corporations have no souls, so the supreme corporation among American institutions, the State, is incapable of charity. It cannot exercise benevolence. This is a natural impossibility for the State. The so-called "charitable institutions" which it maintains are wrongly named. The purpose of the State may be called a selfish one—that is, to protect the mass of the governed from injury from defective and irrational members in the most economical manner. These institutions are managed by paid officials, who serve primarily for wages without charitable motive, while the recipients of their care receive and demand their benefits as a right rather than a kindness.

Whatever is necessary to protect its people from external or internal injury, that the State may do. Whatever will promote the highest prosperity and happiness of the people as a whole, that the State may assist and encourage. As she levies her taxes with an impartial hand upon all alike, so she must expend them for the benefit of all.

She has no right to exact money from the merchants or manufacturers of Philadelphia to expend upon injured miners in her coal fields ; or to tax the farmers of the Cumberland to take care of the sufferers among the iron mills of Allegheny or to bind up the wounds of her railroaders. What law, human or divine, requires the citizens of Scranton to contribute to the cure of a sick Philadelphian or for a surgical attendance upon a citizen of Pittsburg? Hospitals and all kindred local institutions, Homes for the Friendless, and the like are useful within a limited area, and are to be supported and maintained by the community which is benefited by them. No community is obliged to impose upon itself a larger expense for these purposes than it can afford, nor to appeal, under ordinary circumstances, until it has exhausted its own resources, to strangers and the outside public for assistance. A reliance upon others to materially diminish the burden of local duty, degrades and diminishes the Christian charity of the community, and inflicts injury instead of benefit upon its society. The voting of State aid to local charities, therefore, not only violates the fundamental principles of free government, but inflicts a serious and subtle injury upon the community which receives the donation. There is no doubt from the wording of the new constitution that its framers intended to prohibit State appropriations to local charities, except in emergencies ; but the ingenuity of the modern politician has devised a way to evade the intention. Hence, on the plea of charity the average annual tax upon society in Pennsylvania for

the last ten years has been, as shown above to be, $3,347,498. Of this amount over $214,528 annually went to local objects. Yet the last session increased this sum to $690,745.

Suppose by wise economy and judicious management the support of the insane, and of jails and alms-houses, were reduced 50 per cent., which is quite possible and practicable, we think we should thus effect a relief from taxation of $1,215,543 ; and adding the amount wrongfully given away to local objects, $1,430,071 (together with the apprehension of un-limited increase of the last item). The statesman who should accomplish a reduction of almost 50 per cent. in the burden of taxation, while conferring a positive benefit upon the social organization, ought to achieve lasting renown, and certainly would deserve the gratitude of his fellow-citizens.

3

CHAPTER V.

PHASES OF THE PROBLEM.

What Is the Solution?—Punishment by Law Absurd—Deterrence, Reformation, and Prevention Proper Objects of Penal Code— Incongruity and Aimlessness of Poor-Laws—True Purpose and Scope—Economy of Correct System Illustrated.

WE have thus far considered the convict and dependent classes in the aspect of a present and an abnormally growing burden upon society. We have proposed a serious problem for popular solution, and have appealed to an economic and selfish motive to excite a general interest in its study. Christ said, " The poor ye have always with you," and the voice of human nature proclaims with equal truth that the wicked will never " cease from troubling " on this earth. Criminals and paupers will probably always exist in the widely varying gradations of humanity; and Christianity, philanthropy, and political economy alike impose the duty and necessity of helping the weak, sustaining the incurable, and raising the fallen.

A professional criminal is a beast of prey constantly endangering society. As the class cannot be exterminated, we must look to protective measures for security from the obdurate, and to preventive and

34

reformatory influences to diminish as far as possible the numbers of the class. The burden of pauperism must be lightened by a wise economy of necessary expenditures, made in support of the helpless poor, by affording all an opportunity to contribute to the extent of their ability towards their maintenance; chiefly by a united effort of the independent members of society to restrict the constant reproduction of the dependent and defective, and to stimulate and assist the weak, the incompetent, and unfortunate to avoid a public support. Can this be efficiently done?

When we attempt to descend to definite practical measures, we are reminded that the best doctors often disagree as to the remedies, even when entirely agreed as to the disease and the end sought. While careless and thoughtless politicians are allowed to invent and enact shortsighted or unintelligent plans to remedy the most flagrant evils, under a "penny-wise and pound-foolish policy," or to waste their time and the people's money in stopping spigot leaks to neglect of the open bung-hole, little can be expected of value. Our whole system of criminal and pauper legislation needs a complete revision, in order to bring it into conformity with the new principles evolved by the experience of ages and brought to light by the science of modern civilization. Reformation must begin with the laws. Those principles which came into existence as the means of enforcing the power of rulers, have become the palladium and bond of modern society, the very essence of its government. The principles which were reduced to practice in an age of ignorance and barbarism, no longer apply in our advanced social conditions.

The idea of the mere legal punishment of crime, for instance, upon which our penal legislation is based has been found fallacious in theory, false in principle, absurd in practice, and almost a total failure in results. God, the Creator and Ruler, has reserved to himself the sole power of determining the exact degree of blameworthiness in human transgressions of both divine and human law. He alone is capable of inflicting a just and proper punishment upon the transgressor. All human attempts to usurp this prerogative are acknowledged parodies on justice, even as it is understood by mankind. He who steals a loaf of bread to feed his starving child, according to human law, is just as real a thief, and must suffer as mercilessly the penalty, as he who violates the most sacred trust to gratify a morbid appetite. The penalties of crime have been greatly diminished in severity within the present century, and various crimes distinguished by degrees of guilt with distinct penalties; but the inequality and injustice of punishment becomes only more and more glaring thereby. With moral culpability, and its punishment, human law can properly have little, if anything, to do. Its proper object and purpose is the protection of society.

The chief province of penal legislation is confined, we think, by nature to the control of the criminal for the general security, and to his reformation as a preventive and economical project.

These purposes, however, have small recognition in our penal codes, which are chiefly a blind and blundering attempt to prescribe the method of expiating particular transgressions by the imposition of various amounts and kinds of suffering—imprisonment for ten days, thirty days, sixty days, ninety days, six months, one year, eighteen months, two years, five years, ten years, in the discretion of the judge, for certain named crimes, as though it were possible for the criminal to measure off his criminality in just such regular amounts as would require the specified days, or months, or years, or for different criminals to deserve the same penalty for similar crimes, or to be equally punished by imprisonment, where some would enjoy a comfort, and even luxury, of living in idleness, which they never could attain at liberty, and others find utter blasting ruin and misery.

Our present legislation ought to be reorganized upon the principle of confining the criminal at self-supporting labor, in healthful but not agreeable quarters, until he ceases to be a criminal, or dies ; also of keeping him so separated from others in confinement that he shall neither receive nor impart contamination. First offenders, on the other hand, should suffer such inflictions as will discourage repetition of the offence, without running any risk of being criminalized by confinement.

In short, the scheme of the penal code should be deterrent, reformative, and preventive, instead of punitive. The purpose of the judiciary should be equally the protection of society and the restoration of the convict to an honest independence of life, rather than a vindictive meting out of penalty for crime. William Tallack states that an intelligent public and official recognition of correct principles in dealing with criminals has abolished six out of seven jails, and a large percentage of convicts, in the county of Gloucester, England.[1] There can be little doubt but that similar results will follow in every community. They have universally followed in other counties and countries where they have been adopted wholly or in part. The penal laws of this country greatly need a complete remodelling and codification.

For the decrease of the burden of pauperism, legislation, public intelligence, and effort are necessary. Our poor-laws are incongruous, generally intended to provide for obsolete conditions, and framed to maintain the needy, rather than to assist and enable such to maintain themselves. Without harmony with themselves, they are confusing and wasteful by their multiplicity, and false in their purpose and scope. They require to be conformed to the new status of society, with the manifest object of reducing both the number of dependants and the public cost of their maintenance. They should be based upon the biblical principle that "if a man will not work neither shall he eat." Every one receiving public aid should contribute, to the extent of his or her ability, to his or her own support ; society only being called upon to supplement to the extent of the actual inability. This can be

[1] *Penological and Preventive Principles*, p. 33.

best done and most economically by gathering the paupers into homes, or almshouses, by themselves.

One county house only should be maintained in each county; with sufficient farming land about it to raise all articles of food which can be economically produced in the section with the labor of the inmates. A county overseer of the poor should be appointed by the county court, or selected by the people, with sufficient salary to enable him to devote his entire time to their care; to hold office for not less than five years, or as long as efficient. His certificate should be necessary to secure public assistance.

In this country, where work is always to be had, it should be his first duty to bring self-supporting work to the needy, either outside or inside the county house, and to see that none suffer through misfortune or adversity; and second, to enforce the best methods of managing the county home.

Annual conventions of county overseers should be provided for mutual consultation and instruction; and a State official, or overseer of the poor, should be appointed, to whom all should report and be subject. When similar officers shall have been provided in other States, annual conventions of such officials should be held for the study and consideration of plans for the decrease of pauperism and the management of paupers. In agricultural districts the county farms should be model and experimental farms, for the test and development of methods of farming and breeds of stock for the public benefit, so that the community may receive some return for the cost of their maintenance.

By such a general organization excessive costs, due to ignorance and inattention, would be reduced, and the expense of all institutions be brought down to a minimum. In 1890 the various poor-directors of Pennsylvania expended $1,782,849, more than half of which great sum was worse than wasted, in that its expenditure, even when made for the legitimate support of the poor, probably tended to increase instead of curing the evil upon which it was administered. The enactment of a general code, conferring general powers of regulation, administration, supervision, and audit upon a State Board, would undoubtedly greatly reduce the weekly cost of maintenance, and inaugurate measures to reduce pauperism to a minimum. A wise and comprehensive poor-law, embodying most of these features and repealing all the rest of the confusing and antagonistic legislation of the State, was reported to the last Legislature after a very full and careful study of the whole subject at home and abroad. This was done by an able commission appointed by Governor Beaver, of which our late distinguished fellow-citizen, Hon. Lewis Pugh, was chairman. There is no doubt its enactment would have accomplished all the good results possible at the present time from legislation. It would have effected a saving to the people of at least one million dollars a year in taxation.

The politicians and poor-directors, however, who now have the handling of this great sum, by a general movement upon legislators, were able to prevent even a consideration of this wise and humane law, either by the Legislature or by the public.

With some slight amendments of detail, retaining supervision by the Board of Public Charities, etc., it ought to be enacted without delay. The people must interest themselves in this as well as in the measure so longed urged by the Board of Public Charities, which removes the sheriffs from the charge of jails, or there can be no cure of the cancer which is sapping the vitals of our prosperity.

CHAPTER VI.

UNRESTRICTED IMMIGRATION AS AN ELEMENT IN THIS INCREASE.

Alarming Proportion of Foreign Criminals and Paupers—The Necessity and Possibility of National Regulation of Immigration —The Value of American Citizenship and How It should be Protected—The Land of the Bible and the Sabbath—Necessity of Inculcating American Principles—Appeal to the Church.

HAVING indicated how materially taxation may be reduced by wise legislation and improved management of public institutions, let us now consider whether the numbers to be supported at the public expense may not be so reduced as to effect even a greater economy. In this connection it is to be remembered that the transfer of an individual from a class supported at the public expense to the class of self-supporters, benefits society not only by the relief from the burden of maintenance, but by the value of his productive effort, which, besides affording the person a better living, usually yields a profit to society. Every such transfer, therefore, is worth more than double the present public expense.

42

There is, then, a double incentive to our present consideration, and to effort for relief in this direction.

It has been stated that our population, foreign-born or having one or both parents foreign-born, while constituting but about 20 per cent. of our whole number, furnishes over one third of our criminals and three fifths of our paupers.[1] Let us then first examine the foreign element as the most important point of philanthropic attack.

The last census shows, however, that our white paupers, native and of native parentage, were only 29 per cent. of the total in our almshouses, and that the colored native population, constituting about 12 per cent. of the whole, furnish only 8.8 per cent. of our dependents.[2] The ratio of foreigners to natives among the defective classes, so far as we have been able to determine (for the examination among them is both more difficult and less accurately reported than respecting paupers and prisoners), appears to be about the same as among these. In Massachusetts the commitments of the insane of foreign birth or parentage in 1889 were three times the number of natives.

During the last decade there has been an influx of foreigners to the country through our own ports of entry of 5,246,613, equal to an annual average of 524,661 souls; besides the large unnumbered multitude which has flowed over our Canadian frontier. The flood of immigration is constantly

[1] *Census Bulletin No.* 31.
[2] *Census Bulletin, Eleventh Census, No.* 90.

swelling, having nearly doubled in the last decade
the numbers of the preceding. There sweeps in
upon us now each year a greater horde than that of
the Goths and Vandals which overwhelmed the
Roman Empire when it ruled the world. As irresistible and constant a current as the Moslem
invasion which once overthrew and subdued Christendom, it must produce changes and results to which
as Americans we cannot remain indifferent.

Two principal inferences are suggested by these
statements. The first is this: that the principles
and institutions which mould and nurture the American people must be of wonderful and unparalleled
beneficence, vitality, and strength to transform in
two generations this heterogeneous and largely low-
grade mass into wholesome, independent, and reputable citizens. There is, indeed, no grander or more
conclusive demonstration of the excellence of
American institutions possible than is afforded by
our present condition. Notwithstanding the constant injection of foreign languages, customs, beliefs,
religions, scepticisms, communisms, and nihilisms;
nothwithstanding the fact that all nations have for a
century or more been sloughing off their insupport-
ables upon us, together with a moiety of their
ambitious and enterprising people in search of "a
better country," still the bounding current of our
national life has been able to absorb it all; and to so
cleanse, purify, elevate, and ennoble it, that the
American people of to-day stand without a peer
upon the face of the earth in happiness, prosperity,

THE UNION. A GROUP OF DISTINGUISHED AMERICANS.

PRODUCT OF AMERICAN INSTITUTIONS IN STATESMEN.

intelligence, and Christianity! This is not the result of climate or soil, of inherited traits or crossing of blood or races, nor of liberty and the abolition of caste or classes. It must come from the vigor, truth, and overruling influence of the whole body of American thought, customs, laws, and institutions. These united in the bonds of Christianity, have so far been sufficient to cope with and triumph over all these evil elements. But when we notice the growing quantity and rapidly changing character of our immigration, a less satisfactory inference is suggested.

In the forty years from 1820 to 1860 our English-speaking immigrants numbered 2,744,850; our Germans, 1,545,508; and those of all other nationalities, 763,671. From the Revolution to 1820 the arrivals are estimated by good authorities at 250,000, making a total of 5,304,029. Between the revolutionary period and that of the civil war there were only 57,416 more than arrived during the last decade. Over 84 per cent., moreover, of these immigrants previous to 1860 were either English-speaking or German people, attracted to the country chiefly, doubtless, by their love of liberty and their preference for our institutions and form of government, to which they adapted themselves voluntarily.

But how different has the tide been for the last ten or fifteen years? Immigration to the United States during the last three decades has been from the sources shown in the following table, " alien passengers " being included to December 31, 1867.

Sources of Foreign Immigration as Shown by Report since 1860,[1] of the United States Treasury Department.	January 1, 1861 to June 30, 1870.	Fiscal Years 1871 to 1880.	Fiscal Years 1881 to 1890.	Per Cent. Males, Last Decade.	Year Ending June 30, 1891.	In Last Decade		
						Per Cent. under 15 Years.	Per Cent. between 15-40.	Per Cent. over 40.
England................	568,128	460,479	657,488	61.	53,787	23.5	65.2	11.3
Ireland................	435,778	436,871	655,482	51.	55,634	14.1	78.6	7.3
Scotland...............	38,768	87,564	149,869	61.	12,554	24.2	65.2	10.6
Total English-speaking......	1,042,674	984,914	1,462,839	....	121,975			
Germany................	787,468	718,182	1,452,970	57.6	113,531	26.6	62.2	11.2
Austria-Hungary........	7,800	72,969	353,719	73.8	71,039	22.1	66.3	11.6
Russia and Poland......	4,536	52,254	265,088	65.8	74,892	24.7	65.9	9.4
Italy..................	11,728	55,759	307,309	79.4	75,143	15.3	69.2	15.5
Denmark................	17,094	31,771	88,132	61.	10,637	20.	70.3	9.5
Norway and Sweden......	109,298	211,245	568,362	61.	49,392	18.3	73.	8.7
Total New Immigrants....	150,456	423,998	1,582,610	....	281,103			
All Others.............	334,226	685,097	748,134	....	138,887			
Totals.................	2,314,824	2,812,191	5,246,613	....	555,496			

[1] Quarterly Report of Chief of Bureau of Statistics, Treasury Department of the United States, No. 3, 1890-91.

In respect to occupations, but .056 per cent. of the alien arrivals in the last decade are classed as " professionals "; 10.3 per cent. as " skilled " artisans; 39.63 per cent. of miscellaneous trades; 47.34 per cent. are reported as having " no occupation," and 2.22 per cent. as " not stated." Note that the " new immigrants " in the last decade are ten times as many as between 1861 and 1870; that they exceed both the English-speaking and the German; that the percentages of males, of children and aged, is excessive, except among the better classes from Denmark, Norway, and Sweden. Also observe that the immigration from Austria, Hungary, Russia, Poland, and Italy during the last year more than doubled the annual average of the whole decade.

It must be evident, then, to the statistical student as well as to the thoughtful observer of his environments, that we are now not only taking in faster than we are assimilating, but that the kind and quality of our food is becoming more difficult of digestion. The proportion of arrivals from the effete races, of Russian Jews, Moslems, adherents of the Greek Church, and Romanists speaking strange tongues, with prejudices, habits, customs, and religions of the inbred strength of centuries, has suddenly grown to alarming dimensions. These, too, being from the lower classes of their people, are much more difficult of education and transformation, and have a much greater advance to make in order to reach the level of American citizenship than the Anglo-Saxons or Teutons, with some community of race, language or religion, who have hitherto constituted our chief increment.

Their labor being less valuable, is cheaper, and tends to depreciate the wages of our own citizens, which militates against national prosperity, is opposed to the spirit of our institutions, and contrary to the purpose of our government. Here, where the people reign, the object and design of their organization is, necessarily, that most general diffusion of prosperity, which involves the raising of the earnings of the wage workers, who constitute the largest proportion of our numbers, to the highest possible standard.

A continuous tide of cheaper labor than our own, depreciates the value of that with which it comes in competition here, just as it has done in its native land, and so acts as a constant retardant of national progress. Instead of the impetus and momentum which immigration has hitherto imparted to our development, this change in its sources and character converts its influence into a weight and clog. Its inspiration or impelling motive has also declined from an ennobling desire of emancipation from autocratic repression to a mere sordid and selfish wish to share with us the prosperity and wealth which are the fruit of our past struggles; or to enjoy, without cost to itself, the unparalleled privileges and opportunities for individual success with which these struggles have endowed American citizenship. Our present notable position among the nations, the sudden grandeur of illumination which we have shot into the darkened sky of human

A GROUP OF SYRIANS FROM MT. LEBANON LANDED AT NEW YORK.

misery, and hopelessness in other lands, has attracted
the lighter, mobile elements from every direction.
Wretched people from all lands fly toward " Liberty
Enlightening the World," like the insects of a summer night, without purpose, without thought, without care, save to bask in the beams of this new
sun.

Our national growth, then, is becoming adipose
rather than muscular. We can no longer naturally
digest all we receive. Unless assistance can be obtained from a modification of diet, exercise, or efficient medicament, national lethargy, enervation, fatty
degeneration, ulceration, and other fatal disease must
inevitably ensue. While our food was natural in
kind and quantity, we grew and flourished ; the
national vitality and functions being sufficient for
its utilization. Youth, indeed, may ignore the
stomach with apparent impunity, but maturity will
not, and cannot.

What needs to be done, then, now that the danger has become imminent, and threatens our very
existence ? The right and duty of the nation to
preserve itself and protect itself from injury, in
whatever way this danger may threaten it, cannot
be questioned. The national government must
enforce a discrimination as to who shall be admitted
into social and political fellowship. Congress must
regulate immigration as the initial remedy. The nature and amount of restriction possible is measured
largely by the value of the attractions offered. The
price demanded should naturally be proportioned to
the advantages to be obtained.

4

What is American citizenship worth in the world's market? The American citizen, when he obtains this title, becomes the owner of an undivided twelve millionth of 2,306,485,760 acres of the best land on the North American continent, a domain stretching, through the temperate and sub-tropical zones, from the Atlantic to the Pacific,—equivalent to over 190 acres to each voter ; of the usufruct of an accumulation of over $65,000,000,000 of wealth,—of wealth, won through penury and infinite hardship and suffering during a period of over three centuries of struggle with nature and with savages, including all that has been done on the continent to ameliorate the conditions of life—forests cleared, roads made, rivers and harbors improved, habitations erected, cities built, manufactories established, commerce organized. He becomes endowed with an interest in $10,122,635,900 capital invested in railroads, and hundreds of millions in steamers, for the comfort and convenience of his land- and water-travel and transportation ; 715,591 miles of telegraph wire running to every part of the domain ; in schools provided for every child ; colleges and universities founded and flourishing for their higher education ; the benevolent principles of Christianity regnant in society ; and its institutions providing amply for the needy. He finds here a government which is the growth and fruit of all the ages ; the way to the highest place in which, or to the most prominent positions in wealth or social rank, open and unobstructed to him according to his ability and worth ; a government perfected through the trials and vicissitudes of an hundred years; its foundations established by the blood and suffering of the Revolution; cemented, strengthened, and sanctified by the tremendous and soul-trying fires of the civil war, the material cost of which has been already nearly paid. He becomes an owner in its public buildings, its postal service and offices, its armament, its fortifications, its treasury, its army and navy, its history, its glory, and its flag.

The possessor of this inestimable fortune may enfold himself in the flag of the Union, and instantly 63,000,000 of freemen will surround him with the ægis of American power; wherever on land or sea he may wander, when he calls for protection, all the wealth and blood of these millions will be poured out for his defence.

Who then shall presume to question any price we may place upon the privilege of American citizenship? If any refuse it upon our own terms, we have no need to dispose of it, let him stay where he is.

Have not Americans a right to prescribe who shall be admitted to partnership with them in such a possession? Congress, we are persuaded, should enact, that no immigrant shall be admitted into the country, except those of sound and strong physical and mental health, of fair mental ability and intelligence, of good moral character, probable ability of self-support, and of becoming a good citizen. It is citizens, not paupers, the country wants. Why shall Europe make America its almshouse? Certificates of these facts, given, under proper regulations to

secure accuracy and avoid fraud, by the United
States Consul nearest the point of departure, should
be required upon entering the country. These should
be examined and approved by the Commissioners of
Immigration, who should register them, with the
intended destination. The immigrant should be
required to register, and have his consular certificate
viséd at the county office, immediately upon his ar-
rival at his place of settlement, and whenever moving
from one county to another.

This will greatly simplify and prevent fraudulent
naturalization. Any fraud discovered in such certificate, or crime committed during the five years of
his naturalization, or his failure to properly qualify
himself within this period, should render him liable
to arrest, and return to his native place after expiating his crime, if convicted. The examining judge
might be allowed discretion to extend the probation
an additional five years, if this should appear to be
just or desirable. The imperative qualifications
required for citizenship should be physical and mental soundness ; ability of self-support, and to read
and speak English readily ; correct knowledge of,
and real belief in, the fundamental principles of our
government and institutions. All pestilent agita-
tors against law, order, and government should be
denied not only citizenship, but domicile, and be
returned whence they came. The importation of
low-grade contract labor should be prohibited, as it
is men who are wanted. A sufficient registration fee
should be exacted to defray the expenses of the regulation and return of the rejected, and a capitation

TYPICAL RUSSIAN JEWS LANDED AT NEW YORK.

tax of ten dollars to insure good faith, offset foreign aid, and cheapened cost of immigration, as well as to protect native labor. An act embracing most of these features has been introduced, I understand, i though I have not seen it, into the present Congress by the commission appointed to examine this subject by President Harrison. It should be made to include registration here also, for this is quite as important as the foreign certificate. The forms and procedure of naturalization should be made more impressive and thorough. The induction into citizenship should be a grave judicial proceeding, in which undue haste and fraud would be practically impossible, instead of a mere ministerial perfunction.

Having restricted the foreign increment to proper persons, the numbers attracted to our shores will still continue so large, and of such a character as to require intelligent, energetic, and general attention and effort by our patriotic people to properly and rapidly Americanize them. In the natural reaction from the fierce fervor of patriotism aroused during the civil war, there has been of late too great neglect, even among our native population, of the ethics of citizenship. It is to be feared that the rising generation has far less veneration for, and loyalty to, American institutions than its fathers. There is an imperative need for a general revival in the instruction of the people concerning the nature of our institutions, the functions of our government, and the individual responsibility and duty of loyal citizenship.

The things which have made us the grand nation of the earth have been acquired at a tremendous cost, and we cannot afford to fritter them away by neglect.

Much greater than restriction is the need for the instruction of the alien. Associations for the study and promotion of true Americanism ought to be organized in all towns and cities, where little attention is now paid to this or to the emigrant, save by the selfish politician with an eye for votes. Instruction in the use of the English language should have the first place among the purposes of these associations. Knowledge of it must be insisted upon as the prerequisite of citizenship. It is the language of America, of our legislation, our literature, our press, and of our schools,—the only medium of instruction we employ. The settlement of foreigners in communities retaining foreign tongues must be broken up and discontinued. Newspapers, churches, schools, or business conducted in foreign languages should not be supported or encouraged. These associations should have a care for the education of the newcomers in the primary principles of political ethics, without partisanship or sectarianism. They should strive to kindle a spark of love for, and loyalty to, their adopted country in the breast of all. Distinctive societies of foreign nationalities, public processions following foreign flags, are to be disapproved as tending to sustain that loyalty to native land which their members have forsworn and should forget, in the new relations they have assumed. None but the American flag should ever fly above any American public building; but there it should kiss the breeze on all public occasions.

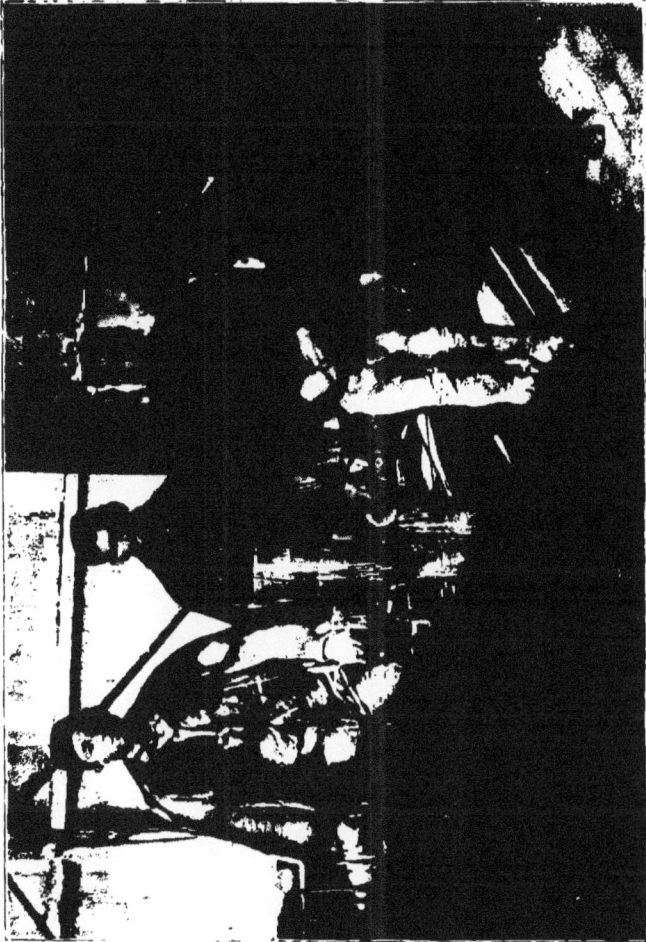

A GROUP OF SICILIANS LANDED AT NEW YORK.

Equally with the English language and the supremacy of the flag, we must insist that America is the
land of the Christian Bible and the Christian Sabbath. While we impose no religious tests either
upon immigrant or citizen; while every one here en-
joys perfect freedom of conviction, and liberty to
worship or not to worship, according to his convictions, whether Protestant, Romanist, Greek, Jew,
pagan, infidel, agnostic, atheist, or pantheist, yet
no man can be permitted to interfere with or change
this cardinal principle of our existence. With the
Bible in hand the Pilgrim fathers first landed on
these shores; with the Bible in hand the boundaries
of these States were fixed; with the Bible in hand
our independence was achieved, and our form of
government established. With the Bible in hand
our officials are inducted into power, and under its
principles of common law are they held responsible.
With the Bible and with prayer, our schools
have hitherto trained our children. Upon Christ's
summary of the law and prophets, which demands
the love of God with all the heart, and the love of
our neighbor as ourselves, and upon the observance
of the Christian Sabbath as a day of rest and worship, our state is founded; and upon these must our
system of legislation and polity be based. It is the
highest, the most imperative duty of the patriotic
American to prevent any sacrilegious hand from
disturbing these foundations upon which our greatness has been built.

As our public-school system is our main hope for
the future, and as an insidious, persistent, and in

many localities successful effort is being made, under the cloak of a pretence of the inviolability of religious belief and preference, to banish the Bible and Christianity from all our public schools, a determined and immovable stand must be made, by every one who loves his country, for their retention in our educational system. Experience has abundantly demonstrated that intelligence without morals, religion, and patriotism contributes to the demoralization of society, and therefore is an absolute danger to the state, instead of a benefit.

The education of criminals renders them only more skilful and successful in crime. So also our charitable institutions, almshouses, reformatories, jails, and penitentiaries, with three fifths of their inmates of the foreign class, must be managed as Christian institutions, designed for the cure and transformation of their inmates into good citizens, as well as for the protection of the public, and their own temporary maintenance. The Bible and the Sabbath must continue their power and sway in them, with potent but unsectarian influence. The associations referred to above must make it their care to see that this is done.

Another vital duty devolving upon the native American and the Association is the preservation, absolutely inviolate, of public appropriations from sectarian objects. This is indeed prohibited in the constitutions of twenty-one of our States, as well as by the spirit and traditions of our general constitution, an amendment to which is now being urged to make this positive. Large sums are annually secured both from the National and State treasuries for sectarian institutions, principally Romanist ; very worthy and excellent in themselves, indeed, but obtained by hidden plans of various kinds in direct violation of this fundamental principle of our government and constitution. These attacks upon the public treasury and welfare are increasing in strength and numbers continually. In our own State they are disguised and subtle as yet. In the National Congress they have been secured more openly. In New York during the legislative session of 1891, under the guise of a " Freedom of Worship Bill," the assault was made direct, and carried through the Assembly without deliberation and with indecent haste by the votes of members afraid, evidently, of offending the foreign voter. The Democratic Legislature of 1892 has enacted a similar bill. This will compel the support by general taxation of Roman Catholic worship in every institution receiving State aid, if a single inmate requires it ; thus imposing the religion of about one tenth of the people upon the public institutions of a Protestant State and community. The necessary result will doubtless be an increase of the bitterness of religious differences ; the restriction of admission to denominational institutions to those of their own faith ; a general scramble by all denominations for State aid ; and the straining, if not the destruction, of the principle of separation of Church and State.

The competition of politics in the ambition for preferment and success has, moreover, led nominees of all parties to truckle and pander to foreign

prejudices and preferences, for the purpose of securing their suffrages, to the serious weakening of
even native defence of our national institutions.
If these questions are brought unequivocally and
plainly before the public attention, there can be
no doubt that the large majority will sustain adhe-
rence to them regardless of party lines or nominees. It is high time that every patriotic lover of
his country should array himself, in association with
his fellows, for the defence of American institutions
against the insidious and indirect assaults which are
being made upon them, or the very freedom of
political action, which has been our boast, will surely
become our destruction.

The necessity for organization has become so palpable and pressing, that already two strong and
powerful national societies have been established to
meet the requirements of the times.   These are "The
American Institute of Civics," and the " National
League for the Protection of American Institutions."
But to secure efficiency, branches of these ought to
be established in every considerable community;
supported and sustained by every intelligent and
faithful citizen, without regard to party.   This seems
to us to be the only hopeful and rational way of protecting ourselves from the foreign overflow which is
pouring in upon us.

Our very prosperity and success as a republic has
become an element of danger.   That very prosperity has in itself become an attraction to the
inhabitants of other lands, who now come to us in-
cited by our wealth, rather than by that love of

A GROUP OF ITALIANS LANDED AT NEW YORK

freedom and religious liberty which actuated the Pilgrim Fathers. In earlier times in the world's history, when national wealth excited the cupidity of neighbors, the invasion was with an armed force and open war; but these insidious millions cross our borders now no more for our benefit than if they came in war. Padrones and other agents collect and import men to be farmed out for their own profit. They will doubtless soon be contracting to supply voters as cheaply as laborers. Foreign quarters are established in our cities, where all the business of their native lands is conducted in their native tongues, and where their imported customs, religions, and habits are preserved. In some of these quarters a native American would hardly be safe after dark, and even the missionaries of churches or of philanthropy seldom dare venture into them for their redemption and naturalization.

Our cities are the weak spots in our social structure. If wholly American, their rapidly growing number and size would constitute a perilous element in our civilization, because the recent immigration seems to concentrate in them. New York is said to contain more Irish than any city in Ireland, and has a population of 80 per cent. of foreign birth or parentage. Chicago has more Teutons than any German city except Berlin; a population of 91 per cent. of foreign birth or parentage. Some Western towns and cities are entirely of foreign population and customs. New Alarus, in Wisconsin, has been a foreign town since 1845, and is now. There are localities in our own State of Pennsylvania, where, for more than a century, the German language and the customs of Germany of one hundred years ago prevail, and the English is an almost unknown tongue. Large tracts of the public domain, of hundreds of thousands of acres, are taken up by communities for the express purpose of retaining their native customs and religions. They come over here in vast numbers, seat themselves, organize, and demand to be let alone to enjoy the freedom guaranteed by a Constitution of which they are entirely ignorant and which they propose to ignore. Even here they claim the right to retain their native language, and to organize their churches, schools, and society in their native manner, after their native traditions. We must insist, with a vigor and resolution we have never yet exercised, upon a thorough and complete Americanisation of all our people.

Next to these demands upon citizenship, the call of the hour is to the Church. Indeed, the call upon it is first and loudest; for our citizenship is but the result of a movement hither of those who desired the establishment of the Christian institutions which she embodies. Every branch of the Church must recognize and respond to this call everywhere. May not the Church add to its many beneficent branches of Christian activity a plan to promote the true naturalization as well as the conversion of foreigners? A general and enthusiastic movement by the churches throughout the land, wisely directed, with the co-operation of the various Home Missionary Societies and Young Men's Christian Associations is the most hopeful, and would surely be the most fruitful means of remedy to be applied to this national disease. By them the great body of their members may be enlisted in a most profitable and efficient work, teaching our language, our customs, our Christianity, to those within their immediate reach. The evil we have depicted is sure to grow unless all these efforts are made for its suppression and cure. If they are made, it can certainly be prevented from increase, and a material reduction be effected in the number of our criminals and paupers.

The Roman Catholic Church especially has a grave responsibility in these respects resting upon it in America. A very large proportion of our immigrants know no other religion. This church exercises over its adherents an unquestioned power which no other attempts. It has a unity of organization, an experience of record for centuries, to guide it. It has an accumulation of property and benevolent institutions more wisely, perhaps more efficiently, managed than any other Christian denomination. But it has failed so far in all these years to identify itself completely with America. It has never made itself, as other Christian churches have, a distinctively American institution, by a cordial adoption and loyal support of those distinctive and fundamental principles of our government, the absolute separation and independence of religion from politics, and the public-school system, which are held as sacredly, and considered as essential to our continuous prosperity, as the principle of perfect freedom of religious convictions. Therefore as a church and organization it is tolerated, but with apprehension.

It not only has failed to merge into our system, but it is very prone to exert its influence and power contrary to our accepted principle of complete divorcement of church and state. It interferes as a church in political affairs, and in our elections, as no other church ever presumes to do. Whoever, for instance, would think of voting for a political nominee because he might be a Methodist, Baptist, Episcopalian, or Presbyterian, as Catholics do? What leader or minister of any denomination would expect to make a single vote by any order or appeal to such a motive among his people? Yet many a public office is filled, as all politicians know, by the direct efforts of priests of the Catholic Church. It is feared that this exertion of religious influence to obtain political power is intended to secure for sectarian objects appropriations from the public treasury, and to procure the eventual abolition of the public schools, by banishing the Bible and religious instruction from them, which appears to be the universal result when they secure a sufficiently strong representation on school boards, and thus impairing their utility and destroying confidence in them.

So long as the Romish Church permits itself here to pass beyond the true province of a religious institution, it will be regarded with jealousy and alarm, and like any other church or organization be properly subject to public criticism and appeal. We appeal, therefore, to the wise and broad-minded men at its head in America, to make this great and otherwise beneficent organization a truly American

REV. JOSEPH C. PRICE, D.D.   PURE NEGRO.
PRESIDENT OF LIVINGSTON COLLEGE, SALISBURY, N. C.
EXAMPLE OF THE RESULT OF NEGRO ELEVATION.

institution, by a complete and evident withdrawal from political ambitions and efforts. By a strong and unselfish devotion of its magnificent machinery to the salvation, elevation, and Americanization of the foreign millions flocking to our shores, this Church may do one of its best works for the race.

Its priests and sisters can accomplish more for the church of their affection, more for the country, more for Christ, than any other organization can possibly effect among them, if they will but divest themselves of this last vestige of foreign prejudice and obsolete notion, as they have of much of their worldliness. Let them join the rest of Christ's church in America with an undivided and purely unselfish effort to make good, honest Christian citizens of these immigrants, as they already have ranged themselves beside them for the Sabbath and temperance, and the battle will be as good as won. It is because they are not a purely American church in these respects, that their hold grows feeble on the second generation. No more convincing illustration of the necessity for this change of policy is needed, than was afforded by the virulent attack made upon the author, when this chapter was first published in the Scranton *Tribune*, by certain local politicians, hoping to make political capital by pandering to foreign prejudice, in a community largely composed of recent immigrants of the Roman Catholic faith.

About nine tenths of the American people certainly, who are not Catholic, are confirmed in their faith in the beneficence of their institutions by the glorious results of the first century's experience under them. They will never yield to so small a minority upon the questions of perfect independence of Church and State, and the public education of the young. These questions are entirely distinct from all religious belief, and disconnected from spiritual and ecclesiastical affairs. We are unable to discover any sound and proper reason for the refusal of the Catholic Church in America to completely Americanize itself by a cordial acceptance of these principles. It would, in our opinion, greatly strengthen itself here by so marching, shoulder to shoulder, with the rest of the people.

Extraordinary emergencies require extraordinary effort. The tremendous tide of immigration now sweeping in upon us, constituted largely of refractory elements with which we have hitherto had little experience, appears to demand of all true lovers of American government, whatever may be their diversities of political and religious conviction, a vigilance, an energy of patriotic service, an exercise of self-sacrificing devotion to our country, never before called for in times of peace. That eternal vigilance, which is the price of liberty, cannot now be relaxed for an instant without peril. The reduction of the unnatural contribution of imported criminals and paupers to our public burdens, important as this is to our continued prosperity, is not the chief incentive to our vigilance. We seem to be threatened with a tidal wave of immigration which may shake the very foundations of our government.

CHAPTER VII.

THE NEGRO ELEMENT OF INCREASE.

Remarkable Disparity between the Proportion of Criminals and
Paupers from the Negro Race—Probable Causes: Social and
Political—Political Status of the Negro in America—Responsi-
bilities of the Government and People—Failure of the South to
Remedy the National Evil—Duty of National Government—
Importance of This in View of the Future Increase and Position
of the Race—Responsibilities of the White Citizen to the Negro
—Absurdity of the Prejudice on Account of Color—Necessities
of Education and Religion—Elevation or Repression.

ANOTHER distinct source of the excessive increase
of our criminals was stated to be our colored population. Our population of African descent numbered
in 1890 7,470,040.[1] They constitute less than 13.51
per cent. of our total population ; yet they contribute one third of our convicts, though only 8.8 per
cent. of our paupers and a still smaller percentage
of our mutes and insane are found among them.
This statement is so anomalous and startling that it
demands careful investigation. It is very remarkable that a certain well defined part of our people
shall produce both an abnormally large proportion
of criminals and an abnormally small proportion of
paupers supported at the public expense,—this, too,

[1] *Census Bulletin No.* 199.

notwithstanding it is well known that this fraction possesses the least wealth, and indeed is almost universally recognized as very poor and improvident. We would naturally expect, from the well-known condition and characteristics of the colored race, an excess of pauperism rather than a reduction of it to almost a minimum, especially when we find an undue proportion of criminals among them.

How can these two contradictory abnormalities be explained or reconciled ? The colored inmates of Northern institutions for the indigent and defective classes seem to receive the same consideration and treatment from those in charge as the whites. Nevertheless, it may be possible that those who need aid, are deterred to some extent from applying for assistance to public charity by a fear that the colored defective may be subjected to the additional discomfort and annoyance which their experience in life leads them to expect from the large number of foreigners with whom they would be associated in the public asylums and almshouses. This apprehension may induce the relatives and friends of many, who, ordinarily among white people, would be committed to a public institution, to make extraordinary efforts to maintain their needy at home. It is quite possible also that directors and officials are less willing to receive colored applicants than white, and to discriminate against them upon one pretext or another. We have never heard of such an instance, and merely give this as a supposition.

The mass of the colored people resides in the milder latitudes of the land, where there is less hardship

in indigence, where nature provides more of the
actual necessities of existence. Here a less expenditure of money and care is required to prevent
extremities of suffering than in the more rigorous
climate of the North. We may then assume that a
smaller number of the unfortunates would be compelled to call upon the public for assistance. The
dire penury of the great majority of freed farm
laborers and plantation negroes is so narrowly
removed from pauperism that there is but slight suggestion in their manner of living of any advantage
to be obtained from almshouse support. So even the
most abject accept their present lot as inevitable or
impossible of improvement. Provision for pauperism
in the South is, besides, less ample and systematic than
in the Northern States, hence the opportunity of becoming enrolled among the pauper class is greatly
diminished. Indeed there exists in the Southern
States generally no special provision for the poor
or defective members of society. The negro is restricted, if not cut off, from the benefits of the few
institutions open to the white people which are
supported by taxation upon white and black alike.
Although his race constitutes the working class from
which the pauper and dependent are everywhere
mostly derived, he is left by the responsible white
people, with a shameful disregard of the example and
demands of our present Christian civilization and
even of Christian humanity, to shift for himself as
best he can.

Actual pauperism indeed is an inability to maintain life and health in a greater degree of comfort

than can be obtained from alms. Tested by this
definition there probably is less pauperism among
the negroes of America, and probably also among
the negroes of Africa, the native land of the palm
and banana, than among the whites in highly civilized
countries with cultivated wants and impaired physical
and mental efficiency. These are the natural ex-
planations for this pauper anomaly.

As an element of the alarming increase of criminality in this country the colored race presents a
peculiar and more interesting study. It is quite
as important and threatening as the foreign element
which we have considered, and it will require quite
as thoughtful, strenuous, and general an effort for
the correction of the evil tendencies which now have
sway over it, although the initial obstacles to be
overcome are less, and the encouragement to success
much greater than with the immigrants. The most
difficult obstacle of all, that of a foreign language, in
the first place, will not be encountered with this
negro problem. They all understand and speak our
own tongue, though the proportion who read intelligently is much smaller than of the native whites.
The census of 1880 returned only 8.7 per cent. of
our native white people of ten years old and upward
in the whole country as unable to write, twenty of
the Northern States having 3 per cent. and less.
Massachusetts has but 0.7 per cent., while fifteen
Southern States have over 10 per cent., and nine of
these over 20 per cent. Of colored persons ten
years old and upward 70 per cent. were unable to
write. Only 8.6 per cent. of colored children attended

school during the year, and but 7.4 of the public schools were for separate colored children. Their ignorance deprives them of the advantages of the educational and elevating influences derived from our literature and periodical press. This induces them to receive with avidity oral instruction, and renders them especially susceptible to the influences of oratory—stump, platform, or pulpit. This characteristic, which opens to them indeed a wide avenue of instruction, exposes them, on the other hand, to the wiles and sophistries of the intriguer and politician, and makes them a ready prey for the designing. They are consequently easily and frequently allured into political and social movements, the inevitable failure of which leaves them stranded in disappointment and helpless want, or inspired with a desperation which leads to crime.

The inbred habits of life, confirmed by generations of slavery, when all were the property of a master, in common with his flocks and herds, his chickens and his provender, have tended to utterly obliterate all consciousness of *meum* and *tuum*. Especially is this true in respect to right of property in the necessities of life, which they are prone to convert to their own uses in whosoever possession they may temporarily be found. Petty thieving has involved by far the largest number of them in the enumerated criminal class. The serious annoyance to the property owners by this general proclivity among them has, moreover, rendered their white neighbors and "justices" more strict and severe, in the enforcement of legal penalities against them, than is customary against the whites for similar offences. The average sentence of penitentiary convicts in the United States in 1890 is shown by the census to have been for a native white, of native parentage, 5 years and 208 days, that of a colored convict 6 years and 183 days; the average penitentiary sentence in Rhode Island being 2 years and 356 days, and in Mississippi 12 years and 116 days. Those sentenced for life in the North Atlantic and Central group of States were 2.1 per cent. of the whole ; and the life sentences in the South Atlantic and South Central group were nearly 3.1 per cent. of the whole. 2.97 per cent. of the sentences in the North Atlantic, were for life and 5.71 per cent. of those in the North Central, while in the North Atlantic 7.86 per cent. were for life, and in the South Central group, 9.78 were for life. Of all convicts serving sentences for less than life, the native whites, of native parentage, had 64,335 years to serve ; and the native colored, 86,359 years. In some of the Southern States the sentences of colored convicts average nearly double those of white convicts for the same crimes.[1]

Compelled often to steal or starve, and without conscientious scruples to deter them, they fall into the hands of those who know no mercy for the negro, and being without either means or knowledge with which to defend themselves, they are convicted, often on slight proof. They are frequently condemned to prolonged companionship with hardened criminals, in chain gangs and mine camps, where their fellows take delight in completing their

[1] *Census Bulletin No.* 106

destruction and making their enrolment in the criminal class permanent.

Petty crimes, which among civilized white people would not be serious in their consequences to the perpetrator, almost universally in the South condemn the negro to the criminal class for life. So, large numbers are held in durance for acts which would not subject a white man even to arrest. No hand is ever stretched out there to save him when once he falls. Apparently no thought is practically given to the reformation of any criminal there. There are not even State institutions for their confinement, but the poor wretch convicted of crime is leased out to the highest bidder for the profit of the State. Convicts clean the streets chained together, or work upon public improvements, or are marched out surrounded by Winchester rifles, to make railroads or work in mines, to live in huts upon scanty rations.

It would seem to be futile to condemn a system which has been so often branded as a "blot upon civilization," and which is so dreadfully repugnant to the common sentiment of humanity, as is the "convict lease system" prevailing in the South. The majorities of Southern Legislatures insist upon retaining it, contrary as it is to all the principles of modern, intelligent penology and sociology. Inspired by the inordinate and short-sighted economy of first cost, it is wholly destructive of hope for the convict, obstructive of the purpose of legal correction of crime, attended with the brutality and inhumanity of the Middle Ages, and cruelty worse than

Siberian or Algerine administration developes. It is a national stigma and reproach more disgraceful and humiliating than any the world has yet charged upon Russia or Turkey.

Our national honor and reputation are involved in the removal of this curse, this legalized crime, from among our institutions. Our rank and position among civilized nations, and the credit of these beneficent American institutions, which we claim to be the most favorable to human progress, are at stake in this matter. That our criminal statistics reveal an augment of crime of such an amount, from so barbarous a source, compromises and conflicts with all our patriotic boasts. No successful effort for the diminution of the criminal class is possible, while such a system is tolerated. No civilized nation in the wide world of Christendom so utterly ignores the primary principles of penology in the management of its convicts, and in its neglect of reformatory measures, as do these States of the South. Their lack of system degrades white and black alike, as did the slavery of which it is the relic and consequence.

The savage code of slavery still prevails there, in a swift and summary visitation of capital punishment, without trial often, for crimes against the person, so that small increment comes from this source. The main augmentation of criminality is from crimes against property; the severe sentences imposed upon youthful transgressors, who for slight and perhaps first faults are condemned to long association with the depraved and vicious; the entire lack of reformatories for youth ; and a prevalent disposition in Southern society to recruit their criminal gangs for the profit of the State, as they ignorantly imagine. To these also must be added another motive, which, horrible as it may seem, contributes to a material extent in this direction. That is, the practice of instigating the arrest and conviction of persons who become politically obnoxious or hostile to the ruling class, in order to deprive them of their voting power. No one will be found willing to admit the truth of this charge. It is too gross to find a defender. But we are assured by intelligent colored men of the South, that negroes are frequently made convicts to nullify their right of suffrage.

The slaveholder's code in regard to the marriage relation between slaves, which recognized little more of sacredness in it than in the breeding of their brute stock, has left a pernicious and baneful influence on the colored race in America, which is the prolific source of many evils. With strong animalism by nature and cultivation, without much knowledge or experience of virtue and continence, and little moral restraint of conscience among the lower classes of them, sexual sins, with all their deplorable consequences, become common. The responsibilities of parentage are but slightly recognized from a sense of duty, although the parental affection is naturally strong in their breasts. Neither their own public sentiment, nor the interference of the whites, operates to restrain the largest license to lust, which contributes its full quota to their criminal class.

They are also particularly addicted to intemperate indulgence in the use of intoxicants, by nature and habit, on account of their poverty and the paucity of their comforts and enjoyments. Licentiousness and intemperance, the two great and prolific causes of criminality among any people, prevail to an unusual and prominent extent in producing the abnormal results which we are considering.

A public sentiment must be aroused in the South which will exert itself to remedy these evils. It would seem to be wise to set about the matter in an intelligent way. The initiative should be taken by the State Legislatures. The country has waited patiently for twenty years in vain for a movement to ameliorate these dangerous conditions. The colored race is here to stay. In fifty years, increasing with the rate of the last decade, which was 13.51 per cent., they will number fourteen millions in the land. Legislators if possible must be made to understand, and act upon the understanding, without further delay, that the highest interests of the State and the safety of our social organization are only to be promoted and secured by wise measures calculated to elevate society, diminish crime, and reduce the numbers of the criminal class; but that it is foolish statesmanship and false economy to endeavor to reduce the present cost of maintaining prisoners at the expense of these primary and essential objects. Neither their own interests nor the national welfare can allow these Southern States to continue to operate their present criminal manufactories, which turn out one third of all the criminals in the country. If they are too blind or ignorant to see and act of their own volition, a sufficient pressure of public sentiment from the North must be brought to bear upon them to induce suitable action.

So also regarding the terrible incubus of ignorance, which the South permits to drag upon the wheels of our national progress, it must be made to take speedy action. We cannot wait longer in safety. What they have done so far was so plainly and forcibly stated by George W. Cable in his discussion of the " Negro Question," that I venture to quote it here. His figures are deduced from the report of the United States Commissioner of Education for 1883–1884 :

" . . . A century of public education has helped to make Massachusetts so rich that she is able to spend annually $20 per head upon the children in her public schools, while Mississippi, levying a heavier tax, spends upon hers but $2 per head. . . . The public-school property of Ohio, whose population is one million, is over twice as great as that of ten States of the new South, whose population is three times as large. . . . With one third more wealth than Virginia, and but one tenth of the illiteracy, Iowa spends four times as much per year for public instruction. With one fourth less wealth than Alabama, and but one fourteenth the percentage of illiteracy, Nebraska spends three and one half times more per year for public instruction. With about the same wealth as North Carolina and less than one eighth the percentage of illiteracy, Kansas spends over five times as much for public education. Dakota makes an expenditure in the year per capita on average attendance in the public schools of $25.77, being more than the sum of the like per capita expenditures by Mississippi, South Carolina, Tennessee, North Carolina, Alabama, and Georgia combined.

" . . . As to comparative wealth, the taxable wealth of Dakota in 1880, at least, was but one two-thousandth part of that of the six States with which it is compared."

Some effective compulsion of public opinion must be applied; or, if that is impracticable, the national government must again intervene. There is no possibility of healing this national sore without the primary tonic of education.

The political position of the negro on this continent is entirely different from that of any other citizen of the United States; and it devolves upon the white people grave and imperative duties. Unlike all other inhabitants of our country, the negro was transplanted to our soil against his will. These people are not responsible for being here. Their immigration was forced and cruel to a degree which long since incurred the universal condemnation of all Christendom; and it was stopped by the international mandate of humanity. For two hundred and sixty years the negro lived and increased here in the enforced ignorance and savage degradation of slavery, until this wrong and outrage became so intolerable to our advancing civilization, that the nation was willing to expend the blood of half a million of men and over three billion dollars as the price of their freedom. Suddenly transformed by this act from slaves to citizens, without its volition or effective demand, without preparation or the imposition of any test of fitness, it would seem to be self-evident, from the mere statement of these facts, that the whole race is, in the fullest sense, the dependent ward of the nation, and must continue to be so considered and treated, until it shall rise in all respects to a level of equality with its white fellow-citizens, and at least have a fair show in the competitions of life.

REV. C. N. GRANDISON, D.D.   PURE NEGRO.
PRESIDENT OF BENNETT COLLEGE, GREENSBORO, N. C.
EXAMPLE OF THE RESULT OF NEGRO ELEVATION.

Its numbers are so great as to preclude the possibility of their return to Africa, even if this were desired either by them or by ourselves. But it is not desired by either. It would be contrary to public policy, if it were desired and possible. We cannot spare their labor or help. Their generations of nativity here have engendered in their natures the same love of our country, the same loyalty to our institutions, the same patriotism, as white citizens possess. Their language and religion are our language and religion ; they are in every political sense as much a part of the American people as any one is, as essential to, and identical with, the nation, as the whites. Poor and despised, weak and submissive as they still are, they constitute in numbers and usefulness a very important part of the commonwealth, which must remain with us ; and, while preserving its race distinction of color, continue to increase in numbers, wealth, intelligence, influence, and power. The problem which this indisputable fact presents is one of the most serious and difficult presented by our social condition to the statesman and philanthropist of the present day. Its wise solution must include the solution of the question we have before us here.

While our government is not founded upon the parental model, and our public sentiment is wisely opposed to conferring upon it parental functions as concerning the people in general, the inexorable facts and logic of its past relations to the colored race have incontestably installed it *in loco parentis* over this portion of our people, which through its

acts have come into our life and family in the condition of children. It is then the duty of the
national government, representing the national
authors of their being as citizens on this continent,
and because of their helplessness, to protect them
in the enjoyment of equal public and political privileges and rights with the rest of the family. It is
clearly a national duty to secure them from injury,
or imposition by those with whom they have been
brought into association; to care for their proper
subsistence and education, until, as a race, they
arrive at a condition of self-supporting maturity,
and are able to make their own way in the struggle
of life, without handicap or disadvantage on account
of the accident of political birth or minority; until,
in short, they have a fair field and need no favor.
We may as well recognize the fact first as last,—that
the colored man is an integral part of our nation;
that he is destined to remain a member of our
national family, without the assimilation and obliter-
ation which follow the additions we receive from
other races by intermarriage and absorption.

The sooner he is fitted for the fullest enjoyment
of all the privileges of equality, political and social,
the sooner all causes of family dislike, quarrel, disturbance, or hatred will be removed. His color
alone constitutes no reason for dislike, and has in-
herently no element of repugnance. Colored and
white children associate as intimately and affectionately as those of the same color. Colored and white
men and women of equal education and similar
tastes mingle without constraint, in one another's

society and may be mutually agreeable. No white gentleman or lady, except in the South, hesitates to associate with a West Indian or South American or negro gentleman or lady of congenial nature, not even as little as a white laborer dislikes to work alongside of a jolly, laughing, singing negro. Even as slaves the colored nurses and family servants were regarded and loved as affectionately by the master's family as if they had been white, probably more so.

The very essence and purpose of this government "of the people, by the people, for the people," is the widest and most general diffusion of intelligence, prosperity, and happiness. Only in proportion as it secures this for every citizen is our system successful and worthy of loyalty; and from whatever direction it fails in this there is a reflux of danger involving its perpetuity, and even the destruction of the blessings it bestows upon humanity, and its hopes of the future. It is impossible that the equal rights of seven and a half millions of its citizens should be longer denied them with impunity or without real danger.

The South has claimed the right to deal with this question in its own way. We left the solution to the Southern people, and they have demonstrated their determination to continue the policy of repression, instead of adopting the national plan of elevation. In the years during which they have controlled and shaped legislation concerning the negro race they have succeeded in reducing the problem to its original simplicity. A ruling white minority, possess-

ing the wealth, stands over a black majority which
is paid for their labor actually less than the fairly
comfortable subsistence which they received when
slaves ; and denies to them every right of equality ;
except the simple name of citizen. This is as hostile
to true Americanism as was slavery. It has become
so palpable, atrocious, and pregnant a national peril,
as to require national intervention. The natural law
of self-perservation, to which we appealed in the
destruction of slavery, as superior to all other law,
demands the securing of equal, complete, and perfect
liberty to every colored citizen in the country ; and
a sensible political economy requires that these seven
and a half millions, valuable and even indispensable
as they now are, should be enabled to add as great
an increment to the national prosperity and power
as they would if they were equal in education and
wealth to the same number of whites.

Congress must then enforce, by suitable legislation, the protection of the colored race in the enjoyment of the rights it has conferred upon it, in the
face of the world ; the rights " of life, liberty, and
the pursuit of happiness," with equal freedom to
that enjoyed by the white citizen. As this race has
received the right of suffrage without conditions,
Congress must provide security for the fullest exercise of it. Above all must arrangements be made to
afford colored children the amplest benefits of that
common-school education which is generally admitted
to be the fundamental essential of national security,
and of the permanence of American institutions.
Neither taxation of their own industry, nor the

HON. JOHN H. SMYTH. PURE NEGRO.
EX U. S. MINISTER, ETC., ETC., WASHINGTON, D. C.
EXAMPLE OF THE RESULT OF NEGRO ELEVATION.

benevolence of the North, is adequate to meet the needs of these emergent millions. Though the latter has been severely strained in the effort for many years, and has provided education for more than seventeen thousand pupils and supplied more than sixteen thousand teachers for colored schools, this charity has clearly proved its inadequacy. Our national representatives have at last apparently reached a consciousness of the necessity of expending somewhat of our treasury surplus upon fortifications against foreign foes ; but the defence of the national integrity and public health, against the insidious and far more threatening dangers to which they are exposed by the growth and expansion of the colored race in ignorance in our midst, has as yet made little impression upon them.

A few millions of the duties received in the protection of American industries could be annually expended in the protection of American industry, by the elevation of the negro to a higher plane of competition and productiveness as a citizen, without injustice to any, and with the highest advantage to all. This would be done, too, in the discharge of what must be acknowledged as a national obligation, and as some part of the compensation in justice due for the unrequited wrongs of the past.

It is of the utmost importance also that legislation in the North should be directed toward the encouragement and assistance of the colored race in reaching a condition of intelligence and comfortable self-support. They are destined to be the farmers and producers of the South. They must become the owners
6

of the agricultural lands, the yeomen of the tropics, the peers in wealth and independence of the farmers of the North and West. As such they will become, much more quickly and much easier, an element of strength, wealth, and glory to the State, than is possible for immigrants from a foreign land. In the independence and honest patriotism of its agricultural population is the strength and power of any people. If the colored man is made contented upon his farm, he will be much more willing to remain on it, and to avoid the town and city, than the white man appears to be. Schools and colleges must be multiplied for their children, until the percentage of their illiteracy is reduced to a minimum; and the cheap education of the press and all the wonderful dissemination of knowledge which that affords shall be opened up to them.

Penitentiaries and reformatories must take the place of the chain-gang and lease-system. And these must be managed according to the principles of modern penology, to reduce the criminal element by reformation, as in the North. Humanitarian institutions for the care and diminution of pauperism must be organized. White society all over the country has the responsibility resting upon it of insisting upon these reforms; and in the North, of educating the ruling whites of the South to the consciousness of their real duties in these respects. The pulpit and press, patriotic and philanthropic citizens everywhere, must impress this responsibility upon the people continually. Their first effort must be made toward the effacement from the general consciousness of all prejudice on account of the accident of color. It is unnatural and absurd in itself, a relic of slavery unworthy of true manhood, an offence against humanity which is hostile to national welfare, and an insult to the Creator. This arrogation to one's self of superiority on account of race hinders the acquirement of that self-respect by the negro which is the foundation of nobility of character, is contrary to the spirit of our institutions, and falsifies our boasted assertion of complete freedom for development in our country. Where brains, intelligence, and personal ability are the only recognized titles to social rank and preferment, distinctions of birth and race can have no logical or rightful place. Let society be taught to ignore them, as regards the negro, as a patriotic duty. Let every colored man be treated, everywhere in public and in private, exactly as if he were white; according to his deserts as an individual, his merits as a man.

But the white people of this country owe the negro more even than this. By the immutable law of just compensation they are compelled to make good to him the value of two hundred and sixty years of unpaid service, in special effort to restore to him the lost advantages of two hundred and sixty years of civilization.

In whatever the colored race are behind the white, in religion, morals, education, prosperity, and charitable institutions, the obligation rests upon the latter, who have enjoyed them in a higher degree, to contribute from their accumulations until both share alike in these blessings, and an equilibrium is

established.   The social equality which is necessary
is impossible while the present disparity continues.
Not only the national and state governments must
discharge their duty, but the wealthy and benevolent whites, North and South, will have to sustain
more liberally the beneficent institutions already
founded for the education and amelioration of the
negro race—such as Lincoln University, Biddle University, and the Hampton Institute, and hasten to
provide ample means for the training of teachers and
preachers sufficient for the whole race.   The situation is so grave that it will require the united efforts
of all to alleviate it.   The common-school education
must be provided from public funds.   The benevolent care for the needy and defective must be enlarged, the services of the philanthropic redoubled,
to work the elevation and reformation of the degraded and criminal.   But all these must be supple-
mental to the necessary legislation.

The Christian Church ought to devote an increased
zeal and multiplied agencies to instil into the recep-
tive natures of the negro race the salutary and cor-
rective principles of our national religion in their
fulness and purity.

The Christian Church has a double obligation
toward the colored people on this continent.   For,
as to them, there is added to the duty of salvation
for Christ, the necessity of christianization for the
sake of the State and civilization.   Missionary enterprises must be greatly increased among the freedmen.
Religious as they are by nature, for the lack of educated direction their faith and belief are mostly

exercised in transient emotion, and to a large extent are without fruitful development in improved and benefited life. Whatever other doors are open in these days for Christian effort toward the work among the colored people of America, every instinct and motive of Christianity, hopefulness, philanthropy, and patriotism call with a voice that must not and can not be ignored.

If adequate remedies are thus applied to this third part of the national disease, there is every reason to expect, and no room to doubt, that the proportion of criminality among the colored population will soon be reduced to a parity with that of the native whites. Such a reduction, upon the basis accepted in the estimates of sociologists, that every individual reduction in the number of criminals is equivalent to a saving of two thousand dollars in public expense, would be worth to the country in the neighborhood of forty million dollars, and a large portion of this annually.

We have considered the colored element chiefly in its relation to our criminal statistics. "The Negro Question" is the momentous one of our national politics. It has well been termed "the running sore of our body politic," sapping more and more the very fountain of its strength and vitality. But it is not our province to discuss it in general here. Those who are interested in a fuller study of the whole subject, we refer to the thoughtful, temperate, and masterly treatise of George W. Cable, published last year, entitled *The Negro Question*, and to the able representation of what the author assumed to be the correct Southern side of the question, made by the late Hon. H. W. Grady, in the *Century* for April, 1885, entitled *In Plain Black and White.* It must be evident to all, that the differences of the two sections of the country upon this subject are fundamental and irreconcilable. They are as incapable of harmonization and adjustment as they were before the war. The whole administration of the South upon it proceeds upon the false and un-American idea of a servile class, to be maintained in a condition of suppression ; an idea which the welfare of our institutions, society, and government cannot tolerate, and must, in some way, totally eradicate, abolish, and extinguish. The American people, this nation, and its free government are irrevocably pledged and devoted to human progress, elevation, and civilization, without regard to tribe or tongue, sex or color, or any previous condition of nativity, servitude, or intelligence. Let this national adjuration enforce the reclamation of the race which it has made free men : for their sake, if it will; for its own sake, if it must.

The negro question is in no sense a question, as most Southern and many Northern people seem to think, whether the whole negro population of the country can be soon, or at all, so elevated that all of them will be capable and fitted for legislators, Congressmen, and rulers. This is no more to be expected in regard to the negro than the white race. We select all our public officials from a class composed of about one tenth of our numbers, while nine tenths live upon daily wages. The question which is urgent

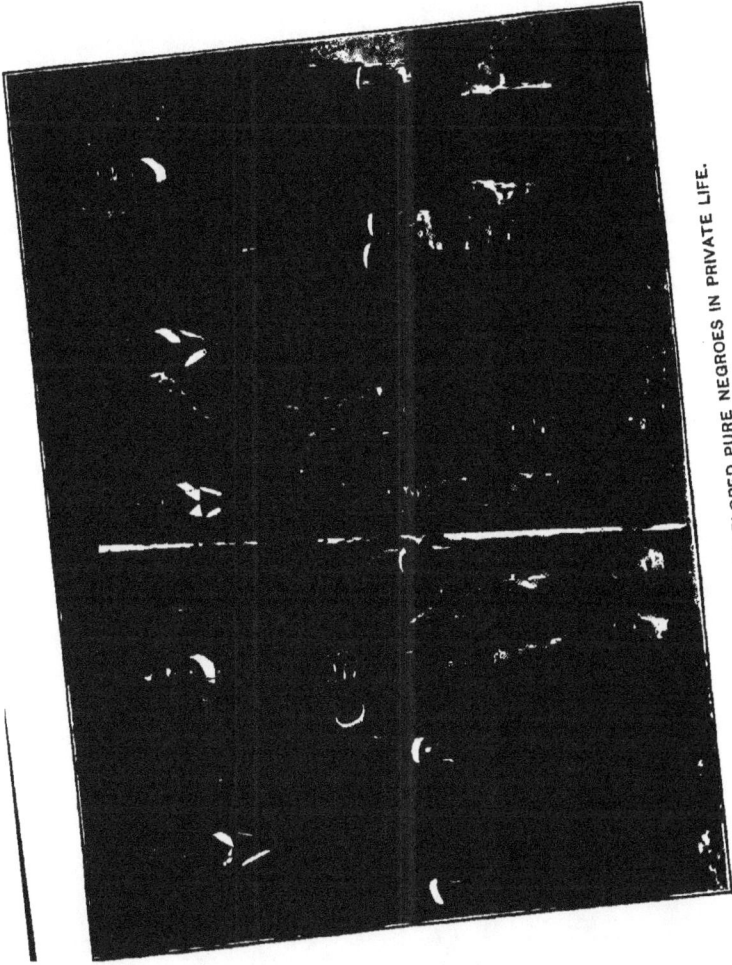

GROUP OF WELL DEVELOPED PURE NEGROES IN PRIVATE LIFE.
THE POLE IS SIX FEET LONG.

and imperative is this: Shall this eighth of our sixty
millions be fitted by education and privileges to make
their fair and equal contribution to public prosperity,
and receive a fair and equal share of its enjoyments
with the other seven eighths? or shall a small minority in the Southern States be permitted to rob the
country of this contribution, and the race of these
enjoyments, for its own selfish, private profit, by con-
tinuing to repress, or neglecting to elevate them?
What answer is to be made?

CHAPTER VIII.

THE URBAN POPULATION AS A SOURCE OF INCREASE.

Contribution of the Urban Population Compared with That of the Rural—Rapid Growth of Urban Population—The.Problem—Its Social Factors in the Three Classes of City Society—Interference with Family Life—Contamination of Children—Neglect of Domestic Duties—Dangers to Youth, of Tenement Life, of the Consolidated Business Systems, of Sabbath Desecration, of Gambling, of Club Life—Evils of Institutional Benevolence.

THE streams of vice and poverty which spring from the three sources to which we have traced them, the native whites, the native colored, and the foreign immigration, flow alike and are augmented alike in their course through the mire and bogs of intemperance, and through the dense population of cities, whose sewage they take up. Intemperance is indicted as the cause of more than 75 per cent. of the crimes committed, while our cities supply about 90 per cent. of the criminals in our public institutions. It may be both interesting and useful then, to consider the effect of intemperance and of urban life upon public morals; to measure them as accurately as possible; to investigate and analyze them, and discover if we can, some means to correct, check, and diminish these contributions to crime and poverty; not only for the sake of reducing the public cost and burden of taxation, but far more, for the benefit of society and the good of mankind. We will confine our attention first to the urban population. The group of States called in the *United States Census* the North Atlantic Division afford the most accurate returns of their criminal population, and exemplify the most advanced treatment of it. These States have been the longest settled of any, and contain the largest proportion of cities. We have arranged the following table to show the relation between criminality and urban population there. The numbers denominated criminals include the inmates of penitentiaries, jails, and reformatories returned in the *Bulletins of the Census of 1890.* The percentage tabulated is that of cities of ten thousand inhabitants and over, of the total population of the several States ; the number of such cities also being given and the total number of criminals :

PERCENTAGE OF URBAN POPULATION AND CRIMINALS
IN CERTAIN STATES.[1]

	Number of cities.	Percentage of urban population to total.	One criminal to every	Total criminals.
The United States....	345	27.6	786.5	79,617
Vermont............	2	7.6	1605.	207
Maine..............	6	17.1	1031.3	641
New Hampshire.....	4	24.7	1137.5	331
Pennsylvania	33	39.1	929.	5,659
Connecticut.........	10	41.8	454.	1,641
New Jersey..........	15	51.	489.	2,948
Rhode Island........	4	57.6	556.	621
New York...........	32	57.8	455.	13,159
Massachusetts........	37	66.	703.	3,182
District of Columbia..	1	100.	548.	370

[1] Collated from the *Bulletin of the Eleventh Census.*

This table is, of course, rather indicative than
absolute in regard to the relation which exists between crime and urban life. However, enough is
apparent to justify closer examination. In general,
and notwithstanding disturbing elements, it will be
observed that the States with more than the average
of urban population have more than the average of
criminals. Also that the distinctively rural popula-
tions of Vermont, Maine, and New Hampshire have
the smallest averages.

The report of the Board of Public Charities of the
State of Pennsylvania, however, affords us an opportunity for a closer examination. The total number
of inmates of the penitentiaries, jails, and reformatories on September 30, 1890, is there shown to
have been 7,320, or one in 718.2 of the population
of the State. Of these the city and county of
Philadelphia supplied 3,200, or one to every 327
of its population ; more than twice the general
average of the State. If now we eliminate from the
record the counties of Allegheny, Berks, Bucks,
Cambria, Carbon, Dauphin, Delaware, Erie, Forest,
Juniata, Lackawanna, Lancaster, Lehigh, Luzerne,
Montgomery, Montour, Northampton, Northumberland, Philadelphia, Schuylkill, Venango, West-
moreland, and York, twenty-three in all, as containing
the principal cities and towns, and on account
of incomplete returns, the remaining forty-eight
counties of the State have a population of 1,673,556
of a distinctively rural character. These counties
are charged with furnishing 401 convicts, and 291 inmates of reformatories on September 30, 1890, a total
of 692 ; which is but one in 2,418 of their population.

The county of Allegheny, where are the cities of Pittsburg and Allegheny, with a joint population of 343,440 out of 551,959 in the county, largely made up by mining and manufacturing towns, supplies 2,023 of the criminal population of the same date, or one in 272.7 of its population. This is nearly three times the average of the State. Philadelphia furnishes about seven and a half times, and Allegheny nearly nine times as many criminals as the average of the rural counties. A similar condition exists in regard to pauperism.

COMPARATIVE STATISTICS OF PAUPERISM BY RURAL AND URBAN COUNTIES AND THE STATE OF PENNSYLVANIA.[1]

	State of Pennsylvania.	County of Philadelphia.	County of Allegheny.	Rural Counties.
Population	5,258,041	1,046,964	551,959	1,673,556
Inmates of almshouses...	9,026	2,877	719	2,075
Inmates of homes, asylums, and other charitable institutions, and receiving temporary aid.........	20,858	16,913	592	5,265
Insane hospitals..........	4,826	1,406	352	2,427
Indigent deaf and dumb.	606	108	86	159
Institutions for feeble minds	800	90	11	58
Other institutions	74	12	5	37
Homes and private families	561	75	31	291
Average daily occupants of hospital beds..........	3,301	2,271	551	30
Institutions reporting.....	183	97	23	19
Totals............	40,052	23,752	2,347	10,342
Percentage of population..	.759	2.268	.425	.618

The above table, collated from the same report, shows the relative proportion of paupers maintained

[1]Collated from the *Report of the Board of Public Charities for 1890.*

at public expense in the State of Pennsylvania, also in the counties of Philadelphia and Allegheny and the rural counties specified above, on September 30, 1890, with the number receiving temporary relief during the year.

This table is not complete as to all institutions, as some failed to report. Also no "temporary relief" is intended for Allegheny County. This is an item of several thousand in Philadelphia, and of 4,630 in the rural counties. If bestowed, it would doubtless increase the percentage of Allegheny considerably. The city and county of Philadelphia had three times the average of paupers in the State, and the rural counties .141 of 1 per cent. less than the average. If we omit the number afforded "temporary relief" in the rural counties as not actually paupers, and because this relief in the country is generally unwisely afforded, the paupers of the rural counties are only .341 of 1 per cent. of their population, only one seventh the percentage of Philadelphia. These comparisons are cited as definite illustrations of our assertion, which will not be contradicted by any one conversant with the facts—that the strictly urban population of our country furnishes about 90 per cent. of the criminals and 75 per cent. of its paupers.

Not only this, but the urban population is increasing with great rapidity. As the civilization of humanity advances, the social instinct seems to grow in intensity. Cultivation, education, refinement, and wealth so increase the wants and desires of mankind that it is both driven by a force like crystallization and drawn as by magnetism to focal centres, which will swell and expand in a geometrical progression. The activities, competitions, conveniences, luxuries, opportunities, and excitements of city life attract high and low alike. When our government was established a century ago, its first census showed only 3.3 per cent. of the inhabitants of the country living in cities of 8,000 and over ; in 1850 this percentage had increased to 12.5 ; in 1880 to 22.5 ; and now, in 1890, cities of 10,000 and over contain 27.6 of our population. During the last decade our urban population in cities of 10,000 and over, now numbering 345, has increased 41.37 per cent. in number of cities and 60.57 per cent. in number of people. This approximates in the increase of population the 80 per cent. increase of criminals in the country. The North-Central and Western groups of States have indeed exceeded this, with an urban increase of 96.07 and 118.13 per cent. respectively,[1] so that the correspondence of this growth with the increase of criminals is in itself sufficient to attract attention.

The recent and novel growth of cities to the enormous sizes that are now becoming common, so largely in excess of the general increase of the population, is undoubtedly one of the potent causes of the abnormal increase of the criminal class. There is no probability that the disproportion between the urban and general census will diminish in the future. On the contrary, as agricultural attractions become less, and the quantity of desirable farming-land not settled decreases, and manufactures and commerce offer multiplied inducements, it is likely to be en-

[1] *Census Bulletin* No. 165.

larged. With constantly cheapening facilities of transportation and intercommunication, permitting the support of more and more people in town and city occupations, it is likely that the close of another hundred years may find 50 per cent. of our inhabitants dwelling in cities. Even were it possible to check this tendency, it might not be desirable to attempt to do it.

The problem then is that of the reformation of city life. There is no sound reason why people aggregated into dense communities by natural instincts, and finding in such communities a mode of living there, superior in physical, intellectual, and moral advantages, should be debased by concentration. Indeed, as those who are first and most attracted to cities are the brightest, most skilful, ambitious, hopeful, and able, the young, the strong and bold, we should naturally expect a constant and rapid improvement in character and morals, rather than a decline of these in the urban population. That we are so greatly disappointed in this expectation must then be due to faulty conditions, which, we think, can be discovered and rectified. It cannot be indefinitely tolerated that society in its highest estate, its most scientific development, of refined cultivation and satisfactory environments, should be rapidly relapsing into vice and immorality. The next step would of necessity be a descent into disorganization. The cycle of modern civilization would complete its round and return, as all others have done, to barbarism, thus leaving the race to begin its struggle again at the bottom.

Our Christian faith rejects such a result as contrary to the will of the Creator, as well as to the scheme and promise of redemption. The upward tendencies of the race in America at the present time are more powerful than the downward. All that makes for good in human life leads upward to strength and vitality, to endurance and power, while the evil debases, corrupts, weakens, and destroys. The vicious and criminal classes are wearing themselves out in ignorance and indulgence, while the moral and wise are lengthening and strengthening their lives. Notwithstanding this, however, the public safety and welfare require the most energetic and immediate effort to correct the evils of our dense society. What are they?

The Creator ordained the family to be the social unit, by a law as immutable as the law of gravitation. Wherever the family relations are distinctly and perfectly preserved, society is safe from internal corruption. Progress, purity, and the millennium are possible. In proportion to the interference with the proper and full development of family life, the welfare of society is endangered, and the elevation of humanity towards its ultimate plane is hindered. Rural life is honest and moral, not on account of any inherent virtue in the countryman, or any other thing in it or him, so much as the privacy and completeness of his domestic relations. Where there is little else to occupy the attention the family becomes the world to its members, and each strives to contribute to the general fund of happiness and hope for the present and future life.

The separate and distinct family is universal in rural life, but the exception as communities become crowded. We shall find, as we pursue our inquiry into the causes of the social corruption of cities and the growth of criminality and pauperism in them, that they are discovered in the various interferences with the integrity of the divinely instituted family which occurs there, in evils which strike the very vitals of social progress. This is the root and germ of a disease with frightful and fatal symptoms. Fortunately, this reduction of the case to a fundamental principle of sociology establishes a basis for unerring diagnostication, and inspires a hope of cure.

Humanity crowded into cities divides itself into three distinct strata in their extreme divergence, although so gradually merging together as to leave no positive line of demarcation between them. At the top of the social scale is the wealthy class, able to live without labor, and to indulge itself in the gratification of most of its desires. Next below is the middle class of workers, living in comfort without extreme luxury. At the bottom all the rest, the largest number of all ; hustled and swirled in the fierce currents of life hither and thither ; packed and crowded into such tenements as are left to them ; mostly unable to procure or incapable of enjoying any but the baser sensual pleasures ; mixed indiscriminately in their habitations, and everywhere with the most vicious of mankind, with everything to corrupt and but little to improve them.

The influences of city life upon these three classes are different in nature and degree. The two upper

are extensively reached by the conservative and elevating privileges of intellectual and religious culture
and stimulation ; the lower but slightly. Wealth,
and the power it confers, tends to engender in the
highest stratum a sense of independence of, and
superiority over, the rules and regulations of human
and divine law. Selfishness and indulgence weaken
the moral sense and physical powers ; the incessant
pursuit of pleasure by individuals disturbs and dis-
rupts family relations ; domestic enjoyment is abandoned for the more exciting attractions of "society,"
and the family home becomes but little better than
a hotel to sleep and eat in when not otherwise engaged. As a consequence, marriage tends to become
simply an arrangement of convenience like the home ;
children are committed to the training of hired nurses
and tutors ; parental responsibilities are ignored or
neglected, and one by one the members of the highest
class sink out of it, by loss of health, character,
or wealth, and it makes its contribution to criminality or pauperism in due time from those ruined
in it. The display of luxury and splendor by
the wealthy also, doubtless, excites ambitions and
desires among those who are unable to gratify
them honestly, which leads to dishonesty and crime.
The inability of many of the young who are in
association with the wealthy, to maintain the expense of a family in the style to which they are
accustomed, operates to discourage matrimony,
and conduces to licentiousness and the increase of
prostitution. It is commonly understood that
social morals and religion are at their lowest ebb

in the upper and nether strata of society the world over.

The great intervening mass of citizens which constitute the social leven, ordained to save the whole lump, are exposed to grave dangers of a different nature in city life. They are subjected to temptations of the most attractive and insidious kinds. Vice clothes itself in its most alluring vesture in great cities. The most capable and skilful of the vicious and immoral naturally seek and find here their most fruitful field of operation, as well as opportunity to hide themselves amid the thronging thousands. Gorgeous saloons for gambling, drinking, and prostitution invite the unwary on all sides, Traps for the innocent are baited with every kind of "entertainment"; names are invented to clothe wrong-doing in the garments of respectability, and the constant, necessary familiarity with the various forms of vice which abound, leads the unwary first to "endure, then pity, then embrace." The density of population affords also opportunity for secret indulgence in sinful practices, without attracting attention. People live for years in houses whose doorsteps are only separated by an iron railing, without knowing one another. Thousands spend their lives in "flats," with other families above and below them, others in hotels and boarding-houses. The husband and father is absent regularly every day at his business, the home deserted ; Sunday, being the only day when the whole family is together, becomes a day of enjoyment and recreation ; religion wanes and dies, and its restraints and elevating influences disappear.

Worse than all, the children are compelled to play in the streets, and to associate with all they meet there; to learn all the evil known by the worst. Here they become familiar with every form of evil and sin. The curbstones and doorsteps of the respectable resident portion of large cities, crowded with children on a pleasant evening, are often a painful sight to a philanthropist. Girls and boys of all ages and kinds, sporting promiscuously of necessity, where every foul nighthawk seeks its prey, lose the lovely innocence of childhood before they reach their teens, and each generation of city growth takes a lower level in purity and morals as its average than the preceding. Parents, too, absorbed in the urgent competitions and activities of business and pleasure, become more and more prone to delegate the nurture and admonition of their children to the day-school and Sunday-school teacher,—often to omit the latter entirely. Family training and duties grow lax as communal social requirements increase. As the divinely-instituted responsibilities are ignored, the conservative and elevating influence of domestic life declines; so the community takes the place of the family.

It is a threatening and dangerous change which substitutes public pleasures for private enjoyments, or a public for a private life in society, obliterating the home from the consciousness and recollections of a people.

An inordinate eagerness to accumulate wealth is inflamed in the ranks of the successful; a speculative spirit akin to gambling depraves honest business principles, and the standards of upright dealing are gradually lowered at the expense of the general average of morality.

This middle class of citizens is moreover largely constituted of new families from the country, seeking wider opportunities for success, or for indulgence. It is continually augmented by the aspiring youth of both sexes, looking for employment. Both families and youth are strangers to the older residents. They are freed from the restraints which have surrounded them in their former homes,—of acquaintance, custom, good habits, friendly advice and influence, and religious counsel and invitation. The youth, especially, enjoying in all their spirited buoyancy an unknown sense of personal freedom, are easily enticed into excesses which would have been repugnant to them in their country homes. There are thousands on all sides eager to introduce them to the forbidden pleasures of the city, and scarce one to invite them within the shelter of improving society, elevating entertainment, or Christian care.

After a laborious day they must return at night to a cheap and cheerless room, or accept the comfort and enjoyment provided so luxuriously for the public. What is the wonder then that the youth fill the theatres, the billiard-, liquor-, gambling-, ill-famed saloons, our jails and prisons, while the old people fill the churches?

The modern disinclination for marriage compels a large influx of girls to the cities looking for self-support; in shops, in counting-houses and offices, where they are forced by disappointment, or by poor

pay and the wily seductions to which they are too
often suddenly exposed, in large numbers, to swell
the "social evil," becoming rapidly one of the most
alarming features of city life. Under such conditions the middle class, must continue to augment its
contribution to criminality and pauperism.

If the life of the upper classes of citizens conduces
to degradation, what shall be said of the lower, and
lowest? What can be expected from the helpless
and hopeless; the dregs of humanity, settled, out
of the ferment of civilization in the cities? Their
want and misery, immorality and vice, have reached
bottom, and can descend no farther with life. The
shocking and deplorable condition of the "submerged" has been forcibly portrayed by General
Booth of the Salvation Army, and other recent
writers. Whole families, (fourteen, even, were
found in one room,) huddled in single garret or
cellar rooms, to feed together on garbage, and sleep
together on rags and straw gathered on the streets;
murderers, robbers, thieves, worn-out drunkards, and
prostitutes crowding together in vile dens; establish-
ing communities which the police scarcely dare enter
after dark; filling single tenements with the population of a village; whole precincts living in actual
if not open defiance of the law of God and man, of
decency, of health, of honesty, social welfare, morals
and religion.[1] Their numbers, constantly recruited
by criminal fugitives from every direction, have no

[1] President Wilson, of the Health Board of New York, published
in December, 1891, a census of 37,358 tenements with 1,225,411
occupants.

thought or study but to prey upon society, and to educate one another in the ingenuities of vice. Few, feeble, and futile are the efforts that are made to rescue or help or save them, and even these are received with a snarl like that with which the hunted street cur takes a morsel from the hand of pity.

Next above these, are found the so-called homes of common honest laborers. Crowded, comfortless, generally dirty; wives and children compelled to companion with criminal neighbors, constantly corrupted by evil communications. The bottle seems to them their only blessing, and opens a wide and easy road to ruin, while penury shuts up every upward way. Skilled laborers and their families in most cities inhabit tenements, common to several families, devoid of privacy and seclusion ; and must permit the children to seek their exercise and play in the streets. Mills, factories, great warehouses, enormous office buildings, collect factory girls, mill-hands, shop girls, type-writers, clerks, office boys, all together in great crowds daily, where they make improper acquaintances, form evil associations, and become the office, shop, and street prey of the designing.

The minions of vice ply them with their seductions, and advertise their allurements among them, as they go and return from work. Considering their youth and inexperience and comfortless homes, the wonder is that so many escape ruin, rather than that so many fall.

Amid such environments society is corrupted chiefly by the frightfully increasing vices of Sabbath desecration, intemperance, fornication, and gambling. To these debasing influences are to be attributed largely the shocking increase of pauperism and criminality from cities. These are the honor des-; troyers; the family disruptors; the youth corrupters; the corroders of vitality; the obliterators of morality; the savage enemies of religion in cities. They assail all classes with equal virulence and assiduity. They are the common enemies of Christianity and humanity, grown already into such proportions and power in our cities as to threaten the public welfare and endanger the State. They have been ignored and tolerated, or unwisely dealt with, so long, that they have acquired a status and strength which displays its arrogance even in the organization of the government which should suppress them. They demand and often receive official protection, instead of police extinction. Public sentiment, even, is half disposed to recognize and accept their presence, as an inevitable necessity. With a contempt bred of familiarity, many question and doubt the possibility of their control or eradication; while their minions and votaries, with amazing audacity, assert and proclaim their immunity from interference. The burglar, the robber, and embezzler might, with equal propriety, make common cause with their pals, and claim a right to exercise, unchallenged, their nefarious professions.

It is high time that society should be aroused from its lethargy concerning these perils. It is absurd that this great people, boasting of its prosperity, happiness, and intelligence, should continue to allow

these prolific causes of vice and poverty to run their
venomous course unchecked through its urban
centres. The results are already appalling. All the
resources of philanthropy, religion, science, and
politics will be severely strained, in the contest with
them. They must all be enlisted for the war, and
the struggle cannot be deferred.

The quiet, rest, peace, and religious observance of
the American rural Sabbath are rapidly disappearing from our large cities; and with them the great
conserving influences which have so largely contributed to our national prosperity and greatness.
The disproportionate tendency of foreign immigrants
to the cities; and their insistence upon importing,
along with themselves, foreign ideas and customs in
regard to the non-observance of the day; the necessity
for the uninterrupted operation of street-cars and
public conveyances; the disregard of the day in
public hotels, saloons, and places of entertainment ;
the demands for Sunday newspapers; the increasing
occupation of the day for recreation by the employed
classes in excursions, visiting, and carousing; the
freedom from restraint allowed those who are inspired
by selfish motives to work on the Sabbath, are all
rapidly tending to break down the sanctity of the
day. The wise and wholesome distinctions between
it and the other days of the week, in the moral consciousness of the people, seem to be fading away.
Sabbath desecrators are strong and urgent, as well
as cunning, in the urban organization. There is
imminent danger of their soon becoming a majority,
obtaining the control of urban government, so gather-

ing power to eliminate the workers' day of rest and the Christian Sabbath from its place among American institutions. The degree to which this has already been accomplished adds a material quota of the urban contribution to the evils we seek to diminish.

Another prolific source of crime and pauperism, in cities, is the gambling spirit which pervades all classes. From speculation in real property or in the paper tokens of property, such as stocks and bonds, and social card-playing for money, down through the gilded gambling-saloons, glittering with an almost regal splendor, and made attractive with almost every luxury of temptation to appetite; through the private poker-rooms of the hotels and liquor-saloons; through skilfully-disguised lottery schemes; plain betting on competitions, on horse-races, on base-ball games; indeed on every undecided event, the desire and effort to acquire the property of another without labor, or without the rendering of a fair equivalent of value, seems to permeate and corrupt a constantly increasing proportion of city people. The inevitable losses which befall the losing half, and the hope of retrieving them where they were made, are the incitements to more frauds, embezzlements, misappropriations, robberies, and even thefts, than are the demands of actual want. There is no good title to property acquired by chance or luck, and its speedy dissipation and loss almost invariably testify to the violation of law and right in such acquirement.

The gambling spirit which seems innate in the lowest conditions of savage life is revived and encour-

aged more in modern civilization among rich and
poor, young and old alike, by the horse-races and
base-ball games which make their annual rounds of
the principal cities, than by any other means. There
is need that strong public sentiment should be
aroused against the sin and crime of betting. This
whole thing is a relic of savage life. It violates the
fundamental principles of social and commercial
honesty, and leads to the commission of innumerable crimes as the inevitable result of indulgence.

Let society set its face sternly against gambling
in all its phases, then, in self-protection. Let efficient
law punish the gambler and bettor as offenders
against social order and public welfare. Like the
appetite for intoxicants, the gambling spirit seems
to grow by indulgence, and when once it fastens
its influence on a person his ruin is almost inevitable.
Those who live by gambling recognize this fact, as
do the dealers in intoxicants. So they make it their
study to ensnare the young and unwary as mere
beasts of prey, heedless of the tears, sorrow, and
suffering they inflict, and careless of the wrong and
cost they impose upon society. Gambling is a crime ;
let the gambler be branded a criminal, and be made
to share the lot of his many victims. The power of
the gambler in politics is sufficient in cities to protect him in open and flagrant contempt of statutes
and public interest. Gamblers control Tammany,
which controls the city of New York, which controls
the state of New York, which controls closely con-
tested national elections, and they are able to
defeat, and have often defeated, parties and candi-

dates inimical to their interests and favorable to social progress.

Another modern development of urban life contrary to nature and prejudicial to good morals is becoming recognizable in the multiplication of "clubs" of all kinds. Some of these are useful as midday resorts for those engaged at a distance from home. Others are unobjectionable when formed for the promotion of a laudable object. But when they become substitutes for home, and are made to satisfy the desires and wants of young men apart by themselves, they deserve the condemnation and discouragement of every Christian, moralist, philanthropist, and patriot.

The *New York City Directory* contains the names of two hundred and forty-two of such clubs as having sufficient prominence to warrant record there. Besides these, there are the unnumbered small coteries, unnamed or unknown beyond their immediate membership, which exist in all parts of the city. This lead of the metropolis is being followed to a greater or less extent in all important cities, and the tendency to club life appears to be growing. Inspired in the inception largely for the comfort and convenience of the unmarried young men abounding in the cities, by providing opportunity and temptation to indulgence of all kinds in comparative privacy, especially for convivial drinking and social gambling, they not only threaten the young there with the dangers of intemperance and gambling, but so ameliorate the loneliness and discomforts of bachelor life as to become an obstacle and hindrance to marriage. It is said that the sales of liquor in some of the most popular clubs in New York exceed those of any bar-room in the city.

But their encouragement to acquire bad habits is a less evil than their discouragement of marriage. To whatever extent they make young men content and satisfied with bachelor life, they hinder his entrance into that relation which has been instituted by natural and divine law as the completion of the social unit, and so become opposed to public policy as well as private interest. One of the main objects of these institutions is to provide a pleasant place in which their members may spend their leisure, to enable them to gratify their need for agreeable company, to supply themselves with the comforts of home, and indulge their private desires.

It must be self-evident, then, that as far as they accomplish their design, they are hostile to domesticity and the family institution.

It should be the first object of a young man upon reaching maturity to render himself complete by the selection and marriage of a wife. A bachelor is but half a social unit, half what he was intended to be, half what he is capable of being ; half in comfort, in happiness and usefulness. Sociologically, the life of a bachelor is of necessity a failure, if not a crime. The bachelor stands but half a chance for success in any respect, relation, or business of life. In these days of competition and emulation, the single man is unable to cope with the pair, which possesses double his power.

A man and woman, with physical, mental, and moral endowments supplementary and comple-

mentary to each other, with an absolute single
and undivided purpose and ambition, without the
possibility of separate or selfish motives, identified
as a social unit, bound together by a natural affection for one another and for the children which
combine them both, whose welfare becomes their
chief incentive, overmatch fourfold the bachelor in
the race of life. Nothing else can supply the value
of a good wife's wit and wisdom and counsel to the
husband she loves; to restrain from mistakes, to
suggest and encourage in noble enterprise, to assist
in all life's work, and above all with kindly hand
detect and check the first steps downward or estray.
With her the husband may confidently discuss and
consider the most secret subjects of his life and
business. No one will watch him with keener anxiety, no one appeal so urgently or powerfully, no one
cling to him so closely.

The hope of the city is in her good wives. No
ambitious young man can afford to be without one.
Nature and Heaven have provided some woman for
every man. It is a duty to society no less than to
himself that the young man should abandon the
club, obey the dictates of nature, and complete himself as a social unit by marriage.

We will discuss the subject of intemperance and
the treatment of criminals more fully hereafter, but
desire in this place to direct attention to a reason
for excessive pauperism in cities, as existing in the
inconsiderate and indiscriminate dispensing of so-
called charity in them. In the city of Philadelphia,
for instance, there is a benevolent institution for

every ten thousand of its inhabitants. Basing their claims for public support largely on the number they relieve, their managers naturally become emulous of making this number as large as possible. As a consequence, it becomes easy for the poor to secure aid from them. Every benefit bestowed, pauperizes the recipient, and so the noble spirit of charity is made to increase the evil it attempts to remove. If an institution can secure support by appropriation from the public treasury, it ceases to that extent to be a benevolence, or charity. Its benefits are demanded as a common property or right. The indolent and improvident exact assistance without even the return of gratitude.

The possessors of great wealth living in cities where so much of human misery appeals to their charity, are, more generally than is supposed, conscious of their responsibilities, and give liberally to those who attempt to relieve it. It is important that an improved system of public charities should be organized in all cities to prevent the abuse of benevolence. The "organization of charity," which has begun under this necessity, ought to be perfected and sustained by law. It should comprehend within its scope the reinstatement of the family unit in its original potentiality in urban life. It must endeavor to adapt the family to its urban environments, and urban environments to the essential family privacy and integrity.

The very plan and method of institutional charity is a mistake in almost every direction. It violates the primordial principle of the social organization

by the effort to substitute communal treatment for
the natural family arrangement. Certain classes of
the indigent may be collected into establishments
intended for their care and improvement, such as the
aged, and infirm, and the imbecile, but the construction of extensive buildings for the accommodation
of large numbers under one management, with a
view to their improvement and reformation, for the
purpose of returning them to society, fitted for self-
support and usefulness, is becoming more and more
manifestly an error.

Humanity confined in an inclosure, as inevitably
finds a common level as any fluid. Nor is that a
fair average level of the combined morality and
intelligence of the mass. The depressing elements
are always the most powerful and numerous. The
most degraded may be improved, but the whole
mass will be infected to some degree with their color
and vice. It is a trite but faithful saying, that one
cannot touch pitch without being defiled. The
general consensus of the wisest students of sociology
is coming to favor a smaller classification and a more
domestic provision for dependants, that which most
closely resembles and reproduces private family
relations in the reduced classification, as most hopeful of wide and permanent success.

CHAPTER IX.

THE URBAN POPULATION AS A SOURCE OF IN-CREASE—*Continued.*

Political Factors of the Problem—Erroneous Principles of Urban Government—Proportion of Urban to Rural Population—Disparity of Density of Population in Cities—Remedial Suggestions—The Restoration of Equilibrium—Importance of Suburban Facilities of Transit—I. B. Potter's Testimony—Results of Bad Country Roads in New York and Good Roads in France—Purification of Suffrage—Improvement of the Police Force—Necessity for Increased Religious Effort.

THESE factors of the problem of city life seem to require the exercise of public power. Law, legislation, and government are needed, which are at present wanting or inefficient. While our national and State governments and institutions are producing results which are the admiration and emulation of the world in the general condition of the governed, our management of the dense aggregations of people in cities is a palpable failure. Indeed, the disproportionate degradation of society in them is not the only indication of this fact. The increased death-rate, the foolish extravagance of public expenditures, the waste and misappropriation of public funds, the corruption and dishonesty of public officials, the inefficiency of the police, the insufficiency of public conveniences, the lack of interest of the taxpayer and voters in local elections, their hopeless submission to the domination of professional politicians, whose only motive is selfish greed, and whose sole ability is to manage elections as "wire-pullers," all testify to the weakness and insufficiency of our system of city government, which Prof. Bryce denominates "the one conspicuous failure of the United States."

It is beyond the scope of our present purpose to attempt the solution of a social problem which has engaged the study of some of the ablest and best-equipped minds in this and other lands without success. If we can here, as we have attempted to do along other lines, put up a guide board indicating the direction of safety and improvement, pointing out the road to be taken to reach the desired end, we shall be content to have contributed somewhat to the economy of the effort which others must expend to accomplish the salvation of our cities.

There have been many cities built on the face of the globe while mankind has been struggling upward,—some of them larger and richer than any of the present age,—which have so completely perished that their very location is either unknown or marked only by mounds of useless debris ; some whose very names have slipped into oblivion, and a soil of potsherds and broken bricks is the only indication of their former existence. So far as history preserves the record for us, their destruction and ruin were the result of the same internal diseases which we have

8

diagnosed as active in our own growing cities. Unless they can be cured by the application of adequate remedies, suggested by the higher intelligence and wider science of modern civilization, the same fate must inevitably befall them as befell those cities of ancient days ; and with them must perish, as heretofore, the nations and people who build them. The subject is therefore supreme.

The first observation we make upon the government of American cities is, that it is instituted in the beginning, contrary to and in violation of that fundamental principle of self-government upon which our successful national and State institutions are based. Our cities are chartered by the State Legislatures. Their legislation and government are largely formulated by an external, superior power, applied from without instead of generated by internal need. We need not pause to explain how this anomaly in American politics has been imposed upon the people. It is sufficient to point out the fact that this great nation of freemen, which has secured for itself unparalleled prosperity and happiness by organizing self-government upon the principle of the New England town meeting, has hitherto omitted and still refuses to confer the inherent right of autonomy upon its cities, the most influential elements of the political entity. It creates them, and restricts them. It organizes them and proceeds to exercise over the organization an absolutism more complete and dangerous than exists in nations which make no assumption of popular freedom. In other lands cities have first achieved a measure of independence, and then accepted or created a general government. Here the order of procedure is reversed.

This is not only contrary to our principles, it not only destroys one side of the united trinity of principle as enunciated by President Lincoln, viz.: " government by the people," and which is a symbol of truth and continuous existence, but it is manifestly, in a popular government, a fatal elision.

It is not to be expected that the rural legislator can understand, or know, or properly provide for the needs of an urban population. Its interests are so intense, so numerous, and so diverse, often of so great magnitude, affecting in so important a manner the rights and privileges of the individual and the welfare of the family, involving questions entirely novel and unknown in country life, that it is almost impossible that any one but a citizen should be qualified to deal with them. Notwithstanding the peril of entrusting the venal, the corrupt, the largely foreign mass of voters in cities with the powers of self-government, however, the first correction to be made is, surely, to confer the most complete autonomy upon the city population ; with simply some wise limitations upon incurring indebtedness, or exercising powers threatening the welfare of society, the State, or other municipalities.

The attempt in Pennsylvania to govern cities by the enactment of general laws applicable to classes based upon numbers, is as ridiculous and iniquitous in practice as it is absurd in conception. Why should 39 per cent. of the people controlling three fourths of the property of the State, living in peculiar envi-

ronments, be subjected to the ignorance, lack of interest, or cupidity of the representatives of the other
61 per cent., who, themselves, are unaffected by the
result of their votes? It is because the State rules
the city that men of ability and prominence give so
little attention to municipal affairs. The appeal for
remedy is to the State, and not to local influence,
therefore interest in self-government dies out of the
breast of even patriotic citizens.

The cities should sustain a somewhat similar relation to the State that the State does to the nation.
There is a far greater differentiation of the seventeen
million of the urban population from the rural of our
country than is found in any other political sub-division. In Pennsylvania nearly two fifths—exactly
2,055,723—of its people living in cities, require
special and peculiar legislation, which they should
be allowed to provide for themselves according to
their respective needs. If they enjoyed this privilege those who have the largest stake in good government would exert themselves to secure it. The
social perils which we are considering would be
treated with the maximum of wisdom and vigor,
because superior wisdom and intelligence, though
confined to the minority, always rules the masses
when it is active and in earnest. Our political experience demonstrates that a majority of voters can
always in time be brought to support wise measures
for the public welfare.

One of the primary objects of good local government in cities should be the restoration of a fair
equilibrium in density of population. The last census

shows enormous differences in the ratios of population to area included in the principal cities, ranging in number of persons to the acre from 4 in St. Paul to 59 in New York. Philadelphia averages 13 to the acre. These ratios have even a much wider range in the closer-built sections of cities, as in New York from 3 to the acre in Ward Twenty-four, to 474 to the acre in Ward Ten ; in Philadelphia from 1 to the acre in Ward Twenty-three, to 163 in Ward Three. The Health Department of New York reported in 1891 a count of 37,358 tenement-houses in the city, occupied by 276,565 families, and 1,225,411 souls. This shows an increase of over 200,000 in tenement population in three years, and an average of 32.8 occupants to each tenement ! The average density of the twenty-two largest cities in the country was 15.92 persons to the acre, so that the greatest density in New York was thirty-two times, and in Philadelphia ten times the average.

Crime and pauperism naturally increase, and church and conservative influences decrease, in a geometrical ratio with the density of the population. It ought to be the province of the government to relieve this social congestion. People do not live in misery from choice, but because they are unable to escape it. Let society, in self-protection, open up the way of escape if it can, and nature will relieve itself. Real estate in cities increases in value according to its accessibility to transportation terminals and occupation centres. The poor abide where they obtain subsistence, because they cannot afford the time and money to live farther away. Offer them cheap and quick transfer to healthier and better homes and they will quickly spread themselves out of their stifling abodes.

It becomes a public necessity, then, to provide rapid and cheap transportation from centres to suburbs. Electrical tram-ways and cable-roads fortunately have been devised as an adequate means of accomplishing this. It would be a reasonable condition of franchise to restrict fares upon roads using the public streets, to two cents within three miles, and to five within ten miles of centres, during the hours between five and eight in the morning and evening. This would tend to diffuse population and reflexively increase the revenue of the roads. As an expulsive measure the Health Department might prescribe the minimum of space and accommodation permissible for individual and family occupation. Capital would thus be compelled to seek more lucrative return from cheaper and better homes, or less valuable lands in the suburbs, and so both ways and means would be provided for a uniform distribution of population. More drastic measures even are warranted if necessary to secure this result. This is one way it may be accomplished, but it must be done some way, to restore the family unit to the " submerged tenth."

It may be remarked in this connection that the improvement of country-roads and the extension of electric tram-ways along the principal highways, with accommodations for freight as well as passenger traffic, would tend to decrease the flow of the popular current from the country to the city.

Very much of the dissatisfaction of the farmer and his children with his lot is caused by the unprofitable return received for his toil, and the seclusion and discomfort of his life. Country life has a thousand charms which would attract, satisfy, and retain a proper proportion of our people if these objections were reduced or removed. It is almost self-evident that no farmer with a smooth, comfortable, and pleasant road leading from his door to a railroad or tramway station, which would rapidly convey his produce and family to the market town, would think of exchanging his farm for a town residence. It is because it costs him more to convey a load of his products to the nearest railway than to transport it thence a thousand miles to market, because during the long periods of bad weather and impassable roads, he and his family are imprisoned on their own limits, shut off from society, from schools, entertainments and all the pleasures of the town, that he is discontented and unhappy. The insignificant moiety of his taxes has little to do with the matter. It is a burden now, as the grasshopper is in old age, for he cannot earn even this. But if he were doing a profitable business, the slight increase or decrease of taxation possible, would be of no moment.

Let us quote from an article of Mr. Isaac B. Potter, secretary of the New York State Roads Improvement Association, in *The Forum* for November, 1891. Mr. Potter is a noted bicycle traveller, who has done more probably to bring this subject to public attention than any one in the country, and will be accorded a high rank among philanthropists as well as among political economists when his work is consummated and appreciated :

" If you will travel one of these roads, going out as near as may be in a radial direction from the market town, you will be interested in noting the gradations of thrift, from good to bad, as your journey proceeds. Leaving the town limits, there will first appear the comely homes and kindred evidences of comfort, which commonly belong to the suburban farmer. The market is just beyond his door-yard, and no condition can be imagined so calamitous as to sever the industrial value of his location. A distance of two or three miles will lead you to a more scattered population, living in homely and more secluded structures, and, in spite of their evident sobriety and industry, surrounded by certain signs of unrequitted toil, while the further progress of your journey will introduce you in due time and with tolerable certainty to a region of hovels and deserted farms. Wherever you go the rule is the same, and it is no exaggeration to say that with the enlargement of concentric circles surrounding every American inland town is to be found an apparently undue diminution of agricultural population, wealth, and thrift.

" In the great State of New York, where the value of farm crops was exceeded last year by those of only two States in the entire Union, the disproportion between the wealth of country and town has become so marked that the officially estimated value of farm-lands last year was less than eight per cent., and that of the incorporated cities and villages more than ninety-two per cent. of the total wealth values within the State."

He quotes Mr. Campbell, of Ohio, as stating that there had been a decline in market value of farm-lands in that State in the last ten years of at least $220,000,000, while the census shows an increase of the aggregate wealth of the State in the same time of $243,000,000, indicating a gain of $463,000,000 in municipal values, against the depreciation of farm values noted. He states the annual increase of farm mortgages to be $8,500,000.

There is no doubt that the inordinate cost of local transport and travel due to bad country-roads is quite sufficient to consume the reasonable profit of agriculture and account for rural discontent. The rural population of France is undeniably the most thrifty and happy of any in the world, domestic life there the most contented, and the family relations the most carefully maintained and sacredly guarded. As a consequence the immigration from France to America from 1873 to 1890, inclusive, has been only 1.5 per cent. of the total arrivals here during this period. France is the only European nation whose people our inducements fail to attract.

Burdened with an enormous and increasing public debt, the necessity of maintaining as great a military and naval power as Germany, she has borne the cost of two wars since our own, and paid five milliards of francs war indemnity, without inspiring in the minds of her people a hope of improving their condition by immigration, because her general government has built over one hundred and thirty thousand miles of good smooth roads, and spends some eighteen million dollars annually to keep them in repair. The territory of France is about equal to that of New England, New York, New Jersey, Pennsylvania, and Ohio, which States waste annually much more than this sum upon their roads in work that is washed away by the first shower. What a transformation would be effected in the condition of the rural population of these States if they were provided with roads equal to those of France, and how sensibly would the congestion of their cities be relieved.

The reflux toward the country has already begun among the wealthy and those who can afford a country residence with city business; it is certain to increase in proportion as the decrease of cost in time and money brings this within the range of possibility for the masses.

A proper protection and purification of suffrage in cities is also essential to their good government. The control of affairs must be wrenched from the hands of professional politicians, who maintain their power by venal and corrupt methods and by partnership and collusion with the keepers of brothels, liquor-saloons, gambling-dens, and with thieves. Last fall the Tammany Society again carried the State of New York by rolling up a larger majority in the city than could be overcome in the country. The 83 leaders of this Society the New York *Evening Post* lately classified as follows: "Twenty-eight professional politicians, 1 convicted murderer, 1 tried for murder and acquitted, 1 indicted for felonious assault, 1 indicted for bribery, 4 professional gamblers, 5 gambling-house or 'dive-' keepers, 4 liquor dealers, 5 former liquor dealers, 3 former pugilists, 4 former 'toughs,' 6 members of the Tweed gang, and 17 office-holders." These "fellows of the baser sort" control the city and State of New York, and sometimes the national elections by the perversion and corruption of, and frauds upon, the right of suffrage, as flagrant and outrageous as any committed in the South. They impose upon the ignorant foreigner, who abounds there; they purchase the vote of the poor, impress that of the criminal, and are always able to base their estimates unerringly upon majorities corresponding to the fund available for use. Similar organizations exist in almost all the great cities. Safety requires special regulation of the act of suffrage by each city for itself, so that the will of the majority of real and actual citizens may obtain control, and keep it.

The recent tremendous tendency of immigration to our cities, magnifies the importance of a careful execution of our naturalization laws; while the magnitude of the multitude applying to the courts for citizenship renders this almost impossible. Our city papers report many instances of immigrants being endowed with the full rights of American citizenship, who have complied with none of the important conditions; who have been in the country but a few months; and who know so little of the language, as to be actually ignorant of what has been bestowed upon them. One of the most valuable results, a registration of all immigrants, whenever, and wherever they make their residence, would conduce to the correction of this abuse.

An autonomic municipality should and would greatly improve its police. It would recognize its increased dependence upon it, and the importance of making it the absolutely safe reliance which it should be. The municipal police is the public executive force, the manifestation of the authority and power of the people's government. Instead of being the tool of politicians, it must be made entirely independent of and superior to partisanship. It should be so organized that it will be recognized and respected by all as the representative and agent of the public in the suppression or regulation of whatever is injurious to the peace, health, morality, general intelligence, and thrift of the community, and its internal safety.

Its officers should be selected after suitable examination as to physical, mental, and moral fitness; held responsible for obedience to superiors, as in the army, only to lawful orders ; and liable to dismissal, only after trial, for the failure to execute municipal law and regulations ; or for the misuse of authority. Instead of occupying themselves chiefly in the arrest of law-breakers, they should make it their first care and duty to prevent crime, and the infraction of the laws ; to keep public places and streets free from obnoxious characters and nuisances ; to return wayward children to their homes and parents ; and warn the latter of their neglect of duty ; and to bring speedy aid to the injured or distressed. A wisely-selected and well-trained police force could accomplish more toward the reduction of public expense of crime and poverty, than any other instrumentality. To its present inefficiency in these respects, in most cities, is to be charged a very considerable portion of the excessive cost to the public of criminals and paupers, and the alarming urban increase of this.

We enter into the consideration of this subject more fully and in detail hereafter. It is sufficient here to suggest the importance and usefulness of a better police administration than is at present enjoyed in most of our cities.

Indeed, in all the departments of city government; of health, highways, light, water, and transportation; the need is not greater for honesty, than for special knowledge, science, skill, and experience in their management. Citizens are learning this, and if left to their own selection, the responsible heads of these departments would soon come to be elected for fitness, rather than for political partisanship. Local politics should be entirely separated from State, or national partisan elections and parties.

Under an autonomic government, whatever else might be found necessary to be done for the cities' welfare, could be readily and quickly inaugurated, as soon as it should become manifest, while it might cost more ability and effort to secure the power from the State, than any citizen, or number of them, could be brought to exert.

The redemption of the urban population, however, is not to be expected from the government alone, although this may facilitate it. Government may restrict and abolish drinking-saloons, gambling-saloons, and brothels. It may punish vice and crime; it may chase immorality from public sight. It must provide for the helpless indigent, and put forth effort to reform the criminal in its hands. But the reformation and elevation of society at large devolves upon philanthropy, patriotism, and the church of Christ.

The increase of urban population has outrun the comprehension and effort of all these agencies. There is need of a great awakening and revival among them. Dr. Josiah Strong, in his great book entitled, *Our*

Country, which ought to be put into the hands of every school-boy and immigrant, gives some interesting statistics on this subject[1]:

"According to the last census there was a Protestant church organization to every 438 of the population of the country ; including, of course, the 27.5 per cent. of urban residents ; but, including missions, in Boston, only one to 1778 of its population ; St. Louis, one to every 2662 ; excluding missions, in Cincinnati, one to 2195 ; in Buffalo, one to 2650 ; in Chicago, one to 3601 ; in Brooklyn, one to 2997 ; in New York, according to the police census, one to 4006. In 1851 Chicago had a Protestant church to every 1577 of its population ; in 1880, one to 3062. Brooklyn had in 1850, one to 1760; in 1880, one to 2673. New York in 1850 had one to 2442 ; in 1880, one to 3048. According to this there has been an excess of growth about 33 per cent. in numbers above the increase of church accommodation in New York. Dr. Strong adds : " These three cities seem to be exceptional only in degree. So far as I have made investigations, there is a general tendency, with variations, in the growth of urban population, to outrun church provision."

" In Chicago there is a certain district of which a careful examination has been made, and in that district, out of a population of 50,000, there are 20,000 under twenty years of age, and there are Sunday-school accommodations for less than 2,000. What wonder that the police arrested last year 7,200 boys and girls for various petty crimes ? There are 261 saloons and dago shops, three theatres, and other vile places, and the Christian Church offers Sunday-school accommodations for only 2,000. In the Fourth and Seventh Wards of New York there are 70,000 people and seven Protestant churches and chapels ; in the Tenth Ward, 49,000 people and two churches and chapels ; south of Fourteenth Street there is a population of 596,878, and only 110 Protestant churches and missions. It was stated by Dr. Schauffler, in 1888, that during the preceding twenty years nearly 200,000 people had moved in below Fourteenth Street, and seventeen Protestant churches had moved out. One Jewish synagogue and two Roman Catholic churches had been added, making a net decrease of religious centres of fourteen."

[1] *Our Country,* p. 185.

Some tithe of the great wealth of our cities must be expended to raise the average of urban church accommodation to a closer accordance with that of the country at large, if we are to hope for an equal average of prosperity and morality in our cities with the country.

The Young Men's and Young Women's Christian Associations must be more generously supported and encouraged in their fruitful work among the throngs of homeless youth in city streets and boarding-houses. Societies to succor the poor and assist them to self-support; to kindle anew the spark of hope in the breast of despair; to enforce parental care and education for children; to find country homes for the little waif and outcast; to aid discouraged families to leave the rookery and tenement and secure suburban residence; to teach English to the foreigner; to instruct the children; to visit the public institutions, the jails, and prisons; and strive to become acquainted with and gain the confidence of the inmates, so that some may be rescued from the ranks of criminality,—all these must be organized and made efficient, and supervised by some general authority, as the common duty of philanthropy and patriotism.

A recent and most promising agency for the redemption of the city is that " Salvation Army " which had its birth in the slums of London. Their dress and ways are not those of the churches, but they are evidently reaching down into social depths and darkness which the churches cannot penetrate. They have rescued and reclaimed and hopefully con-

verted over twenty thousand out of the ranks of the
" submerged " during the last year in America.[1]
Wherever they plant themselves, these consecrated
ones who abandon the world for Christ, the leaven
of Christianity begins to work, even in the ferment-
ing mire of the bottom. Whether their methods
are agreeable to our tastes or not, they are successful.
Let us give, then, our God's speed and our support ;
they are cleansing the very fountains of vice and
want, and saving those who are beyond all other
reach.

[1] Statement of Commander Ballington Booth.

CHAPTER X.

Idleness Due to Inadaptation the Prolific Cause of Crime and Poverty—Result of Inability to Meet Novel Requirements—Industrial Education the Remedy—Polytechnics and People's Palaces
—Especial Need in America—Elevate Idleness to its Work, or
Transport it to Where it Exists.

THAT idleness is the mother of mischief is a trite
phrase, but that it expresses one of the eternal veri-
ties, applicable to all conditions of humanity, each
step of change and progress of the race confirms. It
is the idlers of mankind who fill its poor-houses and
prisons. The industrious and frugal not only take
care of themselves, but are compelled by the instincts
of human brotherhood and the necessities of self-
protection to take care also of the idle and vicious.
A broad generalization of analysis divides society
everywhere into two classes—the independent and
the dependent. The economical instinct, no less than
the divinely inspired one of charity and desire for
the general elevation and regeneration of the race,
impels and compels the former to strive continually
to reduce the members of the latter class.

The conditions and environments of urban existence have not as yet adapted themselves to a natural

9

and fair relation and proportion between these two classes ; or, rather, the two classes have not properly adjusted themselves to these conditions for the maintenance of due proportion between themselves. The social condensation by steam and electricity has been too rapid and forcible for free adjustment. As a consequence, the most capable, intelligent, and alert to take advantage of the novel opportunities have acquired affluence and wealth, while the mass, who are bewildered and impotent, amid the altered requirements of society, is enormously increased. The abilities which were adequate to an honest content where maintenance was secured under simpler conditions become insufficient in the complex competitions of science and skill. Human desire is ever for something beyond, higher and better than what it has. Possession never satisfies. Old fields of labor are deserted as new ones are developed. The occupations of the past have become and those of the present are fast becoming as obsolete as the trade of the flint arrow-head maker. The skill of the former generation is either common or not needed in this, in which, nevertheless, a thousand new calls are made for it.

It is this lack of adaptation, rather than lack of disposition, which augments the ranks of the unemployed in cities, which constitutes the army of the idle there, the swelling source and fountain of the appalling stream that our cities pour into overcrowded asylums and prisons. There is work enough, pay enough, bread enough for all, everywhere ; there is anxious desire to transform work into bread and

content, but the progress and refinements of civilization have pushed work up out of the reach of many,
and their willing hands fall down into idleness, into
want, into crime, into desperation, because they are
found unable and unfit. Health and a common-school
education alone are no longer sufficient, in cities, to
satisfy the needs of all the bread-winners, and so
the great mass of them has become discontented,
desperate ; and, ignorant of the causes, of the whys
and the wherefores, prodded by the spur of want,
like a lumbering blind giant it strikes out in wrath
at whatever attracts its attention. So nihilism seeks
the life of Alexander of Russia ; anarchy schemes, and
the hungry besiege the palace of William in wealthy
Berlin ; communism plots in Paris ; angry workmen
parade the streets in London; "knights of labor"
secretly discuss, combine, strike, and run wild riot in
America. Dissatisfaction with what is, pervades the
workers universally, and even faith in God is shaken.

The throes which convulse the social status of
cities indicate the imminence of a new birth of humanity. If the physicians are prompt and the facilities ample, the deliverance will be safe, and the
result an elevation and advance of the race unparalleled in its history. Neglect, misinterpretation of
the signs, or faulty appliances are full of peril to
society and progress. Adaptation is the panacea of
the present, the balm to ease the new birth and calm
the turbulent waves of popular discontent. It well
behooves the independent, the powerful, the wise,
the wealthy, to act the faithful physician, to provide
and apply this remedy.

As work cannot be brought down again to fit the abilities of those who want it, the abilities of those who want must be elevated to work.

There is demand everywhere for intelligence, science, and skill at large pay, limited solely by ability. It is far beyond the supply. Its growth with accelerating rapidity outruns the supply. New and extraordinary effort is required to quickly increase the supply to equal the demand. More and more of the skilled must be moved up into the rank of the expert, and their places filled by a much greater promotion from the mass of the unskilled, until only enough common labor is left to do the common work of the world. This will solve the whole difficulty, transform commotion into content, eliminate the contribution of enforced idleness from the criminal and pauper class, and tend to restore urban society to a natural condition.

This is not a theory but a fact, abundantly demonstrated by tentative experiments in various localities and in a variety of directions. One phase is well illustrated by the results which have followed the general establishment of " business colleges," in consequence of the enlarged demands of modern business for clerical service. Their graduates have become so plentiful that an advertisement in a city for a bookkeeper, clerk, or stenographer will overwhelm the advertiser with applicants for situations at less pay than ordinary artisans receive. So, also, the learned professions are overcrowded by the colleges. In some American cities, the appreciation of this need has been evidenced by the donation of millions of dollars by various individuals to enable the children of the poor to fit themselves for the fullest employment of their abilities, notably by Peter Cooper, in New York, in the foundation of the Cooper Institute ; by Stephen Girard, in Philadelphia, in the endowment of Girard College ; and lately by the munificent provision made by Mr. Drexel there for the training of the children of artisans, and the bequest of Peter Williamson for this purpose.

Probably the most complete and perfectly adapted institutions in the world, to satisfy these requirements of the age, are the Polytechnics of Quintin Hogg, and the People's Palace, of London, described by Albert Shaw in the *Century Magazine* for June, 1890. They had then become so successful, and had so fully demonstrated their utility, that the Charity Commissioners were about to appropriate three million dollars to the founding of others in the city ; and the writer expressed his confidence that the near future would see from nine to twelve of these admirable polytechnics in different parts of London. They are carefully calculated for the physical, mental, and moral improvement of the children of the poor, between sixteen and twenty years of age, at a minimum of cost to them. To this end gymnasiums, swimming baths, athletic games and careful physical training, night schools, with scientific and theoretical instruction in technical and trade subjects, lectures and entertainments, reading-rooms, libraries, etc., and religious instruction and meetings, are provided, the object and result being to fit these youth for a higher degree of usefulness than would be otherwise possible, to increase their earning capacity, and, in short, to enable them to adapt themselves, if they will, to the advanced requirements of human living.

Such institutions are more imperatively required in American cities than in other countries, because our very declaration of principles guarantee to all the people freedom to find their highest happiness; otherwise there must exist here an oligarchy of wealth, and a slavery of labor, more intolerable than the African slavery which perished in the Rebellion.

Our city life has outgrown the public school. The poor and middle classes of society need more than it provides. Their children need a larger and more practical training to prepare them to meet the demands of these times. Their physique must be improved, their dexterity increased, their associations and ideas elevated, their hands trained to skill in new trades and arts, their minds instructed in the theories, principles, and science of their work, their morals cultivated and strengthened.

All our cities must provide for the adaptation of the rising generations to the probable needs of the coming time, for the general advantage indeed, but especially to reduce the herds of the idle—the prolific source of crime and poverty. This provision cannot safely be left longer to the bequests of the benevolent. It has become a necessary function of government; as imperative as the public school, as palpable and obligatory as the provision of almshouses, asylums, and prisons, and a thousand times better.

A fraction of the sums expended in maintaining these would be sufficient to transform idleness into earning, and largely empty them of their inmates; an ounce of prevention, equivalent to many pounds of ineffectual cure.

It will be necessary to remove those who are incapable, by nature or disposition, of adaptation to a higher life to the simpler requirements of the country, to locations where labor suitable to their abilities is in demand. The time has come when the public welfare requires not only that the advantages of adaptation shall be general and sufficient, but also that the privileges of a constant and even equilibrium of work and labor shall be maintained uniformly, and without friction. The ease and economy of modern facilities of travel and transportation, in America certainly, have not only made great famines impossible, but human idleness inexcusable. If the hands are unfit, and cannot be made fit for the work at hand, let society see to it that they are taken where fit work waits.

We have thus endeavored to emphasize the centripetal social forces of advancing civilization, to expose the dangerous heats developed by this concentration, to direct attention to the unnecessary public waste and dross of the operation. We have explained in detail some of the more prominent sociological extravagances and evils in the upper, middle, and lower strata of the people in cities, and suggested correctives. We have shown the weakness of our urban political organization, the horrors, harm, and needlessness of overcrowded areas; how a more even distribution of population is to be maintained, city government improved, political and social tonics administered, and how idleness, the chief source and fountain of crime and pauperism, is to be reduced and dried up. A full consideration of the conditions is essential to reformation. " Knowledge is the wing wherewith we fly to heaven."

The evils of city life are numerous, insidious, complex, terrible, and stupendous, but not necessarily fatal or incurable. Remedies are known and accessible for them all. This rapid age of energy will brook no delay in their application. Promptitude, faith, and invincible courage may yet redeem this highest development of our civilization from cancerous corruption. Let us then begin at once the attack upon the germs and roots of disease, and cease the concentration of our treatment upon the purulent surface indications.

CHAPTER XI.

WE have attributed the abnormal increase of
criminality and pauperism in the United States
largely to an increase of intemperance. Alcoholic
drink is estimated to be the direct or indirect cause
of 75 per cent. of all the crimes committed, and of
at least 50 per cent. of all the sufferings endured
on account of poverty, in this country and among
civilized nations.

The terrible effects of this curse of humanity are
displayed to all the elements of our population, the
native, the foreign, the colored, and the urban alike.
It smites the citizen and the countryman, without
distinction of either race, color, sex, religious belief,
education, present or previous condition, with its
subtle and virulent poison, and the lovely bloom of
innocence, manhood, nobility, honor, and honesty
fades from face and character, and the horrid signs of

137

sensuality, immorality, and depravity appear. Once inoculated in the system, it creates and nourishes an appetite which grows upon indulgence until it becomes irresistible and overmastering.

The very first effect the habitual use of intoxicants has upon persons is to make them untruthful. No sooner does one begin " to drink " than he begins to lie. He first deceives himself concerning the power of the habit ; he denies the practice to others ; then he begins to lie about anything to subserve his purpose ; next he lies without purpose, and, finally, he lies when the truth would better suit his purpose. The truth is not in him ; it is all burnt out. This is the invariable course and the constant result. Every one who has carefully observed the downward career of one who indulges in alcoholic stimulant is cognizant of this. The inference is common where a truthful person begins to lie, although no other evidence is apparent, that he has begun to drink. All drunkards are liars.

Whatever the physiological effect of alcohol is upon the brain and nervous system, and science demonstrates that it is serious and great, it certainly so disarranges, distorts, and unbalances their natural functions as to first impair and then destroy the power of accurate perception, judgment, and expression. The habitual drunkard probably lies without being conscious of it. Now when the mental and moral faculties are thrown out of gear, the actions of which they are inceptive are erratic ; they no longer follow the straight and direct course of truth and rectitude. Errors of judgment, errors of speech, errors of conduct result. Error is the essence of crime, and of the mistakes of management and life which lead to failure and poverty. When the errors of action become so great and hostile to society as to require repression and correction, they become crimes, and the perpetrators criminals.

Alcohol, therefore, is in fact a natural and actual cause of criminality. It is not simply a contributor, stimulus, and inciter to crime ; not only an accessory before the fact, and author of degeneracy, but the real first cause in all cases where no *alibi* can be proven. This is so rarely possible that Alcohol is to-day cited before the Bar of the Public Welfare to plead to this indictment, which has been framed after due and diligent inquiry and careful examination made as to the facts.

BEFORE HIS HONOR,
JUDGE COMMON-SENSE,

and twelve good men and true, sworn as a jury to fairly try and decide upon the evidence submitted.

THE PUBLIC WELFARE *vs.* ALCOHOL.

INDICTMENT.
A true bill.

Signed,   HUMANITY, Foreman.

In the Court of Public Welfare of the People of the United States.
General Sessions, 1891.

THE PEOPLE OF THE UNITED STATES, SS.:

The Grand Inquest of the People of the United States, inquiring for the Public Welfare, upon their

respective oaths and affirmations, do present : That
Alcohol mixed, incorporated, and disguised in various
enticing and acceptable intoxicating drinks, the same
being brandy, gin, whiskey, rum, wine, porter, ale,
and beer, did in the year of our Lord one thousand
eight hundred and ninety, in the domain of the
United States, and within the jurisdiction of this
Court, corrupt, debase, and deprave 59,703 members of the Body Politic, and cause the same to
perpetrate various heinous crimes against the peace,
prosperity, progress, and dignity of the People, so
that it has been necessary to confine them in Penal
Institutions, and thereby the Public Welfare has
suffered loss and damage, to the amount of
$119,406,000.

And the Grand Inquest aforesaid, upon their
respective oaths and affirmations, do further present, that the said Alcohol, mixed and disguised as
aforesaid, hath, in and before the year of our Lord
one thousand eight hundred and ninety, in the
domain of the United States and within the jurisdiction of this Court, corrupted and incapacitated
for self-support 36,522 members of the Body Politic,
so that they have become a charge upon the People
for their maintenance in almshouses, whereby the
Public has suffered loss and damage to the amount
of $73,044,000.

And the Grand Inquest aforesaid, upon their oaths
and affirmations, do further present : That the said
Alcohol, mixed and disguised as aforesaid, in and
before the year aforesaid, within the jurisdiction of
the Court, hath impaired, maimed, weakened, and

destroyed the soundness of the brains of 48,767
members of the Body Politic, so that it has become
necessary to confine them in Asylums for the
Insane, and maintain them therein, whereby the
Public has suffered loss and damage to the amount
of $97,534,000.

And the Grand Inquest as aforesaid, upon their
oaths and affirmations, do further present: That
the said Alcohol, mixed and disguised as aforesaid,
hath afflicted the aforesaid loss and damage of $289,-
984,000 upon the People of the United States, in and
before the year of our Lord aforesaid, within the
jurisdiction of this Court, against the peace and
dignity and prosperity of the People, and contrary
to the first law of nature and of God, recognized,
obeyed, and maintained universally, not only by this
people and nation, but by every people and nation,
by humanity at large, by every individual of the
race of mankind, by every animal and living thing
that has come from the hand of the Creator, to wit,
namely, the *Law of Self-Preservation.*

Signed : PHILANTHROPY,

Public Prosecutor.

WITNESSES.

E. C. Wines, D.D., LL.D., Rev. Jos. Strong,
D.D., Chief-Justice N. Davis, Hon. M. H. Dickinson,
Hon. Sanford M. Green, Hon. Alfred Hand, Hon.
Robt. T. Porter, Dr. T. J. Morton, *et al.*

Public Prosecutor.—May it please the Court and
gentlemen of the Jury. It is not intended to encum-

ber this trial with evidence beyond the scope of the
indictment.   There are other and much more serious
indictments pending against the prisoner at the bar,
for fraud, embezzlement, theft, robbery, burglary,
arson, assaults, maiming, manslaughter, murder,
seduction, fornication, rape, adultery, incest, sodomy;
for inhuman cruelties to wives and children; for
causing one third of all the diseases of the people;
for causing the death of sixty thousand of our people
every year; for the destruction within the last century of more of the general earnings than the cost
and value of all the public improvements made on
this continent, including all our railroads, canals, and
telegraphs.   These indictments may be tried at
another time; we refer to them only to show the
general animus of the prisoner, and that this indictment is not the only one or the most serious found
against him.   Nor is it for the first offence; on the
contrary, it appears from the records that he is one
of the oldest criminals at large in society; the chief,
the leader, the king of all the vicious and criminal
class.   We have attacked the head in the confident
expectation that if we crush that we shall paralyze
the whole loathsome train which depends upon it.
Neither shall we attempt to excite your sympathies
by a rhetorical arraignment, depicting the soul-har-
rowing incidents and concomitant circumstances of
these crimes specified and charged.   The loftiest
eloquence, the most convincing arguments, withering
invective, the finest arts of vituperation of the grand-
est intellects have exhausted their powers in vain on
this subject.   Your time, patience, and oaths require

a decision upon the facts which are submitted in evidence, and upon these we rest our case.

THE PRISONER PLEADS NOT GUILTY.

Public Prosecutor.—We offer in evidence chemical analyses of the various liquors specified, showing that brandy, gin, whiskey, and rum contain from 40 to 50 per cent. ; that wine contains from 7 to 20 per cent. ; that ale and porter contain from 5 to 7 per cent., and that beer contains from 2 to 10 per cent. of pure alcohol.[1]

That it is the stimulating and intoxicating element of all these beverages.[1]

That the definition of the word intemperance, in this trial, is excessive indulgence in intoxicating drink. Also, the American table of mortality, adopted by the State of New York as the standard for valuation of life insurance policies, giving the " expectation of life " of persons thirty years old as 30.3 years ; also the annuity table of the Equitable Life Assurance Society, showing present cost of annuity of $100 for a male thirty years old to be $1,652.50, and for a female of the same age $1,697.50 ; from which it appears that $3,305 is the cash value of an annuity of $200 to a male of thirty years of age. Also statements of various sociologists and physicians, too numerous to specify, that the foundation of intemperate habits is almost universally laid before the victim has reached the age of thirty years.

[1] *Century Dictionary.*

E. C. Wines, D.D., LL.D., President of the International Penitentiary Congress of Stockholm, author of *State of Prisons in the Civilized World,* etc., etc., *testifies :*

"Intemperance is a proximate cause of a very large proportion of the crime committed in America. Fully three fourths of all the prisoners with whom I have personally conversed in different parts of the country admitted that they were addicted to an excessive use of alcoholic liquors. . . . In a circular letter which I once addressed to the wardens of all our State prisons, this question was put to them, among others : ' What is your opinion as to the connection of strong drink and crime?' The answers were all one way. Mr. Pollard, of Vermont, did but echo the general sentiment, though he put it more sharply than most, when he said : ' My opinion is that if intoxicants were totally eradicated, the Vermont State Prison would hold all the criminals in the United States.' " [1]

William Tallack, Secretary of the Howard Association, London, England, author of *Defects of Criminal Administration, Penological and Preventive Principles,* etc., etc., *testifies :*

"It is unquestionable that, in most countries, the worst sufferings inflicted upon women, children, and dumb animals are perpetrated under the influence of strong drink, for this is provocative of both cruelty and lust. . . . Most crimes must be and are attributable to intemperance. . . . What is the origin, in innumerable instances, of the wretchedness of those homes which it is a calamity for a child to be born into? It is intemperance. And what is the *main* source of that poverty which causes so many children to be either neglected or driven into evil courses? Again it is unquestionably intemperance." [2]

---

[1] *State of Prisons,* pp. 113, 114.
[2] *Penological Principles,* pp. 296, 300.

Chief-Justice Noah Davis, of the New York Supreme Court, *testifies :* " Among all causes of crime, intemperance stands out the unapproachable chief. That habits of intemperance are the chief causes of crime, is the testimony of all judges of large experience." [1]

Dr. Harris, of the Prison Association of New York, *testifies :* " That fully 85 per cent. of all convicts give evidence of having in some larger degree been prepared or enticed to do criminal acts because of the physical and destructive effects upon the human organism of alcohol." [2]

The State Board of Charities of Massachusetts, in their report of 1869, *testify :* " The proportion of crime traceable to this great vice (intemperance) must be set down, as heretofore, at not less than four fifths."

Hon. Sanford M. Green, Judge of the Supreme and Circuit Courts of Michigan, *testifies :* " That it (intemperance) is the parent of pauperism. That it is the chief cause of crime." [3]

John C. Park, District Attorney of Suffolk County, Mass., *testifies :* " While District Attorney I formed the opinion (and it is not a mere matter of opinion, but is confirmed by every hour of experience since) that ninety-nine hundredths of the crime in the Commonwealth is produced by intoxicating liquors."

J. Wilson May, District Attorney of Suffolk County, Mass., *testifies :* " According to my official

[1] Address before the National Temperance Society, 1878,
[2] *The Relations of Drunkenness to Crime,*
[3] *Crime,* p. 37 *et seq.*
10

observation, drinking in some form is directly responsible for about three fourths of the crime that is brought to the cognizance of the county."

Judge White, of Pennsylvania, *testifies :* " After fifteen years on the bench I believe four fifths of all crimes committed are the result, directly or indirectly, of the use of intoxicating liquors. Three fourths of the expense to the State for the prosecution of criminals is attributed to the same cause." [1]

Hon. Alfred Hand, ex-President Judge of Lackawanna County and ex-Justice of Supreme Court of Pennsylvania, in a letter to the writer, *testifies :*

" In the trial of criminal cases in Lackawanna County during ten years it was constantly forced upon my mind, that the great cause of crime, overtopping all other direct causes, has been intemperance. The estimate of crimes due to intemperance, which my observation compels me to make, I place at the minimum, at 75 per cent., and I at one time so stated in Court. It was the same estimate made by Judge Davis, of New York, which I found was fully borne out in Lackawanna County. The exact figures, I am confident, would go above rather than below this estimate."

Hon. Mahlon H. Dickinson, President of the Board of Public Charities of Pennsylvania, *testifies,* by his report for 1890 :

" That 82.7 per cent. of the commitments to the Penitentiaries of Pennsylvania in 1889 were addicted to the use of alcoholic drink ; that over 87 per cent. of those sentenced to county jails and workhouses in that year were addicted to alcoholic drink ; that over 42 per cent. of the youths committed to the Huntingdon Reformatory admitted the use of alcoholic drink, 22.7 of whom acknowledged intemperance ; that of the 5,265 township poor relieved, 408 were recorded intemperate ; that only 66 per cent. of those receiving out-

[1] Address, Pittsburg, May 28, 1889.

door relief because of destitution on account of permanent disability claimed to be abstinent ; that of those relieved for temporary disability only 54 per cent. claimed to be abstinent ; that 110 cases of 1,634 admitted to insane hospitals were directly due to intemperance, more than double the number attributed to any other definite cause, except "ill-health."

The report of the Allegheny County Workhouse, *testifies :* That of 52,783 prisoners received since 1869, over 83 per cent. were addicted to alcoholic drink.

Dr. Thomas J. Morton, Chairman Lunacy Committee of Pennsylvania, in a letter to the writer, *testifies :* "A careful consideration leads me to believe that in probably one half the cases of insanity, or about that percentage, the causes will be found in intemperance directly or indirectly."

Dr. H. M. Wetherell, Secretary of the Lunacy Committee of Pennsylvania, *testifies* in a letter to the writer :

"From my experience and observation of a very large number of cases, and of the records of each year, as well as from my hospital observations, I fully believe that it would be well within the limits of fact to state that one half of all the cases of insanity is attributable to intemperance."

Mr. Fisk, in a report of the United States Commissioner of Education, 1871, *testifies :* "At the Deer Island House of Industry, Boston, 88 per cent. of the committals were for drunkenness and 93 per cent. of the confinements were connected with strong drink."

Charles S. Hoyt, Secretary of the State Board of Charities of New York, *testifies :*

"After an examination made of the inmates of the various poor-houses of the State in 1875, numbering 12,614, that 84.36 per cent. of the males and 41.97 per cent. of the females were intemperate ; and of 4,047 insane examined, 79.21 of the males had been intemperate, and 21.44 per cent. of the females."

Hon. Robert P. Porter, Superintendent of the Eleventh United States Census, *testifies* :

" The number of convicts in penitentiaries of the United States June 1, 1890, was 45,233 ; the number of prisoners in county jails 19,538 ; and the number of inmates of juvenile reformatories was 14,846 ; a total number of inmates in all penal institutions, 79,617 ; the aggregate of inmates of almshouses was 73,045 ; and the total number of insane persons treated in public and private institutions during the year 1889 was 97,535, an increase in nine years of 73.53 per cent. The annual cost per head for the number of insane treated was $161."

Hon. Edward Atkinson, *testifies* : " That the average expense of individuals in the United States for fuel, food, clothing, and shelter does not exceed fifty cents a day, and that the average earnings of all classes engaged in useful occupations must equal $600 per annum."
The taking of testimony is closed.

THE PRISONER IS DUMB BEFORE THE COURT.

Public Prosecutor.—May it please the Court and gentlemen of the Jury. We make no comment upon the evidence. It is plain and sufficient. The indictment charges a minimum sum of damage to the public, much less than is commonly estimated by competent authorities, on account of these persons now supported at the public expense. This sum is found by multiplying three fourths of the number of prisoners and one half the number of paupers and insane by $2,000, which is taken to be the value of each individual to the State when he becomes a public burden.

It is well known that the foundation for intemperate habits is laid under thirty years of age. At this age the average earning capacity of a male in this country is $450 per annum. At an average cost of fifty cents a day for maintenance, or of $138 per annum, the average annual addition of each individual to the general profit or advantage is equal to $263. We admit that intemperate habits have diminished the expectation of life of these individuals one third, and that therefore $2,200 would be sufficient to purchase an annuity of $200 for the diminished expectation. We are also willing to throw off $63 from the annual average profit of these persons to the public, on account of depreciated value of service ; and to assume, in accordance with the well-known estimate of Hon. D. A. Wells, that the value of these lives to the country was but $2,000 each. We ask you to find a verdict of damage of $2,000 each to the people for these lives changed from productive efficiency to a public burden, on account of the ruinous action of alcohol upon them, and to enable you to impose an equivalent fine. We ask that the Court charge that the time of this action is self-evidently in accordance with the indictment ; that the jurisdiction of the Court is unquestionable ; that the law and statute violated are as charged, and so leave the case upon your consciences, gentlemen of the Jury.

Charge of the Court.—The fact of the confinement of the persons enumerated in the several penal and eleemosynary institutions of the country, at the time stated in the indictment, if sufficiently proven, establishes without the necessity of other evidence the fact that they were, and are, within the jurisdiction of this Court, and that the reasons and causes of their confinement must have, of necessity, existed in and before the time specified in the indictment. Moreover, whatever causes the loss or destruction of human energy and productiveness in the social organization, whatever renders it impotent as a contributor to the welfare and prosperity of the community as a whole, or imposes instead of such contribution a tax and burden upon the other portion and remainder of society, violates, and is contrary to the universal sway, domination, and authority of the Law of Self-preservation, the first law of nature. It is, therefore, a proper and undeniable function of the public to lay its hand upon, arrest, and exact compensation from the violator and offender.

If, therefore, you find from the evidence before you, that the prisoner at the Bar has caused the loss and damage to the public welfare charged in the indictment, you will find for the People ; if, however, you find that the prisoner indicted is not proven to be the cause of such loss and damage, or that, if the cause, yet of a different amount, you will so make your verdict. This the law of common-sense.

After consultation the jury present their verdict.

The Court—How say you, gentlemen of the Jury: Guilty or not guilty?

Foreman—Guilty, your Honor, as charged in the indictment.

The Sentence of the Court—Let Alcohol stand committed until he shall have paid the People $289,984,000.

How shall the sentence of Common Sense be executed, and the fine imposed upon Alcohol be collected?

There has been, during the last fifty years, and particularly in the last decade, an astonishing increase of beer drinking in this country. Beer is the common and cheap stimulant of the poor and lower classes of society, which, on account of their larger numbers, furnish the largest proportion of criminals and paupers. It would seem, therefore, when we discover an abnormal increase in the consumption of beer, co-incident with an abnormal increase of criminality, knowing the physical and moral effects of alcoholic stimulant upon humanity, that there must exist the relation of cause and effect between these facts. This assumption is confirmed also by the fact that in other civilized countries, where statistics show no such alarming increase of crime, the per capita consumption of stimulants has not unduly increased. Indeed in Great Britain, where the increase of criminals has been less than that of its population in the decade, there has been a corresponding decrease in the consumption of intoxicants.

The tables appended[1] display the consumption of intoxicants in the United States, and some foreign countries at different periods, and some other interesting data concerning this. From which statement it appears that the consumption of distilled spirits per capita, has not materially changed, even in fifty years, in this country; but the consumption of malt liquors has increased 738.1 per cent., contemporaneously with an increase of 445. per cent, in criminals in fifty years; and 109 per cent. against an increase of population of 24.5 per cent in ten years; more than four times as fast. In the United Kingdom, on the contrary, there has been a decided decrease in the per capita consumption of all intoxicants, and, as elsewhere noted, in criminality. It may also be noted that the Treasury Department reports "From the data accessible to these authorities, the consumption of alcoholic liquors in the arts and manufactures in the United States, would appear to be between 7 to 10 per cent. of the entire consumption. At least 90 per cent. then, of the distilled spirits used in the country has been consumed as beverages."

The monstrous increase of criminality, so far as it is caused by intemperance, must then be attributed to the increase of beer drinking. The temperance agitation, which has been active so many years, and the license system, have signally failed in America to check the rising tide of intemperance, or to restrain the consumption of alcohol within the limits of parity even, with our growth in numbers. The

[1] See Appendix I.

temperance reform has been effective in the classes of society which it has been able to reach as a moral movement. The decanter has been banished from the sideboard, and the wine bottle largely from the table of the educated, "well-to-do" classes of society. But beer sáloons and beer drinkers are constantly multiplying. Political prohibition has proven unsuccessful in most localities for lack of general popular support. The people may come to such a universal intelligence as will enforce prohibitory legislation, but they have not reached that plane as yet. The temperance reform has failed, not on account of any lack of intrinsic truth, force, or need, but chiefly because it has been allowed to become obscured and confused, as a strictly moral movement, against the individual or personal sins of appetite and avarice, and made no effective effort to restrict the multiplication of drunkards by procreation. It has been impaired by a complication with politics and civil legislation, which in America are, of right and necessity, distinct and separate from matters of religion and morals ; but, especially, because it has not extended its influence very much into the intemperate classes of society. It has been embarrassed and impeded, also, by the License and Prohibition ultraists among its promoters, who with violent vituperation and intolerance of adverse opinion endeavor to achieve spiritual success with carnal weapons, and so excite and organize an unnecessary opposition and unpopularity.

The license system is unsound in principal because it gives governmental protection and sanction to a traffic which is an intolerable public injury. It is a mistake and fallacy of statecraft, because it increases an evil it is intended to diminish. European nations have discovered this fallacy in licensing the " social evil," and are abandoning that experiment. We must soon follow their example in this respect in our dealing with the saloon. Absolute prohibition is unsound in principle, because it is an attempt to reform society by ballot : as unnatural and impossible a purpose as to attempt to legislate people into Christianity. The " Prohibition " idea has no logical or authorized standing in American politics. It is contrary to the spirit of American institutions, in the proposed restriction of personal liberty of action which it involves, and therefore it invites the opposition of political judgment and sentiment. As American society is at present constituted it is evidently impossible of attainment, even if all the expected relief could be secured from it, which is doubtful. The mass of mankind will not submit to dictation and interference in matters of taste, appetite, or of morals, however much such submission would conduce to the benefit of either the individual or the mass. The progress of civilization and elevation has always been by gradual advance, by progressive steps, by evolution, rather than by revolution, edict, or legislation.

If, therefore, it is impossible, as it appears to be, to prevent the consumption of intoxicants by law, let us see if we cannot discover some plan which will receive the support of the public, and effect a partial relief, if not a complete deliverance ; suggest some

practical method of legislative action which will promote and assist, instead of impeding the progress of
the temperance reformation of society. Some common acceptable ground must certainly exist where
the great majority of the people will take a stand,
and present an united and invincible front against
this fearful evil of intemperance. It is too tremendous and alarming to be ignored.

Such a basis of action must be harmonious with
the inborn and cherished principles of general liberty
and personal freedom upon which our institutions
are founded. Political action must, we believe, be
directed upon the thing itself, without reference to
the personalities involved ; it must aim at the protection of society from the injury and burden it inflicts,
by securing compensation, as far as possible, for
them. Let us eliminate from the whole subject the
personal equation, when we deal with it politically,
and the strength and vitality will quickly vanish
from the opposition leagues which are now united
upon a plea of self-defence. Legislation cannot cure
the evil, but it may provide protection from its consequences. It may require compensation in behalf
of the public for the damages it inflicts. This is a
legitimate function of government. We propose
that Alcohol, the pernicious element in all intoxicating beverages, *shall be made to pay as it goes.* That
it shall be made to settle its own bill every year,
instead of fraudulently devolving it upon innocent
tax-payers.

Let Congress substitute for our present internal
revenues and tariff laws upon the subject, a tax upon

the percentage of alcohol contained in distilled spirits, wines, and malt liquors, manufactured or imported for use as beverages, of an amount per gallon sufficient to defray the entire cost to the country of maintaining the penal, reformatory, deaf-mute, blind, and insane hospitals, inebriate and idiot asylums, and almshouses of the country, as shown by the reports of the preceding year. The proceeds of this tax should be divided to the States according to their respective expenditures for these purposes. The grievous burden would thus be transferred from the people in general, and laid entirely upon those who of right ought to pay this cost; namely, those who drink.

In the table [1] we have calculated that a tax of $3.00 per gallon of pure alcohol would add to the first cost of distilled spirits $1.50 per gallon, to wine 30 cents per gallon, and to malt liquors 15 cents per gallon, according to the general average of alcohol contained in them. Also that this tax would have yielded, in 1890, a revenue of $268,000,000, which would probably have about equalled the expenditure for the maintenance of criminals and paupers. If it is objected that the entire cost of these classes should not fairly be laid upon alcohol, we answer that the enormous expense for buildings and accommodations already incurred, and of maintenance for centuries, has been paid by the general public,— an expense which it will take alcohol a long time to reimburse. No charge is included in this estimate for the costs of arrests, trials, convictions, or the spoils

[1] See Appendix I.

of prey. This would require an increase of only 60
cents per gallon in the present tax on spirits, and a
trifle over $3.00 per barrel on beer, while it would
effect an actual reduction of duty on wines, the use
of which is already decreasing. It would not be prohibitory on account of an increase of cost of drink to
the poor, although it would probably restrict the consumption, which is the main object to be effected.
It would, in effect, doubtless add one cent to the
price of a glass of beer. There was a very decided
reduction in the consumption of distilled spirits
following the imposition of the present tax. We
should expect a similar reduction if it were increased.
There would be a check to the disproportionate increase of the consumption of beer. Crime and pauperism would decrease *pari passu* with a decrease in
consumption and revenue from the tax, so that a
constant equilibrium would be maintained. The
public appropriation of this revenue to the support
of criminals and paupers would be, moreover, an
omnipresent argument before the people for temperance ; more cogent, practical, and universally applied
than any other that could be made. The whole question of temperance, license, and prohibition, would
thus be taken out of politics. The liquor dealer's
organizations would dissolve, and temperance resume
its appropriate place among the other virtues, to be
inculcated and promoted as honesty, chastity, religion, and charity are.

We are confident that this plan offers the easiest,
soundest, most practicable, and hopeful solution of
the economical and political part of this greatest of

social problems. It is constitutional; it accords with
American principles of government; it infringes
upon no personal or individual rights or privileges;
restricts no freedom of will; interferes with no one's
fancied right to deal in, or use, strong drink. It
simply abolishes the unequal and annoying system
of license machinery and espionage, imposes the
financial burden where it justly belongs, and fulfils
the highest purpose of government, by the protection of the governed.

This done, religion, philanthropy, and humanity
can devote their undivided and unhampered attention to the prevention and cure of intemperance and
drunkenness among the people, with faith and hopefulness. Let us then abandon the misdirected efforts
of the past, and all unite in this one purpose, almost
sublime in the simplicity of its grandeur, *to make
Alcohol pay as it goes.*

Whether drunkenness or dipsomania is a physical
or mental disease, an uncontrolled habit, or a sin,
it is unnecessary for us to discuss, for our present
purpose. Our opinion is that in some cases it is a
disease, in others a habit, and in all a sin. The experience of mankind from the beginning down to the
present has established one thing indisputably, that
the introduction of alcohol into the system excites
a tendency to repetition, and that every repetition increases this tendency; that the tendency, if
unchecked, invariably becomes overmastering, and
results in such a weakening of will-power, moral
consciousness and intelligence, that the victim is
finally reduced to a mere animal, as cruel as a hyena,

and as sensual as a hog. Modern science has likewise positively demonstrated that this tendency to
drunkenness is often hereditary, and may be communicated, like other characteristics, from parent to
child ; and that children begotten or conceived under
the influence of alcohol are inevitably depraved or
unhealthy. It seems also to be contagious and
communicable by intimate association. Unique
among the diseases which afflict mankind, in the
universality and unremitted diffusion of its terrible
ravages upon the race, the iniquity of its uniquity is
tremendously magnified by the fact that it is the
only disease for which there is known an infallible
cure—the certain and practicable specific, abstinence,
voluntary, or enforced.

We have proved that intemperance and drunkenness are the direct or indirect cause of most of the
crimes, and much of the suffering and want of
society. In view of this fact, who can deny the
right of society to legislate logically for its treatment and cure? as it legislates concerning its
kindred affection of insanity. It is, indeed, not
only a right, but a duty of self-preservation, especially where the evil grows so rapidly as it now
does in this country. The present legislation relating to drunkenness is based upon no correct or
general principle, and is entirely inadequate.

In the first place, we believe that drunkenness
should be made a crime in itself by law, as it is in
fact. Instead of this, criminals are permitted often
to urge it in court as an excuse for crimes committed
under its incitement. They plead drunkenness, or

the influence of liquor, with the brazen assurance
with which temporary insanity is offered in extenua-
tion of guilt, when it should be held as an aggravation, because the criminal generally stimulates his
courage and stupefies his moral sense for the purpose of facilitating his crime. If the drunkard were
liable to arrest and punishment for the mere fact of
drunkenness alone, the fear of the law would restrain
many from those first steps which lead to absolute
ruin, if the penalty were sufficiently severe. The
first offence should be punished by solitary confinement for from ten to thirty days, the second from
thirty to sixty days, the third from sixty to ninety
days. The next conviction should consign the culprit to confinement at self-supporting labor in a
State asylum, house of correction and reformation,
if it should be preferred to so name it, not to be
released until a competent authority should pro-
nounce that a permanent and reliable cure had
been effected.

It is a reproach upon our intelligence and civilization that a drunkard must commit some additional
crime before he can be confined, in Pennsylvania,
for even sixty days, when it is known that in most
cases, at least six months or a year are necessary to
restore the drunkard to a normal condition of physical and moral health. Whether drunkenness be a
disease or a habit, it is certainly beyond the control
of the victim. No one can doubt this who has
witnessed the remorse and anguish, or heard the
vows and oaths never to touch the accursed cup
again, which often follow a debauch. These are

as sincere and earnest as any pledges made by man, but broken almost as soon as made. Nor can any one who has heard them doubt the necessity of external aid and treatment of such a sufferer, sufficiently prolonged and enforced to re-establish a healthy operation of the personal will, if this can be effected, or indefinitely, if it cannot be. Our laws afford no means of extending this aid to the victim of intemperance, or of protecting society, or him, from its dangers. We provide institutions for every class of defectives but drunkards, the largest and most dangerous, as well as the most hopeful of cure of any. Hundreds of thousands of our best and brightest minds go down yearly to the drunkard's grave, to a horrible physical and spiritual death, because society fails to do its duty to them and for them. Every one of them, without exception, could be cured and saved. Their blood is upon our heads ; society must answer for it. We must not permit this awful and useless loss to continue. This "government for the people" must take hold of these helpless ones and put them in a place of safety and cure.

Every State should have Reformatories, to which drunkards should be sent, voluntarily, upon application to the court by friends, or upon arrest and conviction, where, under the skilled care of medical men and moral teachers, they should be confined until cured. Those who are unable to pay the cost of treatment and maintenance should be obliged to work at profitable labor, and the excess of their earnings distributed to those dependent upon their support.

11

The record of the Keeley Bichloride of Gold Institution at Dwight, Ills., is given as 95 per cent. of cures out of over twelve thousand cases, most of them the most hopeless and obdurate, with whom every other effort had failed. Whatever may be said against this method of dealing with drunkenness, it certainly succeeds. We have personal knowledge of many confirmed inebriates who have been restored to a normal condition of health and appetite, with no more desire for liquor, apparently, than existed before they began to drink. Some may again succumb to temptation and fall, or the latent fires burst out again ; if so, they will fly again to the physician ; but as months pass and the condition of health grows stronger, faint hopes become absolute faith, and it would seem that at last humanity had triumphed over its arch enemy. It is the duty of the State to supply this or any other tested cure to its drunkards.

Other inebriate asylums in this country, and in other lands, have also restored a large proportion of their patients to sobriety. The Christian Home, in New York, has saved hundreds ; it is claimed by its managers at least 75 per cent. of those committed to it ; the Franklin Home in Philadelphia, and the " Rescue One " mission of Col. W. W. Hadley in New York, have been very successful, relying solely on the saving efficiency of the Holy Spirit of Christianity. The Binghamton Inebriate Asylum, in the sixteen years of its existence, treated over four thousand and restored 61 per cent. of its patients, although the legislation for the purpose was inadequate, and the science of the subject not as well understood as at present. The failure in obtaining the highest success in asylum treatment, hitherto, has been found to be due to the impossibility of retaining the patient under restraint long enough to build up the natural functions of body, mind, and morals, to a condition of health and strength sufficient to resist the temptations to which they originally succumbed. As soon as the inebriate has recovered an apparently normal tone of system he insists upon his cure and liberation, although it is manifestly contrary to reason and common sense that habit or disease of ten, twenty, or thirty years' duration should be permanently eradicated in a few weeks or months.

The medical profession, scientists, philanthropists, and Christians, all who have given the matter proper consideration, agree that quarantining of the inebriate, the application of proper remedies, and time, will, in a much larger proportion of cases, effect a positive cure of this terrible affliction than can be predicted of any other serious ill to which flesh is heir. Where cure is impossible, confinement will at least prevent indulgence and propagation. It seems inexplicable that State hospital treatment should have been so long delayed, or that any reasonably intelligent legislator should now oppose it.

There can be no doubt that State institutions, under proper management and organized with adequate control over their patients, would accomplish more for the relief of human misery and for the public benefit than all the almshouses, insane, deaf and dumb, and blind asylums together effect. Let the next step of the temperance reform then be to secure the enactment of legislation for the establishment of State inebriate asylums and the care of drunkards. These would depopulate in time the almshouses and asylums for the defective, and save each year their cost in the reduction of taxation.

I believe the majority of voters also will favor, generally, as it does in most States, the absolute prohibition of the sale of intoxicants to minors, insane, idiotic, or intoxicated persons, drunkards, those whose relatives or friends or poor directors give notice should not be supplied, United States troops, State militia, prisoners, and paupers; the soliciting of others to drink; the sale on the Sabbath, on election day, or within a block, in cities and towns, or a mile, in the country, of public schools, churches, assemblies of people for religious purposes; fair grounds, military encampments, in jails, prisons, almshouses and public buildings; the furnishing of liquor on pass-book or store orders, for goods of any kind, and the collection of dram bills by law. The majority would also favor making whoever supplies liquor to a person who should commit crime under its influence liable for the damage done, the incapacitating manufacturers and dealers in intoxicants for jury duty, and the requirement of scientific temperance instruction in the public schools.

Let adequate penalties be imposed for infraction of these simple prohibitions and requirements, and then let all the complicated, confusing, diversified and inconsistent license laws be repealed. They have been tinkered and experimented with in this country ever since the first settler landed, and the consumption of alcohol has steadily increased under their protection and fostering authority until the hideous results have become the heaviest burden upon public prosperity, and a nightmare in almost every family in the land.

How many hundred years of experience will be necessary to convince the American people, ordinarily so quick to profit by these lessons, that the license system is not only a failure but a public iniquity? It would seem that an increase of over 100 per cent. in the consumption of beer, and of nearly 54 per cent. per capita increase in the consumption of intoxicants in ten years, should be enough to appall the most indifferent and phlegmatic citizen. Where is this increase to end? When is it to stop? These are questions that touch every heart and every pocket-book in the land.

We have purposely avoided the introduction into this discussion of the more serious evils and losses to the country on account of intemperance, and confined our attention to its influence upon crime and pauperism. The physical, intellectual, and moral degradation of the race, the weakness and disease it imparts to succeeding generations, the harrowing bodily and mental suffering it causes, the direct and indirect cost in cash it inflicts upon the country (estimated by competent statisticians to be at least $2,000,000,000 per annum, with a present annual increase of $500,000,000) all these we leave for others to present. The totals are too great for ordinary comprehension. We simply state the parallel facts of abnormal increase both of criminality and of intemperance, and appeal to our fellow-citizens to make one pay for what it produces of the other, as a fair and just relief of the burden of taxation, and efficient preventive measure ; to retain the present prohibitions; provide for the cure of the drunkard, and repeal all license sanction to the liquor traffic, in the full confidence that Christianity and philanthropy in such a fair field will be equal to the emergency.

There are two things which we have to recommend to philanthropy as a means to reduce intemperance among the people which have not been as yet adequately tried, but which, we believe, would be most effective. The first is this : Supply a satisfactory substitute for the liquor saloon. Man is a social animal. He will go out nights where he can meet his fellows and have amusement and entertainment of some kind, different from what he can find even in a comfortable home with a congenial family. The very poor are fairly driven out of their lodgings for any comfort or pleasure. The door of the saloon is invitingly open to them everywhere. Their innate sense of fair dealing compels them to drink before they leave as compensation for rest, fire, and company, if nothing else impels. But once inside there are plenty of other inducements to drink. It is largely because liquor saloons offer the only free and common resort for the poor, that the poorer classes drink the most, and consequently populate our prisons and asylums. We must accept the situation as it is. We must deal with man as we find him if we are to expect success.

Establish coffee- and tea-houses, social halls, with neatly sanded floors, cheap tables and comfortable chairs, where a good cup of coffee or tea can be had at about cost, say two cents; or any of the non-alcoholic drinks, with oysters, sandwiches, crackers and cakes, pleasantly lighted and warmed; where smoking is allowed, and pipes, tobacco, and cigars furnished cheaply. Let them be supplied with newspapers, periodicals, and games; and whatever attraction, music or entertainment can be afforded, in style suited to the tastes and requirements of the poorest. Let there be apartments for families and women. Then the groggeries would soon lose a large portion of their customers; the reform of life would begin naturally, and the waste of dram-drinking be checked where it is most severe.

This is no experiment. The project has been in successful operation for some time abroad. It is one of the most fruitful and beneficient methods of General Booth, and the Salvation Army, and has been attempted upon a limited scale and in various cities of our own country. We need these social halls multiplied and convenient in all the densely populated quarters of our cities. Alcohol plants half a dozen brilliant saloons in a block, and they are profitable out of the scant and hard won earnings of the poor. Let us have at least one life-saving station to every half dozen false beacons it sets up, and I am confident the result would be grand beyond our hopes.

Another project is also based upon the old adage, that "the way to a' man's heart is through his stomach." I believe that much of the intemperance of the poor is due to bad cooking. An early and hastily prepared breakfast, a dinner out of a tin pail, and a poorly cooked supper after a long and hard day's labor, cannot conduce to comfortable digestion. The inward uneasiness or leaden lethargy of the digestive organs after such a day call for assistance and stimulation; so the poor man leaves wife and children to seek relief in the saloon, where he soon learns to stay until he goes home drunk. Now, if the good wife but knew how to prepare the family meals in a neat, attractive, appetizing, and healthful way, how much of the want, privation, suffering, sickness, doctors' bills, and loss of time might be saved? How much domestic comfort, content, and happiness might be added to the bread winner's family?

There are a hundred different ways of cooking and serving bread, pork, and potatoes, so that with these three items alone one might have a different and toothsome bill of fare every day of the year if the cook but knew how to prepare it. Let us then teach the poor how to cook, and to be neat and cleanly. Neatness is next to Godliness; cooking next to manliness; both should be a part of the prescribed course in every public school.

From twelve years upward every girl should be carefully and continuously trained by competent instructors in the best methods of cooking and serving the common articles of daily food, and in the ordinary duties of family life. How infinitely more important is a knowledge of these things to the after life of 90 per cent. of the girls in our schools, than many of the studies upon which at present they not only waste their time, but which actually tend to unfit them for the enjoyment of the life they must necessarily live. We believe in manual training for boys, too, but when we consider how much the health and happiness of the home depends upon the wife and mother, especially among the wage-workers, it seems incredible that we should so totally ignore any effort to prepare the girls in our schools for their lot in life. Let us change this now, and graduate housewives instead of novel readers, factory-girls, and house ornaments, and we shall accomplish more for the promotion of temperance, the decrease of crime and poverty, and the general good of society, than the public schools have ever yet dreamed of doing.

CHAPTER XII.

WHAT IS TO BE DONE WITH THE PRISONER?

Existence of a Large Congenital Criminal Class—Importance of its Identification and Special Treatment—Segregation Essential to Elimination—Special Penitentiaries Necessary—Criminality but Little Effected by Education or Wealth—Crime a Disease—To be Studied and Treated as Such—Evil of the Arrest—Consideration for Youthful Delinquents—Importance of Reorganizing the Penal Code—Results of Reformatory Treatment in Great Britain—County Jails Nurseries of Crime—Number of in the United States—Evils of Sheriff Control—Suggested Improvement in Management—Regulations and Diet.

THERE has been much thought, study, and wisdom expended in the discussion of this question ; much has been already accomplished in this country and more in other countries by this expenditure, toward the improvement of the condition of criminals and their reformation. Inspired chiefly by a Christian philanthropy, the sociological and governmental object has become greatly obscured and neglected in the discussion. It appears that so far as the public is concerned, in America the results are very far from satisfactory or encouraging. Notwithstanding all that has been said and done, crime and criminals are increasing in a fearful ratio, and the necessity for some more drastic treatment seems manifest and pressing. The people, the social organization, must take consideration of the subject in general, as affecting the public welfare, and threatening the social order, and even its existence.

We may check the abnormality of the increase of criminals in this country by the faithful use of the means we have recommended, but until the millenium arrives, society will doubtless have to deal with its refractory elements,—the products of the impoverishment and degradation of excess and immorality. Let us see if some improvement in our present methods may not be made to contribute materially to the reformation and reduction of the numbers of those which it is compelled to keep under treatment.

The condition of the case in America is this. On the first day of June, 1890, the census enumerators reported 79,617 inmates of our reformatory and penal institutions. It is estimated by the best authorities that not over one third of the criminals are in durance at any one time. We may assume, therefore, that we have in our population at least 238,000 criminals, or persons who have been convicts, and are likely to become convicts again. Morrison [1] gives the police estimate of the crime class in England and Wales in 1891, as between 50,000 and 60,000 persons, contributing but 12 per cent. of the inmates of the prisons.

Every one who has visited prisons and observed large numbers of prisoners together has undoubtedly been impressed, from the appearance of the prisoners alone, that a large proportion of them

[1] *Crime and its Causes,* p. 142.

were born to be criminals. There would seem to be certain recognizable features which differentiate these from the rest of mankind, and set them apart as a class by themselves ; a criminal class, of which it might be reasonably assumed that, although any given individual might be reclaimed and saved, as a class the whole were destined to live and die criminals. Indeed, it would seem that a composite photograph of a hundred or so of them might produce the typical criminal, which would be useful in identifying the relationship of a suspect to the class. These are they who have inherited criminality from parents, who are the product of generations of vice and crime, or who have slid down the plane of transgression and excess to the very bottom of degradation, and whose children will inevitably follow the family calling. They are human deformities and monstrosities, physically illshapen, weak and sickly, with irregular features. They bear a sinister, ignoble, and furtive expression. They have an unbalanced and distorted cranium, are of a low order of intelligence, apparently devoid of the nobler sentiments ; with a depraved if not utter absence of moral sense or conscience. They are as abnormal and anomalous mentally and morally, as physically, yet we know physical anomalies often exist without psychical deformity, and moral obliquity or depravity is found in youth without outward evidence, though they stamp their seal indelibly upon the physique before old age.

Herr Sichart, director of prisons of Würtemburg, found by inquiry extending over several years, and

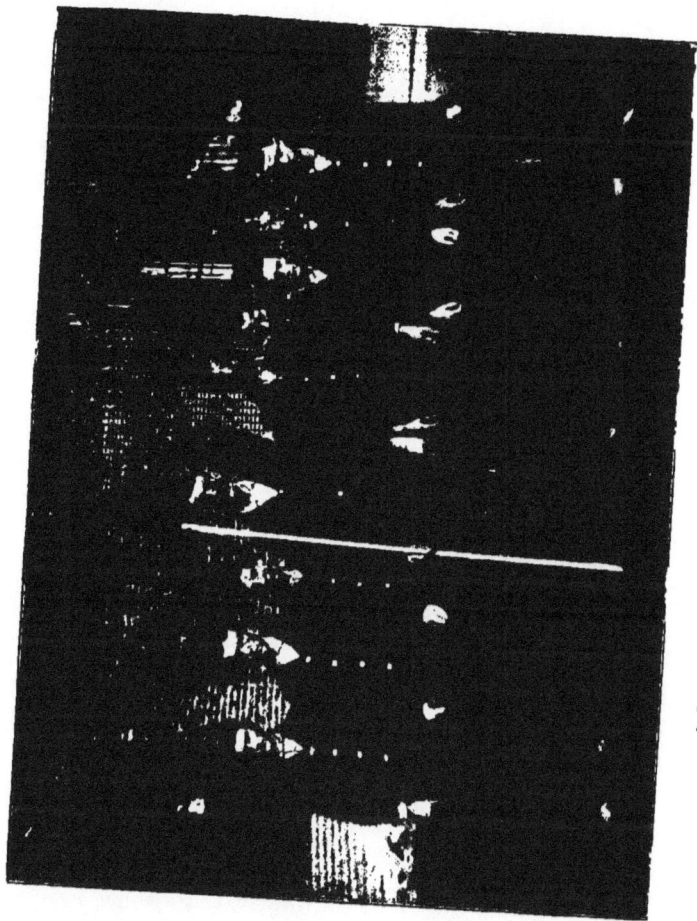

A GROUP OF "INCORRIGIBLES" FROM A REFORMATORY.

THE STAFF IS SIX FEET HIGH.

including 1,714 cases, that "over one fourth of the
German prison population had received a defective
organization from their ancestry, which manifests
itself in a life of crime." Dr. Vergilio says that "in
Italy 32 per cent. of the criminal population have
inherited criminal tendencies from their parents."
According to Dr. H. Maudsley "the idiot is not an
accident, nor the irreclaimable criminal an unac-
countable causality." Of the 527 convicts received
in the Eastern Penitentiary of Pennsylvania in 1890,
ninety-three were upon their third or more sentence.
Seventeen of these had been detected, arrested,
tried, and convicted more than six times. One of
them was to serve his fourteenth sentence; sixty-
eight of these prisoners had relatives who were then
or had been in prison; and 103 were received upon
their second sentence. One was received upon
his seventh conviction for buglary. The convict
who was received upon his fourteenth sentence had
served nearly thirty years in prison since he was
twenty years of age, for burglary, and is the father of
the burglar received on his seventh sentence.[1]
These are fair examples of most penitentiary convictions.

Commenting on these and others, the Hon.
Richard Vaux, president of the Board of Inspectors
of the Eastern Penitentiary, who is recognized all
over the world as the great champion of the
separate confinement principle of dealing with
criminals, and who has devoted a life-time to the
introduction of practical common-sense into penol-

[1] *Annual Report of Eastern Penitentiary for 1890.*

ogy, says : "Where crime is a vocation, the outcome
of inherent, inherited, chronic or constitutional,
moral and physical defects, it is absolutely necessary
to try the best means to produce an alterative that
will reduce, change, or correct the pre-existing cause
of crime." Of the 52,783 persons committed to
the Allegheny County Workhouse between 1869
and 1891, 15,824 were upon their third conviction
and over, 542 upon their tenth ; 135 upon their
twentieth ; 33 upon their thirtieth ; 12 upon their
fortieth ; 5 upon their fiftieth ; and 1 each upon their
sixtieth, sixty-first, second, third, and fourth convictions, with corresponding intermediate numbers.[1]
The cases in the lower courts of Massachusetts during
the year ended Sept. 30, 1860, aggregated 81,255 ;
and in the Superior Court, 2,158, of which 33,290
were committed to jails, and more than half the
cases were recommitments.[2]

In a paper on "Criminal Anthropology" read be-
fore the National Prison Association in Cincinnati,
Dr. H. D. Wey, physician to the New York State
Reformatory, quotes from Dr. J. S Wright :

"The concurrent and unanimous testimony of those who are, from
their experience and knowledge, most competent to judge, is : that
the great underclass of criminals have more or less defective organizations, especially as relates to their nervous system, and more especially
as to their brain ; that they are more or less deficient in moral sense,
showing in this respect the lack of development or result of decay ;
the best and last developed sense, the moral sense, disintegrating first
of all ; that they are perversely wicked and indomitably inexpedient,

[1] *Report of Allegheny Co. Workhouse for 1891.*
[2] W. P. Andrews, Clerk of Court at Salem, at National Prison
Association, Pittsburg, 1891.

committing crimes when doing right would be of more use to them ;
that they are as passionate as the wild beasts of the forest, and as rest-
less as the ocean that heaves with every gust of wind ; that they are
at war with mankind and ever in commotion with themselves ; that
they are like the ship beaten out by the storm—the ship without
compass, rudder, or captain ; they are formed and fashioned by the
hand of an evil genius whose name is bad heredity, and whose handmaid is ignorance ; and that they cannot be very much reformed, and
that their reformation ought to have begun in their ancestors."

In all human probability 99 per cent. of all
the effort and expense society may incur for the
reformation of this class will be wholly thrown
away, and any freedom or leniency allowed them
will be abused to the injury of the benefactor.

The public welfare requires that this criminal
class shall be speedily identified, separated, and
permanently secluded from society for three imperative reasons. First, for the protection of society
from the injury and ravage of criminals. Second,
that the public may save the cost of repeated detections, arrests, trials, and expensive confinements,
and the waste and discouragement of unsuccessful
efforts for their reformation. And third, in order
that the class may be exterminated. The first of
these reasons has apparently been the chief motive
of penal legislation and philanthropic action hitherto, but the last is by far the more important and
imperative.

Criminality and criminals will inevitably increase
faster than the rest of society if the latter are permitted to breed without restraint, for the limitations
which restrict reproduction among the better classes
are inoperative upon them. Neither religion, morals,

marriage, or the burden of supporting their offspring, have the slightest influence in repressing their sensual indulgence.   Indeed, the sexual sense is abnormally developed in them.   They spawn their noxious progeny with as little care as the fish of the sea, and with almost equal prolificacy.   Dugdale in his study of the "Juke" family, traces 1,200 criminals and paupers impregnated with the vicious blood of one ancestor in seven generations, who cost the public over $1,300,000.

Rev. O. McCulloch, of Indianapolis, discovered and identified 1,750 descendants of Ben Ishmael, living in Kentucky in 1790, who had been criminals and paupers, among whom 121 were prostitutes.   In six generations 75 per cent. of the cases treated in the City Hospital in Indianapolis were of the tribe of Ben Ishmael.   Court Pastor Stocker, of Berlin, investigated the history of 834 descendants of two sisters, the eldest of whom died in 1825.   Among these he found 76 who had served 116 years in prison for serious crimes, 164 prostitutes, 106 illegitimate children, 17 pimps, 142 beggars, 64 paupers in almshouses; estimated to have cost the state more than $500,000.

The trustees of the Children's Home in Washington County, O., in their eighteenth annual report state that 66 per cent. of the inmates of their home from that county in the preceding two years had been related by blood or marriage.

It is impossible to estimate the dreadful diffusion of criminal characteristics and tendencies which may be disseminated through the social organism in seven generations by the 238,000 present members of the criminal class in this country. There is virus enough in them to corrupt and poison the entire population in that time. Heredity of character is too well understood and too generally accepted as a fact to require more than the statement. Races, nations, communities, and families preserve their distinctive peculiarities through hundreds of generations. Special skill and excellence in particular trades, occupations, and artifice have been recognized in particular families from the time of Tubal Cain and Moses to the present. Family traits, likenesses, and tendencies are familiar to all, and heredity is acknowledged almost universally as a biological law as invariable as the law of gravitation. But we pay far more attention to the breeding of domestic animals than to that of their masters.

It is time, however, that society should interpose in this propagation of criminals. It is irrational and absurd to occupy our attention and exhaust our liberality with the care of this constantly growing class without any attempt to restrict its reproduction. This is possible, too, without violating any humanitarian instinct, by imprisonment for life ; and this seems to me the most practicable solution of the problem in America. As soon as an individual can be identified as an hereditary or chronic criminal, society should confine him or her in a penitentiary at self-supporting labor for life. Every State should have an institution adapted to the safe and secure separation of such from society, where they can be employed at productive labor, without expense to

12

the public, during their natural life. When this is ended with them, the class will become extinct, and not before. Then each generation would only have to take care of its own moral cripples and defectives, without the burden of the constantly increasing inheritance of the past.

The question of separate or solitary confinement need not be considered in such a prison. There would be no danger from contamination, no objection on account of criminal acquaintance and companionship. The inmates would be compelled to be honest and harmless, and might be converted to a religious or Christian life, but they should be kept close nevertheless. No pardon, no hope of liberty should be possible except in a clear and positive case of mistake in the character, or where, after indubitable reformation, the convict should be made incapable of reproduction.

When upon a third conviction the judicial authorities determine the prisoner to belong to the criminal class, the law should imperatively require the sentence to be the penitentiary for life, whatever the particular crime committed. The main question to be decided should be, is the prisoner a natural or incorrigible criminal? The certainty of the third sentence ending the social life would act as a powerful deterrent upon criminals, and assist in the settlement of the question in respect to any case which even this fear could not restrain.

A board of pardon, consisting of the superintendent of the penitentiary, the sentencing judge, and the Chief-Justice of the Supreme Court of the State, might be given power to correct mistakes of sentence in annual session, when it could be done without danger to the public; but, except by unanimous action, even this should be made legally impossible. The penalty for murder, arson, and rape should also be a sentence to such a penitentiary. This should be constructed with a view to the safe confinement, economical management, and profitable employment of the inmates. Any excess of earnings above the cost of self-support should be applied to the relief of dependants of the convict.

But hereditary criminals do not constitute the entire class. It is constantly recruited from the social lees. Drunkenness, excess, and vicious lives are constantly begetting " defective organizations," which will in turn beget criminals or paupers, as certainly as the child will bear the family resemblance. The laws of heredity operate as inexorably downward as upward, under suitable conditions. The act and fact of reformation is naturally and solely individual. The reformed criminal must reconstruct his entire organism before he can beget reformed progeny. His children are morally certain to reproduce his natural immoralities.

General Booth, the most far-sighted, benevolent, and whole-souled philanthropist of this age, whose life has been devoted to saving men, says:[1]

" There are some cases within our knowledge which seem to confirm the somewhat dreadful verdict by which a man appears to be a lost soul on this side of the grave. There are men so incorrigibly lazy that no inducement you can offer will induce them to work, so

[1] *Darkest England*, p. 205.

eaten up with vice that virtue is abhorrent to them, and so inveter-
ately dishonest that theft is to them a master-passion.   When a
human being has reached that stage, there is only one course that
can be rationally pursued.   Sorrowfully, but remorselessly, it must
be recognized that he has become lunatic, morally demented, incapable of self-government, and that upon him, therefore, must be
passed the sentence of permanent seclusion from a world in which he
is not fit to be at large.".

To quote from Morrison again, "It is hardly possible to do anything with these offenders, and they
unfortunately constitute at least one fourth of the
criminal population." [1]   " The only effective way of
dealing with the incorrigible vagrant, drunkard,
thief, is by some system of permanent seclusion in a
penal colony." [2]

This life confinement should not be confounded
with the " indeterminate sentence " proposal, nor
regarded in the light of a penalty for a single crime,
which it is not; but as the legitimate consequence
of such a continuance in vicious practices, as has
depraved and unfitted the convict for a share in the
public freedom, and made him dangerous to the
social organization and prosperity.   He must be
incarcerated for the public safety.   In a less civilized
and advanced society he would probably be put to
death, and so exterminated.   Our Christian charity
and power may mercifully extend to him opportunity for reformation and salvation, but it must
prevent his perpetuation of his crime-branded lin-
eage.   The abnormal increase of criminals cannot

[1] *Crime and its Causes*, p. 224.
[2] *Crime and its Causes*, p. 226.

PORTRAITS FROM THE "ROGUES' GALLERY."

ILLUSTRATING ABNORMAL PHYSIOGNOMY.

be checked so long as unrestricted reproduction is permitted.

With such an extirpation of the distinctively criminal class, the conservative, elevating, and reformatory philanthropy of modern society will be enabled to cope successfully with the degenerating influences constantly at work in the social ferment. The abnormal increase will be arrested; but without this the task is hopeless, absolutely hopeless. The hand of reformation cannot efficiently reach or touch the loathsome creatures in the miry depths.

As a matter of social economy, the costs of repeated crimes, detections, arrests, trials, transportations to prisons, and maintenance there, would in this way be entirely saved, as well as the consequential damages from future generations. The service of the life sentence need not be rigorously punitive. Its very hopelessness and seclusion would be sufficient in this direction. But it should be sure and certain as a life sentence, and attended with self-supporting labor at least, and profitable if possible. This appears to us to be a perfectly just and righteous solution of the problem, and entirely within the proper power of legislation and government. We think it should be inaugurated without hesitation or delay. Nearly all the authorities and students of penology agree upon the necessity of permanent seclusion of the incorrigible, for the good of society; but none, so far as I am aware, have so far urged this most important of all reasons for it, the natural extirpation of this class. The penal colony would only perpetuate it, but this plan is not to be thought of for America.

Having provided for the extermination of the criminal class, Penological Reform must also consider measures to prevent its reconstitution from society. It is not only necessary that the citadel of crime should be besieged, but that its communications of supply should be cut off. A complete discussion of this aspect would naturally comprehend in its purview the entire subject of sociology. But we limit our present study to the treatment of those who have been detected and arrested, who have thus manifested an inclination to sink below the social average towards the bottom, for the purpose of checking this inclination and restoring them to society.

Major McClaughry, the eminent penologist who had charge of the Joliet prison in Illinois for many years, and lately resigned the superintendence of the Huntington Reformatory in Pennsylvania, to accept the office of chief of police in Chicago, says, "that criminal parentage, and association, and neglect of children by their parents," are the great causes of the increase of criminality in America.

Mr. Charles Martindale says, in the *North American Review*, "that pauperism and crime are the results of heredity, and association can no longer be doubted."

The best authorities abroad fix the proportion of the incorrigible at from 25 to 32 per cent. of the convicts. In America it is undoubtedly larger, because we have so long offered an open haven of refuge to all people, without any application of our proverbial common-sense to penal legislation and management. Without statistical information I should say that at least 40 per cent. of our convicts belong to the incorrigible class.

We now have to deal with the remaining 60 per cent. Notwithstanding all that has been written upon ignorance, poverty, intemperance, climate, temperature, and seasons as causes of criminality, there are but two in the final analysis and classification. Heredity and Heteronomy,—inherited defects, or the corruptions of circumstance and association. Recent studies of the convict in prisons reveal the astonishing fact that the proportion of highly educated criminals to the number of highly educated in society, is greater than that of the ignorant criminals to the uneducated class, and that the number of convicts from the wealthy class is of a greater proportion than that from the poor.[1] Verily,

" Honor and shame from no condition rise."

Neither birth, nor culture, education, affluence, or social position, apparently, secure the individual from the attack of the spirit of evil, any more than they do from the measles, drunkenness, or smallpox. Indeed, the opportunities and temptations to excesses and drunkenness in the higher classes naturally result in degradation and vicious diathesis in the descendant. Until the human race has been brought up to a condition of perfection, to the

[1] See Morrison on *Crime*, pp. 82, 143.

"measure of the stature of the fulness of Christ,"
"who knew no sin," and who had "power and authority over all devils, and to cure diseases," there
will be a proportion in all the walks of life who will
violate the restrictions of human and divine law.
There will be found in the intricate system of co-op-
erating physical, mental, and moral organization,
which is named man, an imperfection, weakness, or
unbalancing of power in certain individuals, whatever their birth or education, which will render them
liable to yield to evil influences and to fall into the
commission of crime. In appendix will be found
some interesting statistics from the census and reports of the State Penitentiaries of Pennsylvania,
New York, Ohio, and Illinois, which corroborate
this view.[1]

The 60 per cent. we are now to treat of are
largely the victims of heteronomy, the subjects of
evil associations and environment. It is fair to
assume in regard to these, that if the heteronomical
conditions are changed and corrected for a sufficient
time, a complete reformation can in most cases be
accomplished, and the prisoner restored to freedom
without danger to the public. Criminality is always
a kind of disease, due either to physical, mental, or
moral deformity, malformation, or vitiation. Crime
is but the symptom. Some are incurably afflicted,
others curably. There are chronic and temporary
conditions; active and morbid, violent and latent
states. It is contagious, and sometimes epidemic.
This is the accepted belief of those who have

[1] See Appendix, II. and III.

given the matter proper study. The argument in support of this conclusion is very fully made by ex-Judge Sanford M. Green, of Michigan, in his book on *Crime*, to which those interested are referred.

The first thing necessary to be determined, then, when an arrest is made, is the character of the disease with which the prisoner is afflicted. Is it hereditary or heteronomic, deep-seated or temporary, habitual or sporadic. This diagnosis is of vital importance, because it is estimated that over 95 per cent. of the arrests made are for trivial offenses, slight aberrations over the line of rectitude; mere sporadic transgressions, resulting from sudden impulse, passion, or accident, which instantly transfer the prisoner from his place in society into the ranks of the criminal. The accidental transgressor should be restored to his place again in society, before he is contaminated by or identified with this class, either in his own mind, or in the public estimation. That is, the effect of the arrest upon this 95 per cent. must be made as slight as possible. Indeed, arrests should be avoided, except in the most necessary cases, as conducing to criminality, rather than restricting it. But if an arrest must be made, the effort of the officer of the law should first be directed to prevent confinement. For disorders, misdemeanors, and the infraction of local ordinances, it would be far better that the prisoner should be taken home or before a magistrate to be fined, or even dismissed with a reprimand, than that self-respect should be impaired by imprisonment, or criminal disposition, acquaintance, and association formed.

The best system that has been devised for avoiding the evils of imprisonment and indiscriminate arrests, is undoubtedly that which has been in successful operation in Boston for more than ten years, which is called the "Probation" system. The city is divided into districts, each having a "Probation" officer in supervision of the persons arrested in his district. It is his duty to get the names of all arrested, examine the history and character of the prisoner, visit his residence and family, and if he concludes that it would be best, and the charge will permit, he recommends his liberation; if found guilty, that sentence be postponed. He keeps him under supervision for a year, assisting him to an honest living if possible, or if he fails to do well orders his arrest and sentence. One district there records 7,251 cases under the probation officer in ten years, of whom only a little over 1 per cent. ran away, and but 6½ per cent. were returned for sentence.

The dread of the jail is the most powerful deterrent to those who have not suffered the degradation of an imprisonment, or enjoyed its comfortable ease. No child under eighteen years of age should ever be sent to a jail. A "jail bird" is branded for life, and without powerful assistance from within and without, stands a small chance of escaping permanent criminality. Fines, restitutions, and compensations, under outside supervision, anything almost, should be substituted for a jail sentence. Where imprisonment is necessary, it should be for first and second

offences of the corrigible, to a State reformatory.
The law under which conviction is had is a law of
the State, and its penalties should be enforced under
State jurisdiction and superintendence.

The State rather than the county is responsible for
the future of the convict. He is adjudged diseased
and needs cure. His case must be wisely studied,
and receive appropriate treatment. He must be
educated into correct notions of right and wrong, be
taught self-restraint by the influences of rigid discipline, and self-command, self-reliance, self-support,
and the habit of industry, by the tonic of hard labor.
His body, mind, and soul must be brought into
rational, harmonious correlation and co-operation.
This can only be accomplished in a State institution
of sufficient importance to warrant capable management; where defects and weaknesses, physical, mental, and moral, can be discovered and possibly reme-
died; bad habits corrected and good inculcated,
by intelligent exercise, education, and religious
instruction.

The laws concerning the punishment of children
especially need a thorough revision. Children are
sent to jail, and transformed there into criminals, in
Pennsylvania and in most States, for mischief of
various sorts, such as trespass, skylarking, stealing
fruit, petty larcenies, riding on railroad cars, and
" incorrigibility " (which last is most frequently
parental incompetence or heartless desire to be
relieved of the support of their children). Such
children should be controlled and punished by their
parents, who should be held legally responsible for

the conduct of their children during their minority. This is the natural way of controlling them, and would be by far the most efficient with the natural parent and child. Abnormals should pass into the reformatory. Children of unnatural or vicious parents, however, should be taken under the care of society, and their parents punished.

Child-saving societies and institutions are the most efficient and hopeful agencies of all for diminishing the criminal class. They ought to be established in all large communities, and be represented and supported everywhere. Through them homes can be secured for children of unnatural parents, or those without proper parental control or support. Christian women can accomplish more, in this direction of philanthropic effort, toward the reduction of crime and for human progress in general, almost than in any other. It is the kind of work to which they are adapted by nature. Legislation should make it obligatory upon the courts to take charge of neglected children, and either enforce proper parental care or transfer them to such an institution as will attend to the rearing of them up into honest and self-supporting citizenship.

The reformatory for youth should be a reform school rather than a prison, in its design and management. The experience of the reform schools of England, France, Germany, Massachusetts, Connecticut, New York, Ohio, and Michigan demonstrate the inutility of prison walls and cells. The grand success of Christian kindness and charity, in dealing with the young, has the seal of promise and experience both. These institutions reclaim on an average 85 per cent. of their inmates, mostly convicts. The percentage would be larger if the incorrigible should be transferred from them to the penitentiary for life.

It•is evident from these considerations that our present penal legislation requires a complete reorganization. Laws are largely the outgrowth of precedents, which stretch back into the earliest times. Thus they are venerated for age and immemorial usage, often when the fundamental principle has become obsolete. Our penal code has been amended, modified, and added to for centuries, but it has grown up about principles which took root and germinated in a barbaric age. Based upon the now absurd theory of punishment for crime, instead of the natural and rational one of correction of the relations of the offender to society, it is utterly unworthy of and abhorrent to our present knowledge and civilization. It should be remodelled, or rather entirely repealed, and a new code enacted, with a chief regard to the person of the prisoner instead of the accident of the crime. It must substitute for the vindictive idea that of disease in the culprit. It must prescribe for the cure of the curable, and the permanent seclusion of the incurable. To this end all definite time sentences should be abolished ; all convicts committed to the reformatories upon an indeterminate sentence, until they are by proper authority adjudged permanently restored and fit for social freedom. The incurable should be transferred to the penitentiary of the incorrigible. By such a system all the unjust and crime-encouraging differences and uncertainties of sentences, which are the inevitable result of the " discretion " of judges of different temperaments, intelligence, and environments, would disappear, and all criminals everywhere receive a uniform treatment. This in itself would produce a powerful moral deterrence upon criminals.

But the most beneficent influence of such a reorganization would appear in the opportunity afforded for an exhaustive effort for the reformation and cure of the criminal, almost impossible under the present illogical and unreasonable system of definite time sentence. It is as manifestly impossible for a judge to predetermine the time required for the cure of a criminal, as for a physician to diagnose the time necessary for the cure of his patient. It is as absurd to sentence a criminal for thirty, sixty, ninety days, or one, two, or five years, as to commit an insane person to an asylum for a similar period. Let it then be made the duty of the judges to commit every prisoner, upon the first or second conviction, to a reformatory indefinitely, and a competent tribunal be established to terminate this commitment by liberation, or transfer to the penitentiary. The periodical removal of the incorrigible from the reformatory will nullify many of the objections raised against the present educational features of reformatory management in America, which have given these institutions the name of " Collegiate Prisons " abroad.

There will then be necessary, in each State, local jails for the retention of prisoners awaiting trial, the reform school for minors, the reformatory, and the penitentiary for chronics or incorrigibles. A simple, uniform, and certain course for the criminal, inevitably devolving upon his personal choice, nature, and responsibility, the quantity and quality of the recompense to be made to society, and the punishment to be endured for the infraction of the law. So, exact justice would be secured, both to the public and convict, which at present is generally disputed, and seldom possible. The penitentiary, reformatory, and reform school would necessarily be under State management, and competent superintendence with the most intelligent system would eventually be secured.

Great Britain supports over four hundred reformatories and industrial schools, through which have been passed in twenty years over one hundred thousand children and youths; and they have been able to close there fifty-six out of one hundred and thirteen prisons and jails within ten years. During this ten years the number of male prisoners there has decreased 28 per cent., and the female 45 per cent., and this notwithstanding a natural increase in population. The British Home Office reports, " It is certain that by reformatories and industrial schools a large proportion of the supply of raw material for the manufacture of criminals has, to a great extent, been cut off." [1]

The foregoing is the system and these are the methods to be striven for and attained in the future. Concerning the treatment of prisoners in our present State institutions, reformatories and penitentiaries,

---

[1] These statements are taken from an address of Hon. Robert Stiles, president of the Prison Association of Virginia.

little need now be said. They are, in Pennsylvania
especially, in charge of intelligent and experienced
managers, who have devoted years of conscientious
study to the subject of criminology and penology.
Men who have well defined opinions, and pursue
consistent and wisely planned methods, intended for
the best and broadest results in dealing with those
in their charge. The separate system in the Eastern
Penitentiary, under the illustrious Hon. Richard
Vaux, and the almost equally well known warden,
Michael J. Cassidy, has been in successful operation
for many years. It is known the world over as the
"Philadelphia" or "Pennsylvania" system, and as
such is being gradually adopted in other countries.
In our Western Penitentiary, the congregate system
has been brought to its highest efficiency under
Major Wright. In both, the reformation of the convict is the main purpose and desire, and the public
costs are reduced to a minimum, ·for the system.
Probably little improvement in results is to be expected from well managed State institutions under
our present penal code. They all do the best they
can with the heterogeneous mass temporarily under
their care, constantly discouraged by the consciousness that many are hopeless recidivists upon whom
all their labor is in vain. In the purview of punishment and reformation, as well as the prevention of
the diffusion of criminal knowledge, taste, and habits,
separate confinement is generally accepted by penologists, as the most rational and hopeful, and consequently the most economical, kind of imprisonment;
certainly so long as the chronic, natural criminal is

to be incarcerated with the sporadic, or accidental. The manifest failure of philanthropic and intelligent management to produce the desired results is chiefly due to causes outside the institutions; to the faults of the laws under which they are operated.

As prisoners are first gathered into jails to await trial or to expiate minor crimes, jail-management effects the larger number, and is consequently the most important factor in this consideration.

There are in the United States, seventeen thousand and fifty-eight county-jails, and only forty-four juvenile reformatories. There is no juvenile reformatory in Alabama, Alaska, Arizona, Arkansas, Florida, Georgia, Idaho, Indian Territory, Mississippi, Montana, Nevada, New Mexico, North Carolina, North Dakota, Oklahoma, Oregon, South Carolina, South Dakota, Tennessee, Texas, Utah, Virginia, Washington, West Virginia, or Wyoming. They have been established in all the States of the North Atlantic census division, and in all but two of the North Central division, while there are but three States which have them in the South Atlantic division; two in the South Central; and two in the Western.[1] It is of interest to note that the census reports of 1890 show four fifths of the negro-convicts in the South Atlantic and South Central divisions, and more than three fifths of the negro juvenile delinquents in the North Atlantic, North Central, and Western divisions.

It is the unanimous testimony of every one who is conversant with the management of county-jails,

[1] *Census Bulletins*, Nos. 72 and 95.

13

that they are nothing more or less than breeders of criminals, where they are, as is generally the case, committed to the superintendence of political sheriffs, who have secured their election for the profit of the office, to be acquired in a single term. Eminent penologists have repeatedly denounced them as a more prolific cause of the increase of criminality than intemperance even. Were the sheriff actuated solely by a desire for the reformation of his prisoners, he could scarcely acquire, during his brief term, a superficial knowledge of the proper duties of a warden. If by diligent care he should obtain this, he would quickly be obliged to give place to a new and ignorant incumbent. Hon. Eugene Smith, one of the vice-presidents of the National Prison Association, describes most concisely, in a paper read at the annual convention of the association in 1885, the evils of sheriff-management, as follows:

"The sheriff is an autocrat in the county-jail; its management is a disagreeable part of his function and is tolerable to him only as it is made profitable. The sheriff's office, speaking generally, represents a bad element, but a very powerful element, in local politics—an element which takes little interest in moral reforms, but has a keen eye for the emoluments of office. Improvements in the county-jail involve the expenditure of money; the sheriff is averse to incurring such expenditures on his own account, and in justice to him it must be said that the people are equally averse to raising the money by taxation. There is no tax that the supervisors of the county are so loth to impose, or that the people so grudgingly pay, as a tax to enlarge or improve the county-jail. The public take no interest in details about the management of a prison; the whole subject is most positively distasteful to them. There is no organized public body that feels much responsibility about the county-jail; and so the whole business is relegated to the sheriff, who exercises a supreme and unchallenged control. The sheriff has a brief tenure of office, he has little knowledge about prison-management, and still less about prison-reform. He takes the jail as he finds it, and administers it as his predecessors have done ; and so it has been handed down from generation to generation. Indeed, the sheriff, even if an earnest and intelligent reformer, would be powerless to accomplish any radical improvement. He could not keep the prisoners in solitary confinement, because the construction of the jail is such that the inmates of cells can communicate with each other almost as freely through the grated doors as when congregated in a common hall. He could hardly be expected to keep the prisoners at hard labor unless some specific appropriations were made for the purpose. The possibilities of jail-reform by the action of the sheriff are only in superficial and meagre particulars."

We foolishly maintain then, in America, forty times as many criminal hotbeds as reformatories, recruiting depots for the criminal class in nearly every county, while more than half the States make no official effort for its reduction. Designed apparently, as a general rule, without the faintest conception of the proper purpose of confinement, with no visible object except security, combined sometimes with cheapness, sometimes with an attempt at architectural display, committed to the management of a professional politician as a reward for partisan service rendered or required, the county-jail is an unmitigated curse upon the community. And yet, quoting again from Hon. Eugene Smith :

" If all the convicts now herded in the county-jails were placed in reformatory prisons under a proper and skilful regimen, it is a reasonable anticipation that 80 per cent. of them could be reclaimed from crime and so trained as to lead a life of honest self-support. As to the economic gain to the property interests of society in being freed from the depredations of so large a fraction of jail convicts, I shall make a statement which will appear startling and extravagant, but it can be fully vindicated by positive figures at my command— *the saving to the community, computed in actual money, resulting from the reclamation of 80 per cent. of our jail convicts, would be sufficient in a single year to rebuild all the county-jails in the United States."*

This is an undisputable fact, and seems sufficient in itself alone to account for the evil we are discussing. We might well afford to destroy and reconstruct all our defective jails at once, as well as our penal code, to effect a reduction of 80 per cent. in the number of those we are supporting continually in and by them. No county can afford to maintain the infamous jails as they at present exist at the county towns. No State should tolerate their influence. However small the number of inmates, they must be confined separately, and without the possibility of intercommunication and association. Under our present laws they will for a time, doubtless, be continued as a necessary evil, but they should be used only for the temporary confinement of prisoners awaiting trial. No convict ought ever be confined within their walls.

Until the whole penal system is reorganized upon a new basis of common-sense, the following principles should regulate their management. I venture these suggestions as the result of careful observation and some study, in the hope that their publication may result in a temporary reduction in the contagion of vice which is now disseminated through the community by them.

First. There should be separation of the sexes, so complete and distant as to preclude the possibility of a single communication by sight or sound.

The necessity of this is obvious to all who know anything of the depravity of the habitual "jail-bird," of both sexes. It is too horrible and ingenious for publication. The entertainment obtained by obscene conversation through soil pipes used as speaking tubes, is beyond the imagination of most people, but these creatures seem to enjoy even this where it is possible, and sign language where that can be used.

Second. Confinement of the accused, whom the law assumes to be innocent until convicted, and detained witnesses, under fairly comfortable circumstances, and entirely apart from convicts.

As some of the accused, however, would be of the depraved and vicious class, it is necessary that the jailer should exercise the utmost diligence that none of such should have intercourse with the others. Untried prisoners, quite free from suspicion of innate depravity, might be allowed intercommunication, but where there is a possibility of corruption, separate confinement should be rigorously enforced. Children and youths should, of course, be kept separate from adults especially, as well as from one another.

Third. Convicted prisoners should invariably be held in solitary confinement, and secluded from intercourse with the outside world. This is important in order that the imprisonment may be irksome, that there may be no distraction of the mind from wholesome meditation upon the folly of their course, and that reformatory influences may have uninterrupted effect upon them, as well as to prevent them from corrupting others, or strengthening one another in vicious thought and knowledge.

Fourth. Convicts should be made to work regularly ten hours a day, in order to contribute as much as possible to their own support, but chiefly that a habit of industry may be instilled into them, and that they may be taught an honest means of livelihood. They should be clothed in a distinctive prison garb, and their diet be made as plain and cheap as is consistent with the preservation of health.

Fifth. Regularity, system, order, and neatness should be enforced in all the operations and conduct of the institution. The convict needs to be taught these habits as the first step in reformation, and they are quite as essential to the proper and economical management of the jail.

Sixth. Visits by friends and companions of convicts should be strictly prohibited, except by a member of the immediate family, at rare intervals. Gifts and presents, calculated to alleviate the discomfort and rigor of confinement, should not be permitted, nor should the *Police Gazette* and such periodicals as criminals delight in ever be allowed inside the walls. It would be better to prohibit newspapers altogether.

Seventh. Convicts should not be permitted to cover the walls of their cells with pictures or hangings, because they are not intended to be a home-like or comfortable place, and because such things may become the breeding places of vermin and noxious things, or hide attempts to dig through and escape.

Eighth. Liquor and tobacco should be strictly prohibited, under all circumstances, to convicts. All

letters sent, or received, should be read by the warden, restricted to necessary family matters, and to
long intervals.

Ninth. All of the work of the jail should be
performed by the prisoners, as far as is possible;
certainly the regular scrubbing and semi-annual
whitewashing, both as a measure of economy and
exercise. Floors and all wood-work in cells and corridors should be thoroughly scrubbed at least twice
a week, and cleaned daily. Every prisoner should
be made to bathe once a week.

Immediately upon the admission of a prisoner, he
or she should be examined by a physician as to
physical health, be given a bath and a clean suit of
clothes, vaccinated if necessary, hair cut, height,
weight, and description taken and recorded, and the
personal effects and clothes, after cleansing the latter, packed up with a description list, and stored for
restoration upon liberation.

Prisoners should be required to rise at five in the
summer and at six in winter, wash and dress, make
their beds, and arrange their cells in order before
breakfast. This, and all meals should be served,
for the separately confined, in the cell. Two hours
after rising, work should begin, and continue until
noon, when half an hour's exercise should be given
in the open air, when possible, before dinner. At one
o'clock work should be resumed, and continued till six
o'clock, with half an hour of open-air exercise. Supper should be at 6:30; at nine all lights should be
extinguished, and prisoners go to bed. They should
not be permitted to sleep in their day garments.

Beds should be straw or husk mattresses, furnished with sheets and pillow-cases and sufficient blankets. The cheapest and best bedstead for jails is made with two wooden saw-horses and three inch-thick boards, a foot wide and seven feet long, which can be washed and kept clean. No other furniture than a chair, a small table, three hanging shelves, wash basin, a small mirror, tooth- and hair-brush, and comb are necessary, or should be allowed.

Work in jails cannot well be made profitable on account of the usually short sentence to be served, but stocking-knitting with machines, carpet-making, mat-making, brush- and broom-making, and, best of all, shoemaking and cobbling, can be usefully conducted. Machinery has so completely taken the place of hand labor in the manufacture of boots and shoes that the old-fashioned shoemaker is hard to find, and it is difficult to get a shoe mended anywhere. If prisoners were taught in jails to make shoes and slippers for the inmates, they might acquire a trade which would afford them a certain support upon liberation, and so a double utility be received from instruction in this. All bedding and underclothing should be made and washed in the jail where the inmates are sufficiently numerous, and, where the character of the prisoners will permit, the outer clothing should also be made by them. The best of them should cook and serve the meals and do the kitchen work. In localities where there should be a market for it, kindling-wood might be prepared and sold, or stone broken for country roads. Industry of some kind should be regularly enforced.

The tendency in all jails managed by sheriffs is toward extravagance and unnecessary attractiveness of food supplies to prisoners. The comfortable quarters, ease of life, and superior food furnished at public expense, makes jail life so desirable to tramps, vagrants, and the large class determined to live without work that "good jails" have become a favorite winter resort for them. They get themselves incarcerated, to enjoy the comforts supplied by a thoughtless public, by the commission of some venial offence, and are frequently known to complain of the unexpected brevity of their sentence. It is absolutely necessary that jail life should be made in all respects less agreeable than that to which the prisoner is accustomed at liberty, to secure any deterrent influence from it.

As a guide for inexperienced sheriffs and wardens, we offer the following suggestions upon the jail dietary. We have obtained from Mr. Michael J. Cassidy, the well-known warden of the Eastern Penitentiary of Pennsylvania, who has had a long and successful experience in the management of prisoners and prisons, the following expression of his views upon the food question, as valuable as any obtainable, and we quote them in full :

"A proper diet for persons confined should not be a fixed diet. Much depends on the location and the condition of those to be cared for. A certain quantity, or one particular sort unvaried, is not best ; as much variety as the produce of the locality in which the institution is located, sufficient in quantity, distributed in accordance with the judgment of the management or direction is better. Some physical constitutions require more than others. A fixed quantity would not be economy. Good and sound articles of food, certainly not fine or specially selected ; vegetables that are in general use, and bread made from sound wheat flour, not high bolted, but that which contains some of the middlings ; meats such as can be made into stews or soup, all grease or fats of the meats used in the food in some way should constitute the general diet. Short-cake or bread, with lard made up in it, one day in the week is very desirable. The following are the daily rations as served at present : Bread is given according to the need of the prisoner, coffee in the morning, tea for supper ; Monday, beef soup, with vegetables, potatoes, turnips, rice, or barley, one pound of beef cooked, cut into rations and served separately ; Tuesday, short-cake and one half pound of bologna sausage ; Wednesday, bean soup and beef ; Thursday, *sauer-kraut* and one half pound of pork ; Friday, Irish stew, beef, unions, potatoes, and barley ; Saturday, mutton soup, three fourths of a pound mutton, and vegetables ; Sunday, meat pie, beef, onions, and potatoes with top and bottom crust, baked in pans in the ovens in which the bread is baked.

"The above may be varied or changed any time. Green vegetables in season, when they are abundant in market, such as tomatoes, green onions, carrots, beets, and pickles, when they are low in price should be supplied. I cannot suggest a more economical method than the above."

The army ration for a ten days' supply of the articles of food enumerated below indicates what is ample for men in active service, and need not be exceeded in the issue to prisoners in jail : Roasted coffee, 12.8 ounces ; tea, 2.4 ounces ; vinegar, 3.2 gills ; molasses, 0.8 gills ; soup, 6.4 ounces ; salt, 6 ounces ; pepper, 0.4 ounces. Three pounds of fresh vegetables are equivalent to one pound of beans, peas, rice, or hominy. Vinegar, molasses, salt, pepper, and soap should be issued in about this proportion to the cell; then the following dietary would be suitable for a week, varied according to location and season. Tea and coffee should be served clear.

A suitable and economical dietary for use in county-jails is given in the Appendix, for the information of those interested in a proper supply of food to prisoners.[1]

By such a management of jails and the prisoners in them, many of the evils which they now propagate may be corrected or diminished, and some reduction be made of their contribution to the general stock of criminals in numbers, as well as of the total and per capita cost of their support.

Permanent seclusion for the natural and incorrigible criminal, and indeterminate sentence to a reform school or reformatory for first and second convictions, except for the most heinous crimes, and special, permanent wardens for all jails, with complete reform of management, are the three vitally essential requirements of modern penology in America.

[1] See Appendices IV. and V.

CHAPTER XIII.

PAUPERS AND POOR-HOUSES.

WE now turn briefly to the subject of pauperism in America. We confine ourselves to America because the conditions of society in this country are essentially different, in respect to the independence of the individual, from those existing elsewhere. It is our just pride that in the United States every human being of sound body, mind, and soul, has an equal and perfect right to, and ability for, an independent existence. There is absolutely no external restriction of birth, circumstance, or law, upon his comfortable self-support, success, or ambition. The human nature is entirely untrammelled and unfettered in the struggle and competition of life. The necessary supply of food, fuel, clothing, and shelter are ample, and obtainable by a reasonable minimum of industry. ` It may be asserted with assurance that no sound man, woman, or child in good health in this country need ever be a pauper. But humanity is the same here as elsewhere, and presents the same examples of widely diversified, and different grades of ability and independence; all the way down from the distinguished accumulator of immense wealth to the helpless imbecile.

The social condition here, as everywhere, in civilized Europe, antique Asia, or savage Africa, is an effervescence, in which strength and purity are constantly rising toward the top, and weakness and the dregs are settling toward the bottom. The condition is constant, the proportions only are variable. Under our institutions, an intelligent sociology can and will produce a maximum of clarification and a minimum of lees, the greatest human advantage, and social economy. The line of separation between independence and pauperism is marked everywhere at the point of ability for a self-support, congruous with the condition of civilization in the community. Our conditions and standards of living are higher than the average, but our institutions are also the most elevating, and the proportion of our population above that line to that below would increase much more rapidly, but for our incomprehensible neglect of rational measures to restrict degeneration, and the constant influx of those who are below it from all over the world. The distinguished Professor R. T. Ely, of New York,[1] estimates the number of paupers in the United States at about 5 per cent. of the

[1] *The North American Review* for April, 1891.

population, or over three millions; and their pecuniary cost to the country one hundred million dollars per annum. Our case is therefore not only special, but serious. Nature requires active and immediate assistance for its relief and convalescence. The subject, notwithstanding our wonderful growth in wealth and general prosperity, is worthy careful and exhaustive study, and courageous intelligence of treatment.

Pauperism has been attributed to various causes; but in America, as in the case of criminals, paupers may be all resolved into two classes, as determined by the cause. Heredity and heteronomy; natural incapacity from deterioration, and the force of environment, developed in habit or misfortune, will account for the whole class. These two classes require quite different treatment. For convenience of consideration they may be separated into three sub-divisions.

First, we have the incapable, by nature unable to maintain themselves without assistance; the physically, mentally, or morally defective; cripples, deformed, deaf, blind, imbecile, weak-minded, diseased, insane, or criminal.

Second, beggars, vagrants, tramps; the incorrigibly idle, dissolute, and criminal, who prefer to prey rather than work.

These two classes are mostly hereditary paupers. They are the victims of congenital defects; the product of ancestral excesses, weakness, or sin.

Third, the unfortunate; whom adversity, destitution, old age, affliction, sickness, or accident, have reduced to a necessary dependence upon charity for the support of life and health, either temporarily or permanently.

These are mostly heteronomics, many of whom a change or improvement of environment will restore to independence.

For the maintenance of the morally defective or criminal pauper, society has been compelled to provide temporarily, at the discretion of judges and juries. We have suggested plans for disposing of these in the preceding chapter. Our States most advanced in civilization have also recognized the claims of the principal defective classes, such as the insane, deaf, blind, and imbecile, for public care, by the establishment of special asylums for their maintenance by taxation. This is a first step imperatively required in every State ; for all classes, where they are sufficiently numerous, to warrant separate treatment. The next should be to secure such management of these institutions and their inmates, as to reduce the public burden of these classes to a minimum.

This object will be attained by such instruction, training, and employment, as will prevent their reproduction, supplement their several defects, and render them as far as possible self-supporting. This can only be satisfactorily accomplished in moderately large State establishments, under skilled and intelligent direction. It is manifestly impossible in almshouses. Irresponsible victims of a congenital misfortune as they are, it is absolutely necessary for the good of all that they shall be prevented from transmitting their incapacity to future generations by marriage. They must be denied that privilege as a price of the assistance they receive from the public, for it is obvious that society might better permit them to perish, than to allow them to perpetuate, through generation after generation, their dependence upon the public. The alarming increase in the number of these, where they are systematically supported by the public, and where, for this reason, accurate statistics are accessible, is undoubtedly mostly due to hereditary transmission of defects and tendencies from parent to child. This unnecessary and unnatural increment should be prevented by adequate police regulations. Legislation should prohibit the marriage of the physically, mentally, or morally defective person, provide for the complete seclusion of these by law, and punish illegitimate sexual intercourse with them by a life-sentence to the penitentiary.

The noble spirit of philanthropy dangerously interferes with the natural processes of extinction of the deteriorated, incapable, and unfit, by interposing public care when they would perish if left to themselves by induced sterility and weakness. The diseased, crippled, or degraded pauper ought to be placed in special hospitals under State management, for cure, and surgical or educational treatment. In this way many might be restored to a condition of self-support, and liberated without danger to society, either from themselves or their descendants. In cases where competent medical authority should decide that defective offspring would naturally ensue upon

A GROUP OF PAUPERS IN AN ALMSHOUSE.

marriage, the patient should be detained in seclusion, and made to devote his life to earning his own and his dependent's support, under public care and direction. In such hospitals the victims of disabling accidents could and should be cared for and assisted, although, of course, without restriction as to marriage. Almshouses are as unfit and unsuitable places for the proper maintenance as these, as they are generally acknowledged to be for the maintenance of the large defective classes of deaf, blind, and insane. In such hospitals also, the weak-minded, the harmless and mildly insane, epileptics, and the incapable crank, could be cared for, made useful, and so prevented from propagating their disability.

Modern philanthropy has provided hospitals in our densest communities for the temporary relief of almost every special ailment; but, so far as we are aware, no State or city has yet established an institution for the permanent treatment and care of these large classes of defectives. A complete and comprehensive plan for dealing with pauperism must, however, include such an institution for each definite ratio of population. A ratio which could be properly determined by an examination of the various institutions where they are now maintained.

The second class of paupers, by our analysis, the hereditary or incorrigible beggar, tramp, vagrant or idler, should be incontinently passed into the State reformatory for convicts, to be treated; and either transformed into honest self-supporters, or transferred into the State penitentiary, for life. The attempt to procure an unearned living, the practice, or habit

14

of securing it, is in itself a theft from society. It is a crime against social order and divine law much more grave and injurious to the public, than any single taking of the property of an individual without his knowledge or consent. It should be made a penal offence, and consign the offender to his appropriate place among other convicts, where such offenders would become subject to the same influences and restraints as have been recommended for criminals, to which class they belong. Such an enactment would of its own motion tend to restrain and reduce the numbers disposed to fall into this class, and by its terror very largely protect society from those outrages which it now frequently suffers from it. It is well known, moreover, that the entire class is largely composed of criminals at large, who would thus be gathered into the institutions intended for them, without the cost or delay of a special crime, detection, trial, and conviction. This would be a result of important public economy, and sufficient alone to warrant the legislation required.

Another considerable and important class requiring special legislation and treatment is composed of those commonly spoken of as "unfortunate girls." It is made up of persons of all degrees of intelligence, immorality, and depravity, from the comparatively innocent victim of seduction to the common prostitute. They are driven to the almshouse or charitable institution by the compulsion of their circumstances. They remain pauperized so long as may be necessary, and depart, leaving their offspring to be reared at public cost ; many returning repeatedly for the same cause, and never leaving better than they came.

Indeed, with this double brand of sin and pauperism upon them, there is but one way to open them,—it is the way which "taketh hold on death." Under present conditions they are not only condemned to the pauper criminal class themselves, but to a continual breeding of criminals and paupers. Their children, "conceived in sin" and brought forth in iniquity, generally inoculated with the virus of drunkards, tainted with physical disease as well as moral corruption, are, if they live, destined by the law of heredity to follow the parental tendency, often so strong and dominant that, even under the most favorable environment and the wisest training, they are unable to overcome it.

The number of these illegitimates added to the population annually is much greater than is generally supposed. If the whole truth could be known, I have no doubt it would be appalling. I have been in almshouses where a stock of two dozen cradles were not considered unnecessary. There were twenty-one born in the Hillside Home of Scranton in the first six months of 1891. The number of children born in the almshouses of Pennsylvania each year, ending September 30th, for the ten years beginning with 1880, as shown by the reports of the Board of Public Charities, was consecutively 406, 355, 416, 435, 481, 436, 383, 376, 391, 365, a total of 4,054, and an annual average of 405.4. In 1889 there was added a report of seven "lying-in" hospitals in Philadelphia and fifteen general hospitals throughout the State, showing 505 illegitimates born therein; which, added to the average, makes a total of 910. In 1890 the total from both sources was 852. The reduction of births in almshouses since 1885 is doubtless to be attributed to improved hospital facilities. If the same ratio prevails throughout the entire population of the country, it would have yielded 10,834 illegitimate children to the United States in 1890. There is no good reason for believing that the state of society in Pennsylvania is worse than the average in this respect, and we are compelled to conclude that the criminal and pauper class is being augmented by births from this source alone at the rate of at least 10,000 per annum, in addition to the legitimates, if we may so call them, or the births to married criminals and paupers. This is certainly an element of large and serious consequence in our sociology. It reveals a condition which must be promptly recognized, adequately dealt with and counteracted. The danger of such an infusion of corruption into our national life-current cannot be safely ignored, for it is as great as any that threatens our welfare.

Scarcely any intelligent or comprehensive remedial scheme has been attempted, except perhaps by the Roman Catholic Church, in its system of "orphanages" for children and "Houses of the Good Shepherd" for the mothers. In these institutions, which are models of good management, the children are reared under kind and religious instruction until they can be entrusted to good familes; and the mothers maintained in seclusion occupied with useful industry until, reformed in character and health, they can be restored with safety to society. They indicate the general direction of the effort which must be made to meet the necessities of the case.

The first object society has to consider in the matter is to stop this illegitimate increase. The second is the reformation of the mother, and of the father, if he can be caught. The third, the rearing of the children into a condition of independent good citizenship.

The proportions of the evil have passed beyond the powers or control of private charity, and urgently demand the exercise of governmental functions. Every State must establish a " House of the Good Shepherd," though not in the ecclesiastical sense, sufficiently commodious for the care of all unmarried pauper mothers, to which the laws should compel its magistrates to remove them, with their children, wherever they are found, as soon as fit for removal; where they should remain at least two years to care for their children, if they live so long, or if they should not, until in the judgment of the matron and committing magistrate it would be best to restore them to freedom. In these houses the mothers should be kindly and judiciously trained, physically, mentally, and morally, with a view to reformation and cure. They should be kept employed, to educate them to honest self-support, and to reduce the expense to the public. The manifestly defective, diseased, or incorrigible should be transferred to the penitentiary for females, while the healthy and reformed should be provided with good situations. When the children arrive at two years of age they should be transferred to nurseries and kindergartens, whence, at a proper time, it should be the effort of the management to remove them into private families, by adoption, or indenture, if they are healthy and sound. These nurseries would afford employment for the best of the mothers.

The State of Pennsylvania requires such an institution to accommodate at least one thousand at the present time. As it would be expected to greatly diminish the evil it would be intended to relieve, the institution need not be of expensive design or construction. The buildings should not be large; they should be detached, for a proper division of the mothers according to moral and physical conditions, and for the care of the children. It should be managed by Christian women of ability and intelligence. Such an establishment would doubtless save the public direct cost of at least two hundred thousand dollars per annum; and more than twice that much in indirect and consequential damage. This, too, would be a constantly increasing benefit, for the number of depraved mothers is increasing, and contaminated children are multiplying continually under our present neglect.

Homeless children are a still larger class of paupers needing special care and attention. The deserted waifs of our city streets, the neglected offspring of the criminal and drunkard, orphans and half-orphans of the indigent, who may be unable or unfit to properly rear them, constitute an important and growing element of our denser communities, and require the immediate consideration of legislators for the protection of society. The pressure of necessity has compelled charitable societies and individuals to establish houses of correction and refuge, juvenile asylums, homes for the friendless, childrens' aid societies, and similar institutions here and there ; but they are managed without any general, regular, or complete system, according to the ideas and ability of their benevolent promoters, and afford but a local and sporadic relief.

The New York Juvenile Asylum, according to its last report, has cared for 28,745 during its existence. The report of the Board of Public Charities of Pennsylvania for 1890 gives the following census of pauper minors in public institutions in the State, September 30, 1890: In Philadelphia House of Correction, 1,005 ; House of Refuge, 735 ; Morganza, 509 ; Huntingdon Reformatory, 332 ; Deaf and Dumb Asylums, 648 ; Blind Asylums, 179; Elwyn Institution for Feeble-minded Children, 800 ; in almhouses, 445 ; reported in forty-seven out of one hundred and eighty-three other institutions, homes, orphanages, etc., excluding Girard College, 7,103 ; a total of 11,756. There were aided by "outdoor relief," during the year, 9,698. There were 78 sent to the penitentiaries ; and 457 committed to county-jails, under twenty-one years of age. For its 6,455 public insane patients, the State appropriated $465,166.14 ; but has absolutely no system for the care of its 21,455 pauper children !

It is of great importance that the States should adopt a systematic and adequate plan of care and

education for this large element of its future con-
stituency, which will not only comprehend the
entire class, but provide completely for its growth
into self-sustaining, useful citizenship. This can
only be assured by the maintenance under the management of Christian women, of homes for all these
children, into which they may be gathered and
trained, until they can be located under the domestic influence of good families in the country. The
subject of child-saving is of sufficient magnitude to
warrant a much more complete consideration than
we can give it here.

We have yet the third class of paupers for whom
to provide. These are the wounded, maimed, exhausted and sick in the battle of life; the true
objects of charity and benevolence. Many of these
have fallen out in the march from inherited weakness, or incapacity, but they have bravely under-
taken the struggle, and are entitled to social and
human sympathy and care. The sterner restrictions
of legislative enactments are unnecessary, except
to secure to them the aid and relief they may be
unable alone to obtain. There are two methods of
bestowing this in common use. One known as " out-
door relief "; the other as " almshouse treatment."

Public " out-door relief " is liable to serious abuse
and imposition. Almost universally it makes confirmed paupers of the recipients, who soon come
to depend upon, and demand it as a right due
them from the public treasury. On these accounts
"out-door relief " is regarded with disfavor by the
public and humanitarians. As the administering

officials are generally unable to properly investigate applications, they encourage fraudulent claims,
waste the public funds, or pervert them to political purposes, thus stimulating instead of reducing
pauperism. The fearful results of careless out-door
relief have been most impressively demonstrated in
the exhaustive and instructive report of Prof. J. J.
McCook, of Hartford, chairman of a committee
appointed by that town in October, 1890, upon
"out-door alms." He shows that Hartford, in
twenty years, had gained 41.1 per cent. in population, 51.8 per cent. in paupers, and 277.9 per cent.
in cost of relief per capita. Its pauper population
had increased, notwithstanding the general prosperity of the city, to 1 to every 16.1 of its people.
This is a greater average than exists in any of seventeen European countries, which averaged 1 in 29.8 ;
England and Wales having 1 in 36, Ireland 1 in 35.7,
Scotland 1 in 57.9. Compared with cities in 1890,
London had 1 in 40.6 ; Manchester 1 in 42.2 ;
Whitechapel (London) 1 in 41.7 ; Philadelphia in
1889, 1 to 78 ; Worcester, Mass., in 1890, 1 to 23;
Berlin in 1885 had 1 in 26.2 ; Dresden in 1889, 1 in
49.[1] The charge upon the taxpayers of the city had
grown to one hundred and eighty-nine dollars per
capita in this time. The reform resulting from his
investigations and recommendations are concisely
stated by Professor Graham Taylor, D.D., in the
Congregationalist of November 26, 1891, and we
quote what he says, as indicating in detail the
restrictions to be imposed upon that kind of relief.

[1] See Appendix V.

" In a single year, with an increasing population, the city of Hartford, Conn., has reduced the ' out-door alms' of its municipal or 'town' charities by nearly ten thousand dollars. This is offset by the addition of only eight inmates to the almshouse, despite the cutting off of seventy-four ' rents,' and the reduction of all payments of rent to a maximum of four dollars per month. Not only has there been no appreciable increase in the demand upon the voluntary charities, but the town expense in caring for the poor in the almshouse has actually decreased ; the burial account, upon which the expense of one in five of all the burials in the town were found to be charged, has been lessened by seventy-six cases ; the coal account was diminished by two hundred and forty-eight tons, and the pauper population has been reduced 18.14 per cent. Notwithstanding additional expenses incurred this first year by inaugurating the new system, the selectmen report a reduction of 9.48 per cent. in the total expense for 'all relief.' The yearly average of this. reduction should be much more marked within the first few years of the reform period. But the saving in the manhood of the poor is worth more to the commonwealth than the money saved.

" This genuine social economy was effected by the adoption in town meeting of the following business methods for the administration of town charity : rent not exceeding four dollars per month to be paid only to families in 'legal settlement,' having one child under fourteen ; investigation and recorded report of all applications for any aid ; not more than one dollar and fifty cents to be given in any case before such investigation ; no grocery orders on stores to be given ; grants of supplies to be made only from storeroom kept by the town and stocked with ten designated articles most necessary to sustain life ; medical treatment only for present existing sickness or injury ; town physicians to be nominated by the Hartford Medical Society ; police court commitments to be excluded from almshouse, which shall be reserved for poor persons only ; revision of rules for almshouse management ; burials paid for by the town to be managed by the town at a cost not exceeding fifteen dollars ; lengthened terms of commitment to jails after third conviction ; fuller statistical and comparative reports to be made of all charity administration.

" Of equal and even more permanent and wide-reaching value are two results attained in the instrumentalities used to secure this reform. First there came the long-belated, but now permanently established, Charity Organization Society, which is an essential substitute for the vicious methods abandoned. But the greatest of all the good accomplished by this whole movement is the report of the special committee on out-door alms, upon which were based the above-given recommendations that were adopted by the town. It contains the most exhaustive tabulation and practical study of comparative statistics bearing on municipal out-door relief that has ever been made in this country. To its author, Rev. Professor J. J. McCook, of Trinity College, Hartford, the country is indebted for the most important contribution on this subject to its sociological literature. His tables of the comparative charity statistics of American and foreign communities, and the appendixes, including discussion of the legal, historical, political, economic, sanitary, and social aspects of the charity problem; make the report a permanent classic in the literature of the subject."

Prof. McCook has kindly permitted the publication in the Appendix of several tables collated by him in the interest of public instruction, to which attention is invited.[1]

In our opinion it were better that public out-door relief should be prohibited by law, except in cases of sudden calamity, and to assist honest, hard-working children to maintain indigent parents at home; or indigent widows to keep their children under their own care. All other proper objects of charity should be provided for either in the almshouse, or by private benevolence. This latter should be allowed opportunity, as a public necessity, to foster the birth and growth of divine charity in the human heart. For upon the development and diffusion of this spirit depends all human progress. In order that private benevolence may be wisely and efficiently administered in these days of steam and electricity, when those best able to give are least able to investigate, because of the incessant pressure of personal affairs

[1] See Appendices IV. and V.

upon their time, a system and organization are necessary. For it must be accepted as an axiom, that every dollar that is given for the mere asking is worse than wasted.

Every city should have an organization of all its charitable individuals and societies, represented by an agent, or agents, to whom all applications may be referred ; and whose duty should be to see that no needy, deserving persons should suffer for want of timely aid. Such aid should be only temporary, and intended to restore the assisted to a position of self-support, by providing work, and teaching how to earn. In this way mendicity may be totally eradicated without compunction to the conscience of any. Where such an organization is sustained, in conjunction with the necessary State institutions suggested, there need be no suffering on account of poverty, and pauperism will be reduced to its minimum. This is not simply a theory or opinion, but has been demonstrated in many places, and repeatedly. The most beneficial relief is that of human sympathy and kindness; a manifestation of the universal brotherhood of man; which not only revives the flagging hope of the afflicted, but gives him courage, with the consciousness that he is recognized as still in the race, and capable of independence, so soon as he is on his feet again. This is better than all material aid, though this must be supplied also. Let us then have organization in every community to look after and help the needy, and abolish, as far as possible, the dole from taxation so often demanded as a right.

How then shall the real objects of charity, our third class of heteronomics be provided for? That is, those whom age, disability, infirmity, or misfortune, have rendered permanently dependent?

Proper legislation might materially reduce the number of these also, by enforcing the support of the aged and children by the next of kin, wherever it is possible ; thus recognizing and enacting the laws of nature in the human code. For there are some (the inspector of pauperism is shocked to discover so many) children who are not only willing, but anxious, to shift the burden of the support of their helpless parents upon the shoulders of the public; as insensible of the claims of filial affection as of duty. Unnatural and hard-hearted parents abound also who seem to regard their offspring as an encumbrance and expense, from which they strive to obtain relief in almost any way short of actual murder ; some who do not even stop short of that. It may not be for the public interest that such parents should be compelled, or that the difficult attempt should be made to compel them to discharge their natural duties, but they certainly should be made to defray the cost when the public performs this for them. Their natural disposition warrants the exercise of severity, absolves the public from considerations of pity or sympathy on account of any alleged inabilities, and they should be held to a strict account.

As the numbers of this third class are great, always have been, and probably always will be, experience and theory agree in an indisputable demonstration

that they must be cared for in public almshouses.
It is unwise and unsafe to attempt regular and permanent relief to them in any other way, for any
other plan inevitably results in neglect and suffering
to the worthy, in great imposture and abuse of
charity, and in the increase of pauperism to an insupportable extent. It must be accepted as an axiom
of public relief that when it is to be continuous and
regular the aid must be rendered in a regularly organized institution. To this the applicant for assistance must be transferred before public support
by taxation can be conferred. As the duty of maintenance rests upon society in general, the response
must be from the social organization, and not from
private charity ; by equal taxation of all, rather than
the benevolence of a few, however large their
interest.

This duty being a just and properly admitted one
in all ages and among all nations, its performance
should be consistent with the best sense of kindness
or charity of the community when the objects are
restricted to legitimate dependents. It becomes
a public duty to be discharged with intelligence,
care, thoughtful consideration, and as much of
human sympathy as can be infused into a public
function or functionary. While the actual performance must necessarily be delegated to paid officials,
it is very important that the community at large
should retain a vital and constant interest in it, and
manifest this by frequent visitation and supervision.
This is more necessary to the community than even
to the well being of the dependent. For society

cannot relieve itself of its responsibility by simply paying the bills. This is the only way even a flavor of charity can be retained in public alms, either as to the giver or recipient, without which the " poor rate " becomes an irritation and its disbursement a graceless exaction.

We have already indicated the necessity for uniform and systematic legislation concerning the poor; for single county almshouses, where a dense population does not make more than one necessary; for paid county overseers, who shall devote their entire time to the administration of the public alms. We have also called attention to other improvements formulated in the law which was presented to the Pennsylvania Legislature of 1891, but prevented from receiving even a consideration by the short-sighted or selfish influence of present officials.

In addition to the general provisions of this law, a Board of County Visitors should be constituted from the most intelligent and philanthropic citizens of both sexes, with rights and powers of visitation and inspection, and the duty of making a public report upon the management of the poor fund in every county. The public should also be constantly urged to visit and inspect the almshouse, and comfort the inmates by their attention.

County visitors should minutely inspect the buildings from cellar to garret, talk with and encourage the inmates to talk freely with them, suggest such reforms and changes as seem necessary, in a kindly way to the officials, endeavor to secure as near approach to the conditions and management indicated hereinafter, as practicable, and keep a record of their observations. Constant inspection and suggestion will promote continual improvement, and finally secure fair results, even where the accommodations have been badly located and unwisely built.

The location, construction, and naming of public poor-houses in America has hitherto been governed by no settled rules or principles, but rather by the caprice of officials of every diversity of intelligence and disposition, so that examples are frequent of almost every degree of excellence and unfitness, extravagance and meanness,—results due, we are confident, more to lack of proper information than intention. The consequence is an enormous waste, in the aggregate, of the public resources, both in first cost and subsequent conduct. We therefore venture to offer some suggestions, derived from a diversified observation, upon these subjects before proceeding to a consideration of the treatment of paupers in them.

The location of the almshouse should be decided upon these considerations chiefly. There should be connected with it at least one hundred acres of good fertile land, for a less quantity does not warrant building and the expense of management. The quantity of land should not be less than two acres for each expected inmate, between fifty and two hundred and fifty. When larger numbers are to be provided for, a proportionate increase should be made in acreage according to circumstances. In agricultural communities the public farm should be made as far as possible an experimental station, where local problems concerning crops, cultivation, and breeding of stock could be solved at the public expense, for the general good. The land should be fertile and fitted for economical tillage, so that it may be made to produce with the inefficient labor of the paupers as much as possible of their support.

All vegetables, potatoes, cabbage, turnips, carrots, beets, peas, beans, green corn and dry, rye and buckwheat, and in favorable localities wheat, needed, should be raised on the premises. The railroads have made it generally possible to buy wheat flour, beef, and pork from the West cheaper than they can be produced in the East. It will be found economical to raise some pork, generally, to dispose of refuse, and sufficient pasturage and fodder for the cows needed to supply butter and milk must be calculated upon. Orchards and fruit-trees should be set out, and plantations of small fruits, berries, and grapes made to whatever extent they can be cared for. Some flowers and ornamental shrubbery will afford pleasant entertainment in cultivation, and appearance to all.

The buildings should be placed upon a high and well-drained position, where proper sewerage may be secured, and where they may be plentifully supplied with pure soft water by gravity to the second story. This supply of water is indispensable, and must be secured by an elevated reservoir where the natural fall is insufficient. Without such a perpetual and reliable water-supply it is impossible to maintain satisfactory conditions or management.

15

They should be within a reasonable distance of a station on a railway or water-way, so as to be accessible to visitors, but remote enough to prevent the premises from becoming a loafing ground for the idle and curious, and to prevent the inmates from easy access to liquor saloons.

The buildings should be permanently constructed of brick or stone, to save the cost of renewals and repairs, and for security against fire. They should never be more than two stories high. The best design we know is in plan in shape of the letter " **T**." A house for the steward and the offices being at the intersection of the cross, connected with a wing on each side, one for males, the other for females, and toward the rear with the building containing kitchen and dining-rooms, by a corridor divided lengthwise by a partition, which continues and completes that separation of the sexes so absolutely essential. The two floors of the wings have a wide hall running the entire length, and ending at a large window from which an iron fire-escape leads to the ground. In the middle of each wing is a large day-room opening to the front, and a passage leading to a separate building in which are bath-rooms, closets, cells for filthy or diseased patients, and which are also suitable for use as an infirmary ; this passage is ventilated on both sides by windows to prevent contamination or odor. In each annex there should be a closet for brooms, brushes, pails, and utensils. In each wing a room is devoted to the storage of the clothing and effects of the inmates, with a framework for compartments, eighteen inches square, along the sides. Trunks and boxes may be arranged in the middle.

Walls should be covered with adamant plaster, all corners rounded, to avoid the angles where cobwebs and vermin are apt to collect, and wainscoated high enough to prevent the hand from soiling the plaster. The cellar and closet floors and washboard throughout, should be of cement. All doors should open outward into the hall, be fitted with such locks that a single master-key will open all, both for convenience of inspection and safety of the inmates, and from sleeping-rooms have an open transom reaching to the ceiling, without glass or frame, for ventilation. The buildings should be heated with steam by indirect radiation, supplied from boilers located outside.

Where fuel is cheap, electrical lighting is preferable, as safest and most easily controlled. The laundry may be over the boiler-house; it should not be in the main buildings. The stairs should be of iron with slate treads. A room should be provided for religious worship and general meetings. Barns, stables, and out-buildings should be far enough removed to avoid disagreeable odors and noises.

Such a plan as this may be adapted to the requirements of any number almost. It is important that the appearance of the whole establishment should express economy and plain utility, rather than elegance or display. Iron bedsteads with woven spring mattresses have been found the cheapest and cleanest. They should have also straw or husk mattresses; two sheets, woollen blankets, a white cover, pillows and pillow-cases, so that they may always be kept clean and appear neat with but slight cost, for the washing should be done by the inmates. Porcelain lined bath-tubs with rounded edges are best and not now expensive; they should be set on legs above the floor and not cased in with wood, but neatly painted outside. Wash-basins and water-closets should also be open underneath, so that perfect neatness may be preserved, and the nuisance of decaying wood avoided. A flue to the chimney-shaft from under the closets will carry away all gases. It is important that the plumbing be done by a skilled and intelligent designer and workman, to prevent future disease and cost. Bath-rooms and closets must be kept neat and clean by frequent scrubbing, or they will soon become repulsive. Small cheap towels, to be used but once, should be supplied to avoid communication of skin and eye diseases.

In these days of cheap and durable porcelain, tin and metal dishes should be banished from the eating tables. But more important than clean white dishes are the services of a good baker and cook; more important to the content of the inmates than plenty and variety of food even, for by them the cheapest articles of diet can be made attractive and sufficient; without them, the most extravagant outlays will be spoiled and in vain.

The exercise of a more careful discrimination as to admissions to the almshouse is not only important in a social aspect, but is in justice due the real objects of charity, who ought not to be compelled to associate with the vicious or depraved, or even kept in the same institution. Much of the repugnance of the pauper to the poor-house is doubtless the out-growth of this understanding that it is the receptacle of so many disreputable persons. It is abhorrent to all that the poor unfortunate, bereft of family, health, and means of support, should be condemned by misfortune to the society of drunkards, tramps, and prostitutes. Wherever these are found in sufficient numbers they should, even now, before the general reformation of our laws is secured, be confined in a workhouse where they can be treated by them-selves.

County workhouses are more necessary than alms-houses, in most parts of the country. By means of these the proper objects of charity may be kept by themselves and the manner of their treatment may not only be greatly simplified and improved, but will become more economical. The attendants will be of a better class, and the sympathies of officials and the community will not be dulled by the exactions of professional beggars. The numbers to be main-tained would thus also be reduced from one half to three quarters in most localities.

As helplessness will then be the chief character-istic of the inmate, attention and care will become the chief feature of the charity, and may be made to express the kindness of the public, instead of its economical impulses. Almshouse management should be actuated primarily and principally by four motives.

First, by a desire to conform to " Heaven's first law " of order and neatness in every detail. Nothing can compensate for shortcomings in these respects, because complete conformity is always possible under all circumstances, and because lavish attention and expenditure will be unsatisfactory to all concerned without this, while content will be assured with even limited allowances with it. To this end the grounds and buildings must be kept in order and repair, grass and shrubs trimmed, walks clean and neat, fences and walks painted or lime-washed, comfortable seats provided for the aged and invalids to sun themselves in cool weather, and rest themselves in shade in hot, and the whole outward appearance of the premises made as pleasant as possible with the labor of the inmates.

Inside, the floors should be oiled every few months and washed twice a week at least; beds and bedding aired daily, fresh mattresses supplied each new-comer, and the straw of those in use changed every sixty days. Sheets, pillow-cases, and coverlets washed weekly, and all beds made up neatly, and alike, each day before noon. A separate bed should be given to each inmate, no clothing, boots, shoes, hats, or personal baggage kept in sleeping rooms, and bed-steads thoroughly washed weekly. Each inmate should be made to bathe and change underclothing once a week. Washing of clothes, dishes, or uten-sils in bath-tubs should be prohibited, bath-rooms and closets should be scrubbed daily, and in hot weather a bucket of water with a pound of dry cop-peras (sulphate of iron) dissolved in it, or a little carbolic acid, should be poured in closets once a week. No vegetables or fruits should be stored in the cellars of occupied buildings, which should be kept dry, and whitewashed every spring.

The cooking should be under the direction of a competent cook, capable of preparing and serving the food in a digestible and attractive manner, properly seasoned ; who also should keep kitchens, storerooms, pantries, utensils, and all employed about them in the most scrupulous neatness. Meals should be served at regular hours, upon neat tables in the dining-room, where some officials should always be present at meal time to see that all are well served and everything in order.

In the Appendix will be found several dietaries in use in various well-managed institutions, which will indicate what experience has demonstrated to be the best provision for the pauper. These, of course, are to be varied according to season and locality, especially in regard to fruit and vegetables. All meats, fish, bread, and butter must be perfectly sound, fresh, and sweet.[1]

Secondly, the benevolence of the public is to be administered with kindness and thoughtful care. The aged, the bedridden and invalid require patience and a measure of indulgence. Their lot is hard enough at best, and should be alleviated in every possible way by the attendants. A competent physician should visit such daily, for comfort and assurance sake, even if no medicines are needed, and prescribe the diet and attention needed by them. Where there are as many as three or four of these constantly, a trained nurse should be regularly em-

[1] See Appendix IV.

ployed with a sufficient number of assistants to care
for all in the house, under the direction of the doctor.
Such a nurse will secure the necessary cleanliness
and neatness in all the surroundings. The people's
money cannot be more advantageously expended
than by the employment of capable attendants.

Thirdly, nothing will contribute to the health
and content of the inmates and the economy of
their support more than constant and judicious
employment. By this they will be able to feel that
they are to some extent earning their own support,
and so much of the bitterness will be removed from
the gall of pauperism.

The males should do most of the farm- and gar-
den-work; raising the principal farm and garden
supplies, do the heavier house work, the repairing,
painting, whitewashing and most of the scrubbing,
and in winter or bad weather be occupied in basket-,
broom-, mat-making, carpet-weaving, shoemaking and
mending.

The females should do the sewing, mending, dress-
making, the washing and ironing, kitchen and dining-
room work, and those with a taste for it could be
occupied with flowers and flower-beds outside. The
old women and invalids should be made to knit
socks, mittens, and do such other light work as
they can perform ; they might be permitted to sell
such articles as may be in demand, and supply
themselves thus with those things they desire
beyond the regular supply.

The officials and attendants should pay sufficient
attention to discover the abilities of the various

inmates, and to make adequate plans to use these to the best advantage. Useful labor will distract the mind from brooding over personal miseries, soothe the suffering, comfort the mourning, strengthen the weak, and bring sweet, soul-refreshing sleep to the tired and forlorn. Better than drugs, more blessed and efficacious than idle rest even, suitable labor is the most beneficial boon public charity can confer upon its objects.

By a studious effort to adapt work to the abilities of the inmate the highest economy of management will be secured. This is the fourth motive principle referred to above. The people's money must be neither wasted nor so expended as to fail of the best results. Poor directors should inform themselves carefully of the best methods of management; of the fair cost per week in the best institutions, and strive to keep their own expenses down to a parity with these.

Successful and economical management can only be secured by a proper grading of responsibility. Poor directors are responsible to the people; the superintendent to the poor directors; the subordinates to the superintendent; each is, and ought to be, supreme in their respective spheres of operation. The superintendent cannot accomplish what is expected of him without strict discipline and system; he cannot maintain either without the unbiassed power of selection and discharge of all employees about the establishment. Even a superintendent of mediocre ability with unhampered powers and control will produce better results than is possible with the highest abilities, and a double- or triple-headed management. Experience has abundantly demonstrated that success in private or public affairs depends more upon that unity of purpose, plan, and action, which can only flow from a " one-man power " at the head, than upon any other element.

Directors may prescribe the general plans and policies, limit the expenditures, provide facilities, buildings, and improvements; fix the rate of salaries and wages, and select a superintendent to manage; but they must leave him entirely free to do it in his own way, to hire and discharge all his subordinates, if they expect him to produce satisfactory results. The slightest infraction of this rule will seriously affect the whole administration, and directors should neither recommend appointments without assuring the superintendent that he is perfectly free to exercise his own judgment and preference in the case, nor interfere to secure the reinstatement of a discharged employee.

It is far better that an individual should suffer injustice even, than that the whole organization should be impaired.

It is the duty of the management to facilitate religious instruction, worship, and consolation to the paupers, according to their respective convictions and preferences. To this end a proper place for Sunday services should be provided, and regular services held in them by ministers and priests of such denominations as are most numerous in the almshouse, every Sunday, upon invitation of the management to those most conveniently located to render such ministry. Ministration to the minority according to their belief and desire should be secured as often as possible. Pastors and priests of sincere piety will always be found willing to render such services without cost to the public. When these become too burdensome upon individuals, the denomination most interested should defray the necessary expense, as a proper and necessary contribution of the church to its poor.

It cannot be tolerated or allowed that any portion of the public fund raised by general taxation should be expended in payment for such services to sectaries. Such expenditures are in violation of one of the most sacred and cardinal principles and fundamental institutions of American government, as well as the constitution and laws of many of the States.

Poor directors are somewhat prone to be oblivious of the fact that they, as a part of the general government, are bound to sustain and uphold its principles in all their actions. If they may appropriate the public funds to sectarian ministers or priests, legislatures and Congress will soon begin to make similar appropriations, and a general scramble of the churches would follow to secure the largest amounts for their denominational institutions. The inevitable result in the process of time would be that the largest denominations would obtain undue wealth and power, and the usual sequestration become necessary.

The practice of defraying the cost of maintaining minor or adult paupers in sectarian institutions from the public poor fund is likewise reprehensible and illegal in States where appropriations to such institutions are prohibited by the constitution or laws. This cannot be permitted, however much better or cheaper the pauper might be sustained in them, than by the poor directors directly. It is an unjust and unfair subversion of funds derived from " Jew and Gentile, Greek and Barbarian " alike, to the support of a particular sect, which, if it desires to support, train, or educate the needy according to its own creeds, should be willing to procure the necessary means from its own adherents.

The strict observance of this principle is necessary, whatever the hardship which may follow in some cases, in order that the general good may finally be promoted by compelling a proper, just, and unobjectionable provision for the needy by the State ; such provision is unlikely to be made so long as the most urgent and impressive cases are constantly removed from public attention by private or denominational institutions.

CHAPTER XIV.

THE POLICE AS A RESTRICTIVE AGENCY.

NOWHERE, probably on the face of the globe, does what is commonly known as the police force occupy so prominent, important, and influential a position and sphere in the social organization as it does in the United States ; nowhere does it sustain so potent a relation to pauperism and crime as here. We do not minify or disparage its power or operations in other civilized nations, however much these may be obscured among them by the display of superior and more impressive authority ; for the potentialities and full usefulness of this element of modern civilization and human progress does not appear to be popularly recognized or appreciated anywhere. In the United States, however, under a social organization for self-government, a government of laws, which are solely the formulated decrees of popular judgment and will, the police and constabulary constitute almost the only incorporate and vital evidence, or general manifestation of the authority and dignity of government ; they represent the concrete absolutism of the laws, and exercise the majesty and power of the people in, among, and before the people constantly. They become, therefore, to the people here, not only the agents and representatives of self-government, but the express force and soul of government, the general and popular conception of government itself. This increases the power, dignity, and influence of the police officer in this country immeasurably above what exists elsewhere. It is his province here to bring the popular power into direct contact with and control over the people. From the manner in which he does this the masses form their opinions largely of the worth and value of the rule to which they submit themselves. His action thus becomes a potent factor in the conservation or destruction of popular government, and extends its influence beyond the direct effect of its exercise to the very sources of its power. The legislation which the people enact for their own benefit is committed to him for execution, and it fails or accomplishes the wish of the people according as he discharges his duties. The most necessary and wisest laws are useless without his faithful execution, and the simplest regulations and ordinances may be made imperative or obnoxious by his neglect. Success of administration, and popularity of government both depend, therefore, very largely here upon the efficiency of the police.

The protection of society from the violence of mobs and the insane rage of riot, to which it is always more or less exposed in dense communities, devolves, in the United States principally, if not altogether, upon the police. With our system of city, State, and national government, the only regular military force being under national orders, small in numbers and scattered in detachments over a wide extent of territory, circumstances as well as law prevent its being called into action until local authority has failed, and there is no force organized to meet sudden emergencies of popular excitement, at the time when it can be most easily and successfully allayed, but the police.

Our cities, besides, are becoming the resort and refuge of the worst elements of immigration as well as of our own population. Criminals, anarchists, and ferocious human beasts of prey from all over the world seek to escape foreign espionage, and to ply their ungoverned vocation amid our crowds of freemen, because they expect to enjoy a liberty here denied them under the sterner governments of other lands. The very immigration which swells and increases our national growth and power beyond its natural increment becomes thus a source of new danger, and magnifies the importance of police supervision.[1] It introduces another element, also, of disturbance and danger to our peace and natural order, by importing into our social organization the prejudices, feuds, and hostilities of foreign nationalities, religions, and

---

[1] The New York *Tribune* of March 20, 1892, says, under date of Paris, March 19th, in relation to anarchist deviltries there, "Thirty have fled to London, and are seeking funds there to reach New York."

clans, liable to blaze up into conflict and strife in our midst from the embers of antagonisms kindled in other lands and times. We are transplanting the hates and strifes of other peoples upon our soil, as well as the acknowledged enemies of all law and order, the communist, anarchist, and nihilist, and thereby exposing ourselves to imported disorders which have no natural origin here. We must depend upon our police to control these elements, to protect us from the attack of the vice of the whole world, from the burden of the pauperism of the whole world, from the ignorance, corrupted intelligence, depraved philosophies, wrath, malice, and hate of the whole world, as no other people is compelled to depend upon them.

The police are, particularly in this country, the eyes and ears, as well as the hands, of the body politic; not only the means of governmental apprehension, but of discovery; the agents of prevention as well as of cure. It devolves upon them to observe the very beginnings of error, failure, and sin in society; to note the sources, the inception and conception of crime and poverty; to watch their birth, growth and development; to become familiar with causes and occasions, to recognize the necessary remedies. They seldom feel called upon to interfere; indeed, the principle of their action is not to interfere before the overt act, when correction becomes necessary and prevention is no longer practicable. The intimacy and constancy of their contact with society and its elements should enable them to stretch out the helping or the warning hand of government when it could be efficient, when the needed slight change of direction can be given the individual faced the wrong way, before the club, the handcuff or the lock-up have become necessary. Indeed, an interference which would be resented from a private person, however gently or kindly made, would be received not only without objection ordinarily from the policeman, but it would carry with it the weight and influence of the wisdom and will of society. A word or an act which would make no impression without authority, with it might be effectual in saving many a youth from ruin. If the police then could be enlisted as conservators of morals as well as preservers of the peace, they would become a power in the community of inestimable utility, and the necessities of their harsher activities would be greatly decreased. The task of training the twig is lighter than bending the tree. If they could be made to devote their chief care to the children and youths when they are beyond the parental eye or control and be placed in a position representing with authority the organized parentage and domesticity of the community outside its homes, upon the streets and in public places, many of the dangers of city life would be alleviated. Their parental functions might be extended for the general benefit to the relief of the poor from suffering, to the ministrations of charity, to the restrictions of intemperance, the arrest of drunkenness, the correction of evil tendencies and the rescue of those in peril of moral corruption and ruin. They are already required to know the various saloons, traps

and pitfalls set for the feet of the unwary, as well as
the criminals and human life hunters that infest the
streets. Set as they are to watch over the welfare
of society, they may properly be expected and required to protect the ignorant and innocent from
contamination as well as from direct assault.

Modern civilization appears to have revolved in
its cycle to the section of tribal supervision again,
to have reached a social condition where the power
and authority of the whole community must be exercised over the children of all. It seems to be necessary that the old patriarchal system should be
revived again in some of its fittest features in our
denser communities, to supplement and perfect the
delimitations which the new environments impose
upon the family. The power of the city home is
growing weaker, the influence of city streets and
public places upon the rising generations of all
classes and degrees is being disproportionately magnified in every way, by the decreasing part of daily
life spent in the homes, and by the increasing attraction and entertainment offered to the public. These
things greatly enlarge the duties and opportunities
of those to whom society commits the charge of its
common possessions and the frequenters of its public
places. Many children of the city are under the eye
of the police much more of their time than they are
under any other charge or care, yet society only requires of its police protection from actual violence,
ignoring the greater and more far-reaching injury
and damage certain to follow the neglect of its
children and youth.

In view of these considerations it will be well to study the present conditions and possibilities of the police force, to discover how it can be best made to fulfil the demands of the times, the requirements of government and the expectation of society. These are subjects quite as grave and important as the enaction of wise laws; indeed, just now more depends upon faithful administration and vigorous execution than upon legislation even. Another reason for such a study is found in the tendency of the public mind toward an extension of the police system over the rural part of the population. It is probable that the time is not remote when all constabulary functions will be devolved upon a uniformed and systematically organized police force in the United States. The country constable and justice of the peace, as at present chosen and paid, supporting themselves upon fees for the performance of their duties, are becoming more and more generally recognized as a social abomination and public nuisance, which must before long be abated, together with the sheriff's control of jails for the public welfare. In the cities the constable has ceased to be regarded as more than a court messenger, and the police are depended upon for order and safety. The necessity for a regularly employed and well organized State police force, sufficiently strong, when concentrated, to control riotous strikers and protect property and willing workers for a longer period than the members of the National Guard can be expected to suddenly leave their occupations, has been notably illustrated by the shocking experiences

this year at Homestead, in Western Pennsylvania.
A couple of thousand well drilled policemen could
have been concentrated and camped there for an
indefinite stay, without serious inconvenience to
themselves and to the great discouragement of the
strikers, as rapidly as the guard was. The policeman is becoming continually more prominent in a
sociological aspect, and it is time careful attention
should be given to his selection and duties.

The *personnel* of the force is of the first importance. As he is to be popular representative of the
majesty and authority of our government, the
policeman ought to be suggestive, and, as far as
possible, typical in appearance of the dignity and
invincible authority of the government. He should
be a man of imposing health, strength, and stature;
expressing morality, firmness, decision, and power,
in his demeanor; and always manifesting consideration for the public weal in his actions. It is necessary then, that he should be a man of good character
and morals, of strong physique, sound intelligence,
judgment, and patriotism; an American citizen by
birth or lawful naturalization, with a good knowledge
of and hearty sympathy with American government
and institutions, and capable of becoming familiar
with our laws and local ordinances.

While he should be a young man when appointed
on the force, he should still be old enough to warrant
the possession of discretion and courage; between
twenty-five and thirty-five should be limits of age.
He should be above the average height, and of proportionate weight and strength, in order that fewer

may dare resist him. It would be well to adopt a minimum height of 5 feet, 10 inches, and 150 pounds as a minimum weight; but no man should be appointed or considered for appointment, until after he shall have passed a satisfactory examination by a compe-. tent surgeon as to physical health and strength; nor till after he has produced conclusive evidence of good character and habits. As he is to represent among the people the honesty and honor of society, he must exemplify before them sobriety, sturdy incorruptibility, and dignity of character. These are valuable and rare qualities it is true, but obtainable, though not cheaply; the pay of the police must be sufficient to secure them. The old soldier said to his colonel in mitigation of an impending sentence for drunkenness, " You cannot expect all the civic virtues, and temperance included, for $13 a month."

An appointment upon the force should be for life or good behavior, and should relieve the officer from further solicitude concerning his position. Dismissal should never be possible, except as a result of a fair trial before a competent court, upon charges and specifications, for unfitness or misconduct. Appointments should never be made on account of political service, rendered or expected. The force must be absolutely independent of partisanship to be efficient; it cannot be tolerated that it should be prostituted to political purposes, or to influence elections. More than officials in general, it represents and has the care of the whole body of society, irrespective of party, or including all parties. The very fact that it could be made so powerful an instrument in carrying elections renders it essential that it should be entirely independent of politicians, both in respect to appointments and promotions. Politi- cal indorsement or influence ought always to be fatal to any application for place or advancement. Politicians must evince enough patriotism to at least keep hands off from the police. No political corruption can be more debasing or destructive of our free people's rule, than the subordination of the popular agents of government to partisan pur- poses. They must be as far above suspicion even as Cæsar's wife.

To insure this, it appears to be necessary that all appointments to the force should be regulated by legal enactment. This should prescribe the essen- tial qualifications of physical, mental, and moral character, age and record, to be determined by a board of four commissioners, not more than two of whom should belong to the same political party; and that the selection should be made, according to the need of the service, from the list of applicants whose examinations have shown the best qualifications. Promotions should be similarly regulated, and depend upon seniority and ability combined. Service and merit stripes should mark and reward faithfulness, and be attended with increase of pay. The rules for appointment and promotion adopted by the Board of Police Commissioners of Milwaukee, Wis., have been so successful in securing the desired objects, that we quote a very concise and complete summary of them read before the Fourteenth Annual Con-

ference of Charities at Omaha, by Col. F. J. Ries,
Chief, for the benefit of other places.

"Applicants for patrolman must not be less than twenty-five nor
more than thirty-five years of age, at least 5 feet, 7 inches tall, must
be citizens of the United States, must be able to speak the English
language understandingly, and must have resided in the city of Milwaukee at least three years immediately preceding the application.
Every application must be in the applicant's own handwriting, and
state his age and place of birth, weight, chest measure, place of residence, occupation, schooling, how long the applicant has resided in
the city, what trade he has learned, if any, and by whom employed
the last three years. Applicants must also state what language, if
any, besides the English, they can speak understandingly. Each
application must be accompanied by the certificates of at least three
reputable citizens, each certifying that he has been personally acquainted with the applicant for at least one year last past, and
believes him to be of good moral character, of correct and orderly
deportment, of temperate and industrious habits, and in all respects
fit for the police service. As a safeguard against partisanship, it is
provided that certificates signed by office-holders will not be considered. Every applicant must answer such questions and submit to
such examination as to physical strength, capacity and activity, and
also as to educational qualifications, as the board may deem necessary
to ascertain his fitness for the service. The educational tests consists
of reading from print and manuscript, handwriting as shown from
copying from manuscript, writing from memory the substance of
matter communicated orally, arithmetic—addition, subtraction, multiplication, and division of whole numbers and decimals applied to
United States money. They will also be questioned about city government, location of streets, public buildings, and such general
matters as strangers in the city inquire about. They must also submit
to a thorough medical examination by a surgeon appointed by the
board. Those passing a satisfactory examination are then certified
by the board as eligible as patrolmen, and, after due inquiry and
satisfactory evidence of their good character, are appointed by the
chief, subject to confirmation by the board, as fast as vacancies occur.
But the appointment is not yet final. For the first sixty days they
are on probation only, and if, after two months of active duty, any
one proves himself unfit for the service, he will be dropped from the
force. If, however, he gives satisfactory evidence of becoming a

good and competent officer, he is retained on the force, so long as he performs his duties faithfully, and will only be discharged for neglect of duties, disobedience, or other conduct unbecoming an officer. All promotions to higher grades are made within the force. Here again, as in the case of patrolmen, the honors are bestowed upon those who, in connection with their record while in the service, are found by competitive examination to be best qualified for the place. Under the rules governing promotions, the chief shall give due notice of all examinations for promotion, and any officer who is eligible and who wishes to be a candidate for it may notify the chief in writing of his wish, and the chief will make such provision as shall be necessary, so that the examinations shall not interfere with the good of the service. The rules regulating promotions are as follows : Promotion to the position of roundsman will be made from patrolmen who have been in the service not less than two years ; promotion to the position of sergeant will be made from roundsmen ; promotion to the position of detective will be made from roundsmen and sergeants who have been in service not less than three years ; promotion to the position of lieutenant will be made from detectives and sergeants ; promotion to the position of captain will be made from lieutenants. The inspector is appointed by the chief, subject to confirmation by the board, while the chief is appointed by the board. Thus, it will be seen that every precaution is taken to keep politics and favoritism out, and retain good officers in the department." [1]

It certainly will be possible to secure a good reliable *personnel* on the force in this way, but good material alone will not constitute a perfect police, or secure its highest efficiency. Wise and firm instruction, drill, management, and discipline, and adequate faculties of operation are quite as essential, both as relating to the individual members, as well as to the force as a whole. It will be necessary to have every recruit drilled by a competent instructor, in what are known in military service as the "setting up exer-

[1] *Report of the Fourteenth Annual Conference of Charities and Correction*, Omaha, p. 120.

cises,'" by which he will be taught to stand erect, to pace his beat with a soldierly carriage of the person, and an expression of decision and power. He must be instructed in boxing, wrestling, handling his club with dexterity, and firing his revolver with accuracy, in the best methods of overcoming resistance in arrests, preventing and quelling disturbances, rendering assistance in accidents, protecting pedestrians on the streets, stopping fast or reckless driving, and runaway horses, the management of crowds, the care of property at fires, action on the discovery and giving of fire-alarms, and in other contingencies likely to arise. He should be required to exercise regularly in a gymnasium, for the development of strength and agility and the preservation of health, and to study the laws and ordinances he will be required to enforce.

His tour of daily duty should be eight hours, with four hours additional for meals, special details, instruction, etc., during which twelve hours, he should be dressed in the neatly fitting uniform of the corps. The superior officers should endeavor to inspire him, by precept and example, with a respect and love for the service, and a proper *esprit du corps.* He should be made in every way to feel perfect confidence that his place is assured for life to the age of retirement, unless abridged by misconduct or incompetency. A life-insurance and pension-fund should relieve him from anxiety for himself and family in case of disability or old age. Experience should teach him to expect exact justice and impartiality of management and inexorable firmness of discipline from his supe-

riors. Such vigilance of inspection and care should
be exercised by the superior officers, that no infraction
of orders, regulations, good morals, neglect or failure
of duty, should escape detection and punishment.

The force as a whole should be drilled together,
and instructed in operations as a united body against
mobs, both with clubs and with rifles, on public
occasions, and in parades. These parades are necessary to stimulate the *esprit du corps,* for instruction
of the force, as well as to impress the public with the
power of the force to cope with opposition. All promotions should be from the next inferior rank if it
contains proper ability. The measure and test of
efficiency should not be the record of the arrests made,
so much as the observance of law and freedom from
disturbances and need of arrests on the beat or in the
precinct. Every arrest should be recognized as a
serious expense and damage to society, as well as
to the individual arrested, and the effort should be
to avoid rather than to multiply them.

The usual organization of a good police force with
rank in the order named is as follows: First, the
chief, in command of all; second, inspectors, one
for every four captains or less, required ; third,
captains, one for every one hundred patrolmen;
fourth, a lieutenant for ever fifty patrolmen ; fifth,
detectives; sixth, sergeants for every twelve men ;
seventh, roundsmen ; eighth, patrolmen. The duties
of these officers are so well stated by Col. Ries that
we quote again from his admirable Omaha paper.

" The officers of each of these ranks are charged with specific
duties. It is the duty of the chief of police to cause the public peace

to be preserved, and to see that all the laws and ordinances of the city are enforced; and, whenever any violation shall come to his knowledge, he shall cause the requisite complaint to be made, and see that the evidence is procured for the successful prosecution of the offenders. He is also responsible for the efficiency and good conduct of the force.

" The duties of the inspector are to assist the chief in his various duties, and to have charge of the force in his absence. He has particular supervision of the detectives, who are especially charged with the apprehension of persons charged with criminal offenses, and the prevention of crime by the arrest of known thieves and criminals.

" The captain has supervision of the patrol service of the city. He is required to visit each police-station daily, inspect the men and the books of the station, and satisfy himself that good order prevails. He is also required to instruct the men in such military tactics as are useful for the police service.

" The city is divided into three police precincts, each having a police-station. Each of these precincts is in charge of a lieutenant. It is the duty of the lieutenants to see that the patrolmen perform their duties faithfully, investigate all complaints made by residents of their precincts, cause the prompt arrest of offenders, and maintain discipline among the men under them.

" The sergeants and roundsmen are to assist the lieutenants in supervising the patrolmen, see that the latter are on their several beats, and report any delinquency they may discover.

" The patrolmen are to obey the orders of their superior officers, and are charged with the duty of becoming thoroughly acquainted with their beat, so as to be better able to protect life and property and maintain good order. They are to treat citizens and strangers making inquiries with civility, and give all proper information in their power. It is also their duty to report all saloons on their beat, and see that no liquor is sold without a license, nor to minors or common drunkards, report all street lamps which are not lighted at night, see that signal lights are displayed at street obstructions, report all defective sidewalks and streets, prevent fast driving, serve official notices, collect delinquent personal taxes, and perform numerous other duties of minor importance. In the performance of their duties, they are to maintain decorum and attention, command of temper, patience and discretion. They must refrain from violent, coarse, profane, and insolent language, and never interfere idly or unnecessarily, nor make an arrest unless they can prove some specific act against the person, but, when required to act, do so promptly and with firmness. It is also their duty to assist and succor sick and injured persons, summon medical aid when necessary, have such unfortunates conveyed to their homes, and be at all times on the alert to relieve suffering as far as possible." [1]

There will also be required at station-houses a police matron to care for female prisoners and children, a police surgeon, an electrician, and other employees, according to circumstances.

As to what is the proper and most economical number for the force in our cities there exists a wide divergence of opinion and practice. New York maintains an officer for every 443, at a cost of $2.90 to each head, of its population, the largest and most expensive force in any of our fifty largest cities, while Scranton, Pa., may boast of the smallest force, an officer to every 2,023 of population, and Binghamton, N. Y., the cheapest, at a cost of 21 cents per capita, of these cities. [2] If public opinion, Dr. Parkhurst, and the recent indictment of the New York police by the Grand Jury are to be credited, neither large numbers nor high cost secure efficiency or satisfactory results.

The police force cannot well be proportioned entirely upon a population ratio. The streets to be patrolled, the area, the amount and kind of property to be protected, the character of the population, the peculiarities of location and the exposure to special

[1] *Report of the Fourteenth Annual Conference of Charities and Correction*, p. 116.

[2] *Census Bulletin*, No. 100, *Eleventh U. S. Census.* See Appendix.

dangers must all be taken into consideration and given their due influence in this determination. The Milwaukee police, to which we have referred above, numbered in 1890 one for each 1,187 of the city's population; it had a patrolman to each 244 miles of its streets, 10.13 patrolmen to each square mile of territory ; cost but 60 cents and made only 1.75 percentage of arrests per capita of population.[1] In a population half German and but one quarter native, itself largely composed of citizens of German birth or decent, such is the excellence of its organization and discipline that it suppressed a dangerous German socialistic mob without firing a shot, a few years ago, and has a general reputation of being the most efficient force in this country.   We may, I think, assume as a general rule, that one policeman to each 1,200 people will be sufficient, if properly selected and disciplined, for most localities. In the Appendix will be found a table of some of the Census police statistics of 1890 of our fifty largest cities making complete returns.   It will be apparent from a glance at this table that we directly waste millions of dollars annually upon our police by bad management, and that, too, without securing even a moderate approximation to the benefits which should be secured from it.   The table may be studied with profit by all our urban legislators.

Large cities must necessarily be divided into sections convenient for direct supervision and control. A police sub-division of this kind is known as a

[1] *Ibid.*

precinct, which should be in immediate command of a captain or lieutenant. Each precinct should have its station-house centrally located and speedily accessible to all its patrolmen, where a capable commanding officer should always be present, and a sufficient reserve force for use in emergencies. The patrol-wagon should be housed adjacent and kept packed with ropes and stakes for use at fires; a canvas to catch people jumping from windows, a stretcher for injured persons and some temporary surgical appliances for use in cases of accident. On each patrolman's beat there should be a sufficient number of signal-boxes connected by electric signal wires with the fire-alarm system, the patrol-wagon and station-house, and with the latter by telephone, so that every officer can place himself in speedy and full communications with headquarters, summon assistance, the patrol-wagon for arrested persons, without being obliged to leave his beat, and give such information and receive such orders as may be necessary. Our modern electrical appliances, lights, wire signals, and telephone, may be made, if intelligently used, to both greatly reduce the cost and increase the completeness of police protection.

The use of the patrol-wagon to convey arrested persons to the station-house is incomparably better in a philanthropic aspect than the shocking spectacle, so common before it came into use, of a struggling, resisting victim, bloody from clubbing, often loathsome, profane and obscene, dragged along the sidewalk at the head of a procession of youths and children, a spectacle so degrading that it is a question if such arrests do not injure more than they benefit society.

Each station-house should be in direct and constant communication with general headquarters, reporting all occurrences in the precinct. All verbal or telephone reports should be, of course, reduced to writing and preserved on file.

By the assignment of a patrolman to each twelve hundred ratio of the population, it would be quite practicable for the officer to become personally acquainted in a short time with every resident of his beat, to know their names, circumstances, employment, habits and tendencies. He would thus be able to report and prevent suffering from poverty or misfortune, and the abuse of charity by imposture. He should know who might be leading an idle or vicious life, without visible means of honest livelihood, those who were falling into evil habits and practices, and warn them or those who should be responsible for them, and readily recognize strangers or wandering criminals entering his section. These he could report to his captain, so that they may be watched. In short, he could make himself a perfect reliance and safeguard of society, and not only protect his charge from depredation but from the evils of a growing pauperism and criminality.

Provision should be made by general State legislation for a systematic interchange of information and reports between the chiefs of police of its several cities, and a uniformity of surveillance over criminals, convicts at liberty upon probation, and suspected persons. Similar intercommunication and co-operation might also be secured by law to the general advantage between cities in different States, and in this way the benefits of the uniform police systems of foreign nations could be introduced here. One the most useful of these, the liberation of convicts upon probation, to finish their sentences at useful and self-supporting labor, as members of society under the eye of the law, is practically impossible in this country without such harmony of co-operation among our various police organizations.

There is but one thing more needed, in addition to proper material, correct organization, and adequate appurtenances, to render our American police worthy the confidence and reliance of our people. The prerequisites which we have specified are neither novel nor impracticable; they have been tested and proven, nor is this final quality doubtful or even difficult. It is expressed in one word, which describes the means of all success, if it is rightly understood, the common term, Discipline.

The discipline of the police involves, of course, the instruction, training, and obedience of every member; but more important far than these, knowledge, good character, correct disposition, determination, and competent will-power in the head, the chief. It resolves itself from all its various ramifications at last back to the power of one man, to his ability to comprehend his duties, and his courage to perform them. The weakness and failure of our police has been due far more to the lack of discipline at the head than in the body. Does any one doubt what the result would be if the Mayor of New York, or of any city in the United States, were to say in such a manner as would carry conviction to his chief of police, " If I find any brothel, gambling-saloon, policy shop, illegal liquor-selling, or public immorality within the limits of this corporation after to-morrow noon, your official head will go into the basket " ? The order would be at once transmitted to the captains, to the sergeants, to the patrolmen, and the thing would be done. If there were failure anywhere, one would be put there with the manly power to do. It is because the executive will not execute, that society suffers. Dr. Parkhurst is right in charging the shameful atrocities of the corrupters of society upon the high officials of the public. There can be no reasonable doubt that they are either incapable or corrupt. It is not for the executive to wink at or be blind to violation of law, to modify, interpret, or take counsel of his hopes or fears, but to execute and enforce the laws as he finds them. If he cannot do this, let the people who placed him in power take him in hand and discipline him, compel him to act, or to give place to some one who will act.

It is for the leaders and makers of public opinion, the pulpit and the press, to stir up the people to move in this matter. The people are the source of power, and no stream will rise higher than its source. They have made the laws, let them demand their execution with a voice that is certain. The laxity of our officials has become insupportable, the evils

17

which they permit to afflict us, and which threaten to overwhelm all we hold dear, and all our hopes of the future, demand instant action. While we listen to the delusive enchantments of physical prosperity and national growth, millions of remorseless *teredos* from the lower depths are honey-combing the hull of our ship of state; the pleasant breezes which belly the sails of her proud progress towards a higher civilization, and the haven of perfected humanity, are smoky with malaria and miasma from thousands of social hell-holes, neglected sinks of iniquity, centres of corruption, and pools of pollution. Their subtle and insidious poison is rapidly debasing our politics, enervating our national vitality, weakening our moral fibre, and rendering us incapable of that decision and exertion which the exigencies of our condition require.

We need wise laws, but our greater need is strong, courageous, incorruptible executors of the laws we have made, and an inexorable enforcement of discipline by the people upon their chosen officials, and by the public servant in turn, upon the people. It is not enough to elect an agent to do the people's will, and leave him free to do his own will, without other compulsion than comes from a little newspaper criticism and badinage. He must be compelled to do his duty. The power and force of the popular will must not be relaxed short of actual consummation; it must press on with a vigor which will not be resisted. If a mistake is made in the selection of the official, the mistake must be corrected; and that repeatedly until the object is attained.

The public officer who accepts the suffrages of his fellow-citizens does so under an honorable agreement with them to honestly execute their will, and when elected he solemnizes this compact by an oath to faithfully enforce the laws. If he fails to do these things, he is faithless, dishonest, and perjured, and should be ostracised as unworthy of confidence and respect, and unfit for the association of reputable people. No man capable of properly discharging the duties of high office would or could face such a social ostracism. It is the just and sure method of enforcing popular discipline.

The lack of personal discipline and self denial is the cause of most of the individual failure and ruin in society; the lack of family discipline is the great source and cause of social depravity; and the lack of political discipline accounts for most of the flagrant evils which torment society. Discipline requires effort, it is incompatible with ease and indulgence. It is easier and more agreeable to drift, but Niagara is below. The condition politically is desperate, but not hopeless. A slight revival of the patriotism and heroism of war times, a little Napoloenic will in office, a few popular assertions of the majesty and might of the majority at the polls, and the political atmosphere will become as clear and invigorating as a June morning after a thunderstorm.

If the American people can be made to discipline its officials, they will be obliged to discipline their police among others, and so the main desideratum of efficiency will be secured. If they will not or cannot do this there is small need of any reform, for the end is nigh, and degrees of evil or good are immaterial. But with proper discipline, a police force, such as we have endeavored to describe, may be made an all-sufficient agency in the reduction of criminality and pauperism to a minimum. It might be extended beyond the limits of incorporated cities and towns and made advantageously to cover the whole country. One of the principal benefits of such an extension of police supervision would be, that the evils resulting from the practice of the country justice and constable with their fees could be abolished. This would be another long step in advance in penological reform. The "fee system," from the nature of things, ranges those who profit from it in the very ranks of transgression, and tends to encourage lawlessness and crime, upon which it depends for business, instead of repressing and reducing them.

Upon a carefully selected, wisely organized, and firmly disciplined State police force extended over the whole country and in hearty and faithful co-operation with its own different members, we may confidently depend for the most efficient service in the reduction and control of the dangerous classes, the suppression of riots and disorders without the expense and inconvenience of assembling the militia, which we have endeavored to show are so burdensome and threatening to our peace and prosperity. We have explained how such a force may be made the handmaid of benevolence and the minister of philanthropy, as well as the guardian of our property and our persons.

But if the force is to be maintained in a condition of excellence, society itself has important duties to perform to it. From the very nature of the case, and the exigencies of his occupation, the policeman is very largely separated from the common, elevating, and religious influences and intercourse of society. It is his duty to become familiar with vice and crime, to know the corrupt, debased, and criminal members of the body politic. The evil disposed court his favor in all ways, they strive to be friendly with him. His power and disposition to resist the influences of "evil communications" are therefore being constantly weakened, while the attacks upon his moral character are continually multiplied. Extraordinary effort is consequently necessary by the better portion of the people to keep him up to the plane of his original selection and entry into the service. Society has apparently largely ignored its responsibilities in this respect hitherto. It has sent its messengers down into the pitch and mire of its slums without the provision of any special means for preventing their defilement, or preserving their moral cleanliness and health. It compels them to treat and handle its corruption without supplying them with the disinfectants and antiseptics necessary to their own safety. It is manifestly impossible that the best selected police force can continue to be long reliable anywhere under circumstances of such neglect.

Humanity, philanthropy, and religion must follow the policeman on his mission with an untiring and increasing care, both for his own sake and the

success of his effort. Counter attractions must be
opposed against the special allurements to which he
is exposed. Pleasant resorts must be provided for
his off duty hours, where the better things of life
may be contrasted with the debasing pleasures with
which his duties make him familiar, and intellectual
and moral influences may be brought to bear upon
his character. Particular effort must be made to
keep up his connections with all the higher influences
of social life, with the educational and religious
enterprises of the people. He must be kept in
touch with good society, in sympathy with the best
social movements, and in connection with the
Christian church. He needs the support, strength,
and inspiration of the church and the Divine Spirit
more than ordinary men. His church should look
out for him with unusual solicitude and zeal, to
counteract the evil of his daily environment. It is
quite as essential to preserve as to select and train
our police.

We commend the police force to the thoughtful
consideration of the people as an agency capable
of the largest and most beneficent development in
the amelioration of the evils of society in America,
worthy of the utmost care and attention in organization and maintenance.

CHAPTER XV.

DEGENERATION AND REGENERATION.

Summary of the Results of Investigation into Causes—Universal Abnormality of Criminals and Paupers—A Condition, Not a Disposition, Confronts Us—Fostered, Rather than Ameliorated, by Present Methods—Remedy Proposed, Advantages and Objections—Failure of Regenerative Methods in Humanity for Three Thousand Years—Supreme Vital Function of Marriage: Evils of Social Neglect of Its Regulation in General and in Detail — Dr. Strahan's Evidence — Threatening the Republic — Principles Which Should Govern the Regulation of Reproduction—Grandeur of the Results to be Expected—The First Step of Decided Progress in the Regeneration of the Race.

WE are impelled in conclusion of this general consideration of these grave and growing factors of the problem of public prosperity in America, to add a few observations concerning the actual and natural cause, common to both, of criminality and pauperism, which are universal and inevitable in civilized society governed by its prevailing sentiments. We have been convinced by our study that most of those characteristics which have hitherto been treated as causes, such as ignorance, intemperance, poverty, disease and defects, are symptoms indicating a social state or condition of crime and pauperism, rather than causes of them. It was not our original intention to go below surface indications, or to attempt

to treat of anything besides the dangers of the public, and the methods of protection proposed for the
social organization.   But so many writers have of late
years been threshing out the wheat of valuable knowledge without winnowing it, that we are constrained
to attempt to concentrate into a concise and intelli-
gible summary, the results of the exhaustive and
diversified investigations of learned men and philanthropists into the causes of the great increase of
crime and pauperism, and the failure of the wonderful modern advance of civilization and growth of
Christianity to check this.

The wide range of these investigations, and the
interesting and useful results obtained, are very
fully and impressively epitomized in Havelock Ellis'
book entitled *The Criminal*, published in 1892.
Those who desire more of the details than we
can offer here may refer to it with profit.   The
patient and laborious researches of distinguished
penologists and professors into the physical and psychical symptoms and characteristics of criminality in
all ages and among all peoples, are there carefully and
thoughtfully presented for consideration.   The size,
shape, convolutions, and weight of the brain, the
size and shape of the cranium, the physiognomy as
a whole, the features in detail, the form entire and
the members separately, the hair and hairy sur-
faces, the organs; the senses of feeling, taste, smell,
sight, and hearing; speech, language, appetite, digestion, circulation of blood, temperature, nervous
sensitiveness, mental disposition, capacity, education, habits, customs, peculiarities, family history,

religious convictions or belief ;—the hereditary and heteronomic influences of a large number of criminals have been examined, and compared with what may be termed the normal type.

But with all this care and research no general rule has been discovered by which the criminal can be positively identified before the crime. Indeed, the most universal as well as the most surprising and anomalous peculiarity of criminals recorded is one which unites them with, rather than differentiates them from, the better members of society, namely, a strong religious sentiment.[1] They even implore the help of God in the execution of their crimes. This sentiment, in conjunction with their dominant characteristics, seems to constitute the most general abnormality of the class, but of course is without value as a distinctive definition. The variations among criminals are apparently as wide and numerous as in the human race in general.

While, however, no single peculiarity has been identified as a universal characteristic, these examinations have demonstrated beyond question the abnormality of all incorrigible criminals. Every member of the actual criminal class diverges in some essential respects from the normal type of mankind. His physical constitution is a serious variation from, if not an actual deformity or malformation of the complete, healthy, human being, aptly illustrating the truth of the reversed Latin adage, "*insana mens insano corpore*"; so that abnormality becomes in itself an indicative character-

[1] *The Criminal*, p. 156.

istic of the class. Conversely, there is never found
in the criminal or pauper class, except by accident,
a normal, well developed, healthy adult. At least
not in America, where the will of the majority is
recognized as rational law by all rational beings, and
the opportunities of self-support are ample for the
healthy and strong.

We believe it is established beyond controversy
that criminals and paupers, both, are degenerate ;
the imperfect, knotty, knurly, worm-eaten, half-rot-
ten fruit of the race. In short, both criminality and
pauperism are conditions and not dispositions. The
mind, the intellectual faculties, and the soul, the
moral faculties,—which are the motive powers of
character, which constitute the man,—have their
home in his body, to which they are conformed,
which they represent, and by which they are limited and controlled in their operations, as well as in
their conditions. A normal character is not to be
expected in an abnormal physique, nor a sound and
healthy character in a diseased constitution. This
is one grain of intellectual wheat that needs to have
the chaff blown away from it, until it may show
clear and distinct to the public eye. Whatever the
cause of the condition, heredity or heteronomy, the
sins of former generations, or of this, the result and
fact is what confronts us, and demands attention.

Omitting then from our present consideration the
subject of secondary causes, let us limit ourselves to
an effort to change the condition, for the condition
requires distinct and different treatment from its
causes. Vaccination will avert small-pox, but it is

folly and wickedness to vaccinate a patient and let him go free, after he has broken out with the disease. We are to prescribe for the case already infected. Here is a gangrened member of the body politic: the question is not how it came to be so, but what shall be done to stop the spread of the poison, and save the life of the patient. There appears to be a remarkable confusion in the minds and practice of many penologists and philanthropists, of the methods of prevention, with remedial measures—a persistence of reliance upon vaccination after small-pox has developed. By thus confining ourselves to the treatment of the diseased member we shall greatly simplify our study, and limit it within comparatively narrow bounds. For while the causes of degeneracy are many and diverse, the rational treatment of a common, well-known case, is simple and plain. The gangrened member must be cut off from the body politic, or physical, and the system toned up to health. We do not propose to turn the criminal and pauper over to the executioner, as is done in some nations, but we do propose, in the utmost kindness of heart toward them, as well as toward society, to show how they may cut themselves off naturally by the processes of exhaustion.

The laws of biology, that "like begets like," that imperfect seed in parentage cannot produce perfect offspring, that "breeding in" intensifies and magnifies parental peculiarities, that certain inherited defects or deficiencies induce criminality, and result in pauperism, are well known, and generally accepted to be as invariable and immutable as the law of

gravitation. It is as absurd to expect healthy, normal children from abnormal parents, as to look for
figs from thistles, perfect fruit on a blasted tree,
sound and full-eared grain from imperfect seed, a
"two-ten" trotter from a pair of plow-horses. The
offspring of degenerate, degraded, defective, or diseased parents are of the necessity of nature below
the normal standard, physically, mentally, or morally,
at birth—even if not malformed or tainted with a
diseased diathesis, neurotic, tuberculous, scrofulous,
intemperate, or other. Some may be rescued from
their inherited tendency by intelligent and favorable
care and cultivation ; but without extraordinary attention nature will reproduce in them—it cannot do
otherwise—an aggravation of parental defects. From
criminals and paupers can only come more criminals
and paupers. Another grain of wheat worthy of
recognition.

These are moreover compelled, by the equally
inexorable laws of "selection" and "association," to
"breed in" with their own classes ; wherefore their
progeny progressively deteriorates and degenerates.
In a state of nature, or freedom from artificial
restrictions or influences, this degeneration rapidly
results in extinction, by the inability to survive of
the weak, and the sterility of survivors. This is
nature's way of protecting its types, and of evolving,
by the "survival of the fittest" and the destruction
of the unfit, improvement and perfection in vegeta-
ble, animal, and human life. There is no such thing
as a criminal or pauper class among what are called
savages or uncivilized men.

The civilized man is the product of the survival through all the ages, of the strongest, most stalwart and capable savages. In the progress of his civilization, the development of the sentiment of human brotherhood and the principles of Christianity teaching him to love his fellow as himself, has caused an interference with the natural law provided for the extinction of the unfit by impelling the strong and independent to maintain and care for the weak and defective. At the same time advances in the sciences of hygiene, medicine, and surgery enable many of the unfit to survive the tests of childhood and disease, the rigors of which they ameliorate, and which in a state of nature would be fatal. It is necessary when humanity thus restrains and limits the operation of the laws of nature that it should supply a correlative supplement to prevent disastrous consequences. If civilization and philanthropy cannot permit nature to accomplish its inexorable decrees in its own way, they must provide some other way for its irresistable pent-up force to expend itself or finally be overwhelmed.

By carefully providing for its degenerates and abnormals in comfortable prisons, asylums, and almshouses, giving them the advantages of the highest knowledge and science of living, society unwittingly aggravates the evil it seeks to alleviate. It maintains alive those who would perish without its aid. It permits their reproduction and multiplication. It fosters, with more attention than it gives its better types, the establishment and increase of an abnormal and defective class. It not only perpetu-

ates by care but encourages by permitting unrestricted " breeding in " among them the unnatural
spread and growth of a social gangrene of fatal
tendencies.   It is assuming oppressive and alarming
proportions which begins to be felt in the whole
social organization.   In terror our advancing civilization begins to inquire if there be no way of coun-
teraction consistent with its highest benevolence, by
which this abnormality of abnormalism may be
avoided, criminality and pauperism restored to
natural proportions, or to that ratio of increase
which may be the inevitable result of ignorance and
excess of living.

We believe that the progress of medical and
surgical science has opened up such a way entirely
practicable, humanitarian in the highest sense, unobjectionable except upon grounds of an absurd and
irrational sentiment.   The discoveries in the use of
anæsthetics and antiseptics have rendered it possible
to remove or sterilize the organs of reproduction of
both sexes without pain or danger.   This is the simplest, easiest, and most effectual solution of the whole
difficulty.   It promptly and completely stops the
horrid breed where it begins and obviates the necessity of permanent seclusion otherwise imperative.
This is another grain of wisdom to be separated for
a profitable use.

The sentimental objections to this remedy when
examined in the calm judgment of reason appear to
have no sound foundation.   These organs have no
function in the human organism except the creation
and gratification of desire and the reproduction of

the species. Their loss has no effect upon the health, longevity or abilities of the individual of adult years. The removal of them, therefore, by destroying desire would actually dimish the wants of nature and increase the enjoyments of life for paupers. A want removed is equivalent to a want supplied. In other words, such a removal would be a positive benefit to the abnormal rather than a deprivation, rather a kindness than an injury. This operation bestowed upon the abnormal inmates of our prisons, reformatories, jails, asylums and public institutions, would entirely eradicate those unspeakable evil practices which are so terribly prevalent, debasing, destructive, and uncontrollable in them. It would confer upon the inmates health and strength for weakness and impotence, satisfaction and comfort for discontent and insatiable desire.

Neither should the purpose of this operation, the prevention of reproduction, be objectionable to the subject. The abnormal does not want children, has no affection for them, and gets rid of them as soon as possible if they come. If this were not so their offspring, being abnormal, weak, sickly, diseased, deformed, idiotic, insane, or criminal, doomed to a burdensome and suffering existence or an early death, are a curse rather than a comfort to their parents; so that in no sense could the deprivation of these organs inflict injury or damage to criminal or pauper. On the contrary they would be enabled thereby to enjoy many comforts and privileges, and be relieved from many restraints at present necessarily imposed upon them. The range of their enjoyments would in fact be greatly enlarged, both in confinement and at liberty. Many indeed might be allowed freedom who are now closely confined. The adoption of this proposition then would seem to be an unmixed blessing and benefit.

But even if this were not the case, society would seem to have, justly, the right to secure to itself relief from the undue burdens of crime and pauperism by thus preventing its multiplication, as a fair price for its care and expense in preserving the unfit from suffering and destruction. Such a limitation of the unnatural increase of these classes would certainly reduce, in a short time, their public burden and cost more than one half, by mere reduction of their numbers. This would be a social economy in the neighborhood of sixty millions of dollars a year in the United States, equivalent to an annual addition to the wealth of the people of a dollar a head.

Besides, this would remove the necessity for a separation of the sexes in public institutions for permanent seclusion, permitting a single instead of a double plan of construction and management, thus greatly diminishing the costs of installation and administration of them. Such a regulation would almost completely eliminate from the catalogue of crimes the long and numerous list of crimes and vices of lust. It would arrest the most prolific cause of progressive debasement and degradation in the criminal and pauper classes, both at liberty and in confinement, and remove an almost insurmountable obstacle from the course of their reformation. For all who have had the charge of them are shockingly impressed with the knowledge that excessive and unnatural pandering to the sexual passion is their most universal, uncontrollable, and debasing vice. They yield to this like senseless brutes, into which they soon transform themselves by indulgence.

These considerations alone seem to devolve upon society, upon the sovereign people, the law-makers, not only the right, but the duty, to complete and perfect its supervision and support of criminals and paupers, by effecting that sterility among them which, by its care, it prevents nature from producing. Such surgery is as wise, beneficient, and merciful as any that is performed. It should be recognized and esteemed by all intelligent persons, to be as necessary, safe, and unobjectionable as vaccination or the extraction of an aching tooth. The incorporation of regulations for such treatment of confirmed criminals and paupers into the legal code would certainly become a greater blessing and benefit to mankind than any other hygienic or surgical discovery has ever been, however beneficent vaccination and the use of anæsthetics may have been to the human race.

As a deterrent, this treatment would surely be more effective than all the other penalties of the code together. For it must be acknowledged that however much the individual and society might be thus benefited, that common sentiment which amounts to an instinct almost, under which the abnormal has found protection hitherto, is one of the strongest and most influential of nature. But it was divinely implanted to secure the progress and advance of human-

18

ity in numbers and development, not its degeneration and destruction. Ignorance, error, and inattention have permitted the perversion of a divinely-bestowed instinct to a controversion and opposition of its purpose. Humanity actually thus sins against the Creator and nature, in its contributory negligence of such perversion.

The remedy we suggest would certainly be effectual, an immeasurable benefit to the human race, the exercise of an inherent right which really injures none, and moreover it appears to have become an imperative duty which society owes to its own preservation, which may not be neglected without actual sin.

Society arrests and confines the leper, the victim of smallpox, yellow-fever, cholera, or typhoid, and treats them according to its own will, with or against their consent. It does not hesitate to remove a gangrened limb, a diseased organ from the person, if it is necessary; it shuts up the insane, the imbecile, the criminal, for the public protection; it inflicts punishments of various degrees; compels men to labor without pay, for its good, in durance, even deprives them of life if it pleases; assumes arbitrary control of the life, liberty, and happiness of an individual, if it considers it necessary for the public welfare; and no reasonable being questions its right or duty to do these things. At the same time it allows its deformed and diseased in mind, body, and soul, to disseminate social leprosy and cancer with impunity, while the skill of its surgeons could prevent the infection by an operation almost as simple as vaccination. It seems inexplicable that the remedy should have been so long delayed.

The charitable institutions, insane asylums, jails, and penitentiaries are all full to overflowing. They cannot be built fast enough to meet the multiplying requirements of social neglect. The demand is constant and urgent for more and larger ones. The most generous plan is found inadequate before it has been fairly completed, and the pressure of necessity greater than when it was begun. Society is working at the wrong end of the subject. It might as well try to sweep back the rising floods of the Mississippi after they have spread over the plain, instead of stopping the broken levee. It is a Sisyphean attempt to bail out the Ship of State with sieves. The leak outruns the capacity of her pumps; the deeper she settles the more the yawning seams pour in their flood.

The more we discover concerning the condition and customs of the earlier civilizations of the race, the Assyrians of Nineveh and Babylon, the Egyptians of thousands of years ago, the more probable it appears that there has been no material increase, in our present boasted civilization, in the proportion of humanity having ability to exist satisfactorily without manual labor. This proportion in America does not exceed ten per cent. of the population. It is probable that royalty, nobility, officers of the army and government, priests, learned and professional men, artists, manufacturers, merchants, and other members of the " upper class " of society numbered as many as ten per cent. of the people of Nineveh,

Babylon, and Thebes. If this was the case, there has been no change in the relative proportions of these two classes of humanity in the last three thousand years. It is reasonably certain that the number of those who now have that superior ability which elevates them to the level of the " upper tenth " is not very much larger now than then. The whole mass of humanity has moved upward greatly; there have been constant accessions to the " upper tenth " from below, and a constant waste there by exhaustion, but the ratio of those who are endowed with that perfection and excellence of capacity which enables them to rank at the top, remains about the same as it was in the beginning. This is a fact of tremendous significance in sociology, in many directions outside of the purview of our discussion, in which it is very suggestive. For we believe the true objective of philanthropy to be the individual rather than the mass. The first interest of every one is himself ; the highest enjoyment of his own existence here and hereafter. If one finds himself or herself incapable of attaining his desires, then his interest centres next upon his children who shall come after him. No general progress is so satisfactory as personal or family success and advance in the social scale. Besides, as the number of individual advancements increases, the general average is moved upward. So we say the true objective of philanthropy is the increase of the " upper tenth " to a fifth or a half, which modern mechanical inventions would seem even now to make possible. It is the insignificance of the number of the " upper tenth " and its constancy that galls and irritates the ninety per cent. of workers below. " We are better off than we were," say they, "but the distance between us and them is just as wide as ever it was. The way is open, it is said, but some unknown force holds us back ; we cannot walk where we would ; we hate it, and those who can go where we cannot." Hence riot and bombs and dynamite.

We have referred to that other extreme of humanity which is just becoming recognizable as the " submerged tenth," composed of the criminal, the pauper, and the children of despair, as the product of degeneracy. It is equally significant that ancient civilizations knew no such class. There were beggars and cripples, but not sufficiently numerous to require or receive public care. While the " upper tenth " continues stationary, the " submerged tenth " grows, and its weight drags with accumulating irksomeness upon humanity. Philanthropy has been hitherto almost engrossed with its care, to the neglect of its cause. We believe that there is a common cause and a single remedy for both these social complaints : the lack of growth at the top, the rottenness at the root of the tree of humanity.

It is an astonishing and incomprehensible fact to the student that society, among all the plans and projects it is continually devising for the benefit and elevation of humanity, has in our modern civilization utterly overlooked and ignored the one vital social function upon which improvement of the race depends. Marriage, which constitutes the social unit, which creates the family, whence the genera-

tions succeed one another in upward or downward
progress, has been left by philanthropy, by church
and State, except by the recognition and solemniza-
tion of the fact itself, almost as entirely unregulated as
it was in the days of savage life, as it is among wild
animals. The union of the pair upon whose fitness
will depend the physique and character of the next
generation is submitted by society to "natural selection," and "chance." If otherwise influenced at all, it
is solely by material considerations of selfish, temporary importance rather than those affecting the
real object and purpose of the union, the children
who are to come of the union. It is doubtful if one
in a thousand of those who marry ever take this
subject into consideration in their selections. If
they were to do so indeed, there would be no proper
method available to determine the questions needing
settlement. So this seriously vital function is settled by caprice and "chance." The chances remaining about the same, the results have been about the
same for thousands of years, save for the multiplication of the unfit.

That is, the same as far as this one result is evident. There are signs of a general degeneracy
attracting public attention, which are worthy of
more serious consideration than they receive. Besides the increase of the "lower tenth," idiocy, imbecility, suicides, drunkenness, insanity, and all forms
of mental, moral, and physical "constitutional"
defects are coming to be common in all ranks of
society.

Stature is decreasing, the proportion of normal

perfectly healthy people diminishing, the general average of physical endurance and vitality becoming lowered, the number of children reared growing notably smaller; hair, the common indication of vigor, is disappearing, and bald heads becoming numerous early in life; weak nerves, weak stomachs, weak hearts, weak heads are ordinary ailments. All these are indicative of a general deterioration, which must be due to faulty breeding, to the supreme folly of chance marriage, ignored and unregulated by the social organization.

The law that "like begets like" is by no means confined to criminals and paupers, but operates inexorably in all classes and conditions of people. A taint of hereditary drunkenness, insanity, suicide, epilepsy, idiocy, deaf-mutism, cancer, syphilis, gout, rheumatism, tuberculous or scrofulous diathesis in the blood is a symptom of degeneration, likely to be intensified by propagation in succeeding generations until the tainted family becomes extinct. Intermarriage with those tainted diffuses weakness, deformity, and abnormality through the social structure, deteriorates and contaminates all who issue from such unions. These things are well known and completely established. We have not space for the argument here. It may be found conclusively stated in Dr. Strahan's valuable treatise on *Marriage and Disease*, which ought to be read by every young person contemplating marriage before the affections have become engaged.[1] The law of

[1] *Marriage and Disease*. A study of hereditary and the more important family degenerations. S. A. R. Strahan, 1892.

heredity in respect to these more distinct forms of degeneration are now so well established, and the frightful consequences of their neglect so apparent, as to demand legislation for social self-preservation. There can no longer be any doubt that the degeneration of the race is due to the continual reproduction of humanity tainted to a greater or less degree with these common diseases and defects. Not only that all, absolutely all of the crime and pauperism, but most of the suffering and unnatural afflictions, sicknesses, loss of children, untimely deaths, and social loss and waste due to these, are to be attributed to misalliances of, or with, tainted stock. The evils and necessities of divorce, with the insoluble problems concerning its regulations which perplex legislators, are made imminent and pressing by the continual linking together of the unfit. If only those were united who ought to be, there would be no need of divorce, no demand for its regulation. Let any one of mature years reflect upon the history of the families of his acquaintance, in the light of the knowledge he has of the habits and fortunes of their parentage, and he will be able to assign a probable cause for most of the troubles and afflictions that have befallen them, as well as of the failures and unhappiness, to inherited taint or peculiarities.

The diagramic history of eight families given below are taken from Dr. Strahan's book, to which we have referred, and illustrate the evil we denounce more impressively than argument. They are fair samples of what is constantly occurring all about us.

CASE No. I., p. 49.
J. E——'s FAMILY.

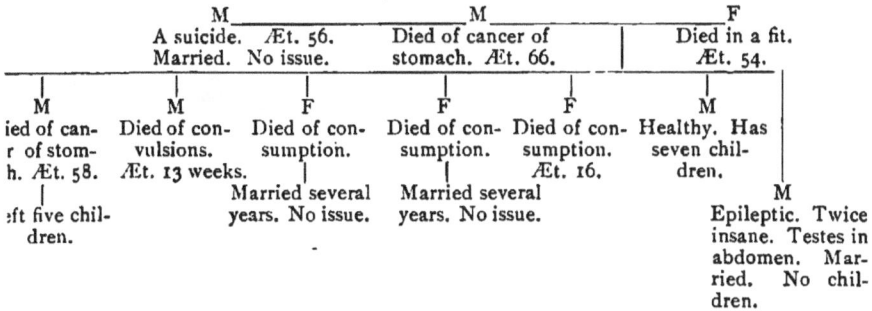

M	M	F
A suicide. Æt. 56. Married. No issue.	Died of cancer of stomach. Æt. 66.	Died in a fit. Æt. 54.

M	M	F	F	F	M
ied of can- r of stom- h. Æt. 58.	Died of con- vulsions. Æt. 13 weeks.	Died of con- sumption.	Died of con- sumption.	Died of con- sumption. Æt. 16.	Healthy. Has seven chil- dren.
ªft five chil- dren.		Married several years. No issue.	Married several years. No issue.		

                                                                    M
                                                    Epileptic. Twice
                                                    insane. Testes in
                                                    abdomen. Mar-
                                                    ried. No chil-
                                                    dren.

No. II., p. 108.
K. S——'s FAMILY.

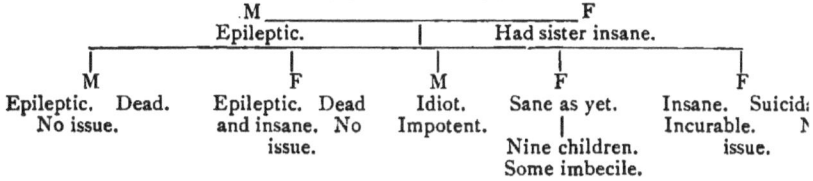

M	F
Epileptic.	Had sister insane.

M	F	M	F	F
Epileptic. Dead. No issue.	Epileptic. Dead and insane. No issue.	Idiot. Impotent.	Sane as yet. Nine children. Some imbecile.	Insane. Suicidª Incurable. ℕ issue.

No. III., p. 125.
Father, a drunkard,

Son,
A drunkard, disgustingly drunk on his wedding day.

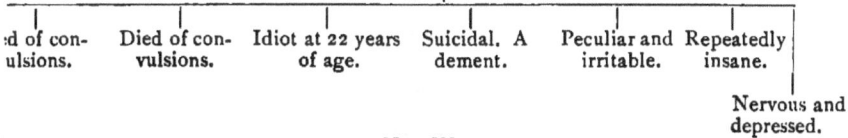

ªd of con- ulsions.	Died of con- vulsions.	Idiot at 22 years of age.	Suicidal. A dement.	Peculiar and irritable.	Repeatedly insane.

                                                                    Nervous and
                                                                    depressed.

No. IV., p. 137.
M
Died mad.

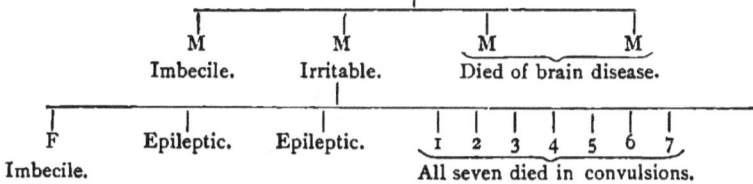

M	M	M	M
Imbecile.	Irritable.	Died of brain disease.	

F	Epileptic.	Epileptic.	1	2	3	4	5	6	7
Imbecile.			All seven died in convulsions.						

No. V., p. 137.   No. VI., p. 166.

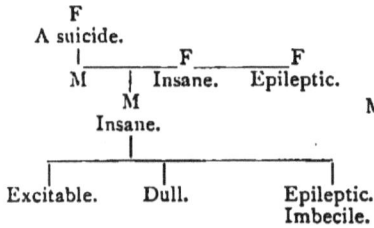

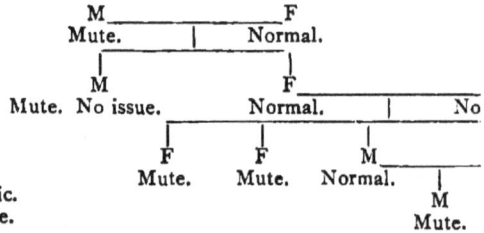

No. VII., p. 231.

J. G. A——'s Family History.

	Paternal side.	*Maternal side.*
First Generation.	Grandfather. A drunkard. Grandmother. Normal.	Grandmother. "Odd." Grandfather. Normal.
Second Generation.	Uncle. A drunkard. Uncle. A drunkard. Uncle. An epileptic. Father. Excitable and irritable.	Uncle. Epileptic. Uncle. Rheumatic, totally cripple, and his daughter Uncle. Rheumatic. Aunt. Rheumatic. Mother. Died in asylum.

Third Generation.
Daughter. Has had rheumatism and has heart disease.
Son. Now insane.
Son. Died a few days old of convulsions.
Son. Now a chronic maniac in an asylum.
Daughter. Suicidal melancholiac ; died in an asylum ; no issue.
Family extinct.

No. VIII., p. 303.

S. H.——'s Family.

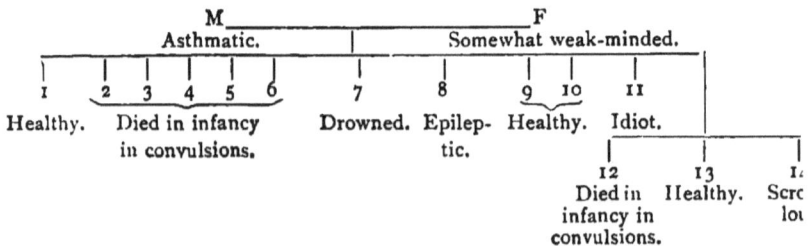

It is not alone the dictate of wisdom and prudence, but the supreme instinct of self-preservation which impels society to a more careful and effective supervision of the institution of marriage. It has been left too long already to " chance the usual way."

This unique act of human existence, equal in solemn supremacy to birth and death, between which it has been committed by the Creator, sole link of this holy trinity, between the two eternities, alone of them to human control; humanity's only exclusive property of the three, its object of the first, its refuge from the last; with blind and inexplicable heedlessness is left by a self-satisfied civilization to " chance," or to a settlement by those whose judgment or decision would not be trusted, even in the ordinary affairs of life, to inexperienced youth.

" Natural selection" is a bewitching theory, like the theory of Free Trade, which requires impossible circumstances for its satisfactory operation. The choice and mutual attraction which ordinarily induces marriage in our present social conditions is generally the result of the close and frequent association of two individuals in a small society. Each selects the most desirable of the present acquaintance without thought, beyond the present gratification, of fitness or the future. If a large portion even of mankind could be offered to each individual under similar circumstances for marriage, it is possible that natural selection might be successful; as this cannot be done, the theory becomes impracticable, false, and fatal.

This pernicious principle of social free trade not only permits the unrestricted dissemination of corruption and imperfection in the race, but it allows, if it does not actually encourage, the propagation of immature and exhausted offspring. The degeneracy due to the former is probably exceeded by that which results from the latter. The marriage of immature children, and those whose vitality is weakened by age or excess, cannot possibly produce healthy and strong offspring. Stock breeders are familiar with this fact in respect to animals, and it is quite as certain in the human race.

Dr. Strahan says: "The distinctive characteristics of the two classes might be roughly summed up as follows: The children of immature parentage are specially liable to death during infancy from wasting, scrofulous, and convulsive affections. They are liable in a remarkable degree to idiocy and imbecility of a low type, and to physical deformities and imperfections. Large numbers of them succumb to tubercular disease about the ages of puberty and adolescence, and few of them attain even advanced middle age. The genital organs are ill-developed and often deformed, and a great number of them are sterile. They are also notorious for their lack of energy and courage. Hence, the class of criminals to which they give the greatest number of recruits is that of thieves and other petty offenders.

" The children of the senile are as a class ugly, small of stature, and stooping, which, together with the absence of subcutaneous fat, gives them the look of old age while still young. Idiocy is less common among them than weak-mindedness, amounting to imbecility, which is often accompanied with more or less perversion of moral feeling, and a plentiful supply of low cunning. Many of them die between the ages of puberty and adolescence of tubercular disease, few of them live past middle age, and great numbers of them ultimately become insane and criminal. They are nervous, irritable, passionate, and horribly cruel, and are the perpetrators of most of those fiendish barbarities, the recital of which from time to time shock the civilized world."

This conclusion is based upon a wide and long personal experience, and the investigations of many distinguished sociologists of Europe. It commends itself as true to any intelligent observer. The magnitude and extent of this evil, however, may not be as generally appreciated. It is a serious fault of our legislation that no statistics of the age of marriage are available in this country. We may fairly assume, however, that they would be similar to those of England in this respect. According to the Annual Report of the English Registrar-General, there were married there during the year 1889 94,040 males of 21 years of age and less, and 42,170 females of 20 years and less. Of these, 33,526 lads of from 21 to 15 years married girls from 20 to 15 years old. There were 11,525 men from 45 to upwards of 85 married, and 7,676 women between 40 and 50 years of age.

It is probable that the disposition towards unfit marriage is excessive in America, because less legal formality is required here, and because of the large

---

[1] *Marriage and Disease*, p. 259.

element of negro and foreign races in our population, ignorant and without care for results. It is certain that the evidences of faulty generation are multiplying everywhere about us. The holocaust of infants reported in the mortality records of our cities, the weak and puny children in our public schools, the stunted and crippled youths we see on the streets, our overcrowded asylums, the growing burden of pauperism and crime, the alarming increase of divorces,—all are to be attributed to the lack of the necessary public supervision of marriage, the most important of all social relations. Grave as these evils are, they do not constitute of themselves the most serious aspect of this neglect.

The decay of republics has always, and must always be due to the degeneracy of the people. The great and strong and rugged race which wrests itself from the domination of its rulers, assumes self-control, organizes its own government, formulates constitutions, enacts laws, is fit and able for these achievements. Consequently the inspiration of its action, as well as its first care, is to secure the greatest freedom of the individual from governmental interference. Fostered by this original impulse, it grows, as we have, in numbers, wealth, and power, until its organization has become a mighty element of the existing humanity. Then the luxuriant fruit begins to bend and strain the branches which have borne it. The people outgrows the early institutions of its childhood. New limitations and restraints upon the individual become necessary for the protection of all in the changed conditions of its society. Contemporaneously the general consciousness of invincibility weakens patriotism, the inheritance of liberty cultivates license, the original freedom changes to neglect of the social unit and encourages debasement, until the whole people to whom the government was committed become incapable of its exercise. The initial and chief condition of good government is purity at the fountain-head. When the people of a republic have become degenerate, it is *in articulo mortis*. It must either crumble into ruin, because the bond of its union is incapable of sustaining its own weight, or some strong hand snatches the reins from a heedless people and assumes control. Our question, then, is one of life or death to the republic. How is this government "of the people, for the people" to be perpetuated "by the people," this spreading infection of degeneracy to be checked?

Society has willingly expended, and continues each year to expend, vast sums of money and great labor in the support of religious institutions, preachers, and churches for the moral elevation of the people. It submits cheerfully to pay the largest share of the public tax, and contributes immense amounts in addition, benevolently, to promote their intellectual progress. It founds and supports medical colleges, stimulates physical culture by encouraging athletic games and sports, and advocates the improvement of the physique in every imaginable direction. Religion and philanthropy join their forces in ceaseless and exhausting effort to stem the resistless tide which appears to be sweeping the race over the cataract of extinction, sustained by faith in the eternal promise of a millenium rather than encouraged by any palpable success. They contend valiantly against overwhelming results, ignorant or oblivious of the easily controlled causes.

Let it once assume the regulation of the propagation of the race with wisdom and faithful efficacy, and all the other burdens and labors will become light and full of promise, hope, and fruit. It must control this vital function of marriage for the public welfare, as well as for the private good of the individual. This control is sanctioned and required by the divine right of self-preservation, and has become an imperative duty to the race and to God—a duty supreme in impulse and in consequence.

Nor is its performance impeded by great difficulties. The tentative measures which have been enacted, the previous license, the consent of parents or guardians for minors, the prohibited marriage of the idiot and raving maniac, have secured unanimous approval. So, eventually, the common-sense of mankind will endorse the enactment of whatever provisions are essential to the common welfare.

We recommend, as the next step, the enactment of a code regulating marriage fully in these respects, and by some such methods, as follows :

First. It should be required that a license must in all cases be obtained from a county official before a legal marriage can be made.

Second. Severe penalties should be imposed upon any who perform the marriage ceremony without the presence of the prescribed license, which should have a blank upon it for the marriage certificate, with the ages, residence, parentage, nativity, and race of the parties ; the signature of witnesses, and the certificates of one or more reputable physicians, under oath, testifying to a knowledge of the following facts, derived from personal acquaintance with the persons and families of the parties, or from other satisfactory evidence :

That they are both of proper marriageable age, in good health, sound and complete physically, neither intemperate, criminals, nor paupers ; whether either parents or grandparents were lunatics, drunkards, idiotic, epileptic, congenitally blind, deaf, or deformed, or of syphilitic, cancerous, scrofulous, or tuberculous constitution.

The license papers should be issued in duplicate, and one copy with all blanks filled should be filed and recorded in the county clerk's office. A false certificate by a physician should prevent the further practice of his profession. The law should strictly prohibit the marriage of females under twenty, and males under twenty-five ; of males over forty-five with females over forty who have not passed the period of child-bearing (for outside of these limitations of age it is generally understood healthy children are exceedingly improbable, if not impossible) ; of habitual criminals, paupers, tramps, and vagrants ; of the insane, idiotic, epileptic, paralytic, syphilitic, intemperate, cancerous, scrofulous, and tuberculous ; the congenitally blind, deaf, defective, or deformed ; the children . or grandchildren of parents possessed of these taints, or of suicides, which is of itself presumptive evidence of degeneracy.

The infraction of this law, or the cohabitation with prohibited persons should be punished by the permanent seclusion of both parties in the penitentiaries provided for life confinements.

This is neither a complicated nor impracticable scheme. Consider what the results would be. In the brief course of one generation all the inherited rottenness and corruption of the ages would be purged out of the people. The criminal and pauper class, as a class, would become extinct. Penitentiaries, jails, almshouses, insane asylums, idiot, deaf and dumb and blind asylums would be largely depopulated. Intemperance, the fruitful mother of all evil, sin, and suffering, would become a rare vice ; suicide, the refuge of conscious incompetence, which has increased at the rate of thirty-three per cent. in twenty-five years in England,[1] and quite as much here, would be an almost unknown crime ; the growing burden of inordinate taxation and benevolence for the dependent would be lifted from society ; the evils of divorce would cease, chronic diseases would disappear almost entirely, and temporary ailments be robbed of more than half their terrors ; more than half of the poignant grief and affliction over the untimely death of children would be avoided ; health and strength and ruddy cheeks would delight the eyes and hearts that now grieve over puny forms and wan faces; doctors' bills would no longer drain the family

[1] *Marriage and Disease*, p. 88.

resources; the earning power of the next generation would be magnified, its capacity for intellectual improvement and education increased, its susceptibility to moral and religious influence and government intensified, and the whole race rebound from the depression of its past with a buoyancy and power equal to the full development of its age of steam and electricity.

More than this even, the wisdom of these regulations and these notable results would so improve the public consciousness as to powerfully influence its "natural selection" with a desire for the improvement of the species. The most favorable combinations would become a subject of general study and knowledge; the propagation of higher grades would be a universal motive; the union of the fittest would produce great and noble characters in abundance, capable of leading the race to higher and grander planes of operation; not only would the "submerged tenth" cease to fetter the feet of progress, but the intermediate "eightieth" would surge upward with a power as natural and irresistible as the tide of the ocean.

Let society, under the compulsion of the necessity which is upon it, cut the Gordian knot of its bondage with this sword of justice; take the control of its destiny into its own hand, regulate its reproduction with the wisdom of its experience, and the "ills which flesh is heir to" will vanish with the mists of its night of suffering and sorrow, dissatisfaction and jealous rage, before the glorious dawn of its millenial day of comfort, hope, peace, and promise.

CONCLUSION.

LET the people, the people who make the laws, who choose their legislators, consider the facts we have thus endeavored to make apparent and impressive, the enormous burden and drag upon our public prosperity of pauperism and crime, as shocking in its magnitude as it is appalling in its needless growth in our land, and vigorously undertake the solution of the problem of reduction and elimination with their characteristic shrewdness and energy. We believe the task is full of promise rather than hopeless in America, where all the conditions of nature and government are favorable and propitious. We have endeavored to indicate concisely the direction to be given public efforts in order, most assuredly and quickly, to secure the largest results. Neither patriot, philanthropist, Christian, pagan, capitalist, nor wage-worker can afford to ignore the subject any longer.

The problem is resolved into three elementary phases, those of prevention, of reformation, and of extinction,—the last the most important of all.

The efforts to be made in these different directions are of equal importance, necessity, and promise, but of wide variation in their character, magnitude, and results. As they concentrate in purpose, they must increase in intensity and vigor. Preventive measures are like a net which must be dragged through the entire social stream. Reformatory treatment is confined to those only who are enveloped in it. The "unfit," the abnormals, the sharks, the devil-fish, and other monsters, ought not to be liberated to destroy, and multiply, but must be confined and secluded until they are exterminated.

The marriage of the criminal and defective must be prevented; and, indeed, marriage of all those afflicted with constitutional defects should be prohibited. Society must take cognizance of the reproduction of the race and correct the tendencies to degradation, as a measure of self-preservation. It is idle and foolish to waste energy, sympathy, and money in the hopeless effort to cure and restrain what should never have been permitted to exist. Physical degeneration must be corrected to promote regeneration.

APPENDIX I.

Comparative statement from the eleventh census, showing the quantities of distilled spirits, wine, and malt liquors consumed ; the average annual consumption per capita of population in the United States during the years 1840, 1880, and 1890 ; the increase in fifty and in ten years ; and the product of a tax of $3 per gallon of the pure alcohol contained in the specified liquors ; together with the addition this tax would make upon the gallon of liquor sold.

Year Ending June 30.	Distilled Spirits Consumed (proof gallons).	Wines Consumed (gallons).	Malt Liquors Consumed (gallons).	Total Consumption (gallons).	Total Consumption per Capita of Population.			
					Of All (gallons).	Malt Liquors (gallons).	Wines (gallons).	Distilled Spirits (gallons).
1840.............	43,060,884a	4,873,096	23,310,843	71,244,817	4.57	1.36	0.29	2.52a
1880.............	67,526,694	28,320,541	414,220,165	506,076,400	10.09	8.26	0.56	1.27
1890.............	87,829,562	28,956,981	855,792,335	972,578,878	15.53	13.67	0.46	1.40
Increase in ten yrs.	24,302,868	636,440	441,573,170	466,502,478	5.44	5.41	D.10	0.13
Percentage of increase in ten yrs.	36.9	2.24	109.	92.2	53.9	65.5	D.	9.2
Assumed percentage of alcohol..	50	10	5					
Gallons of alcohol consumed in 1890	43,914,781	2,895,698	42,789,616	89,600,095				
Prod't of tax of $3 p. gal. of alcohol	$131,744,343	$8,687,094	$128,368,848	$268,800,285				
Tax per gal. liquor consumed	$1.50	$0.30	$0.15					

a. Includes use as burning fluids.

A comparative summary of the consumption per capita of population in the United States, United Kingdom of Great Britain, France, Germany, and Canada, of distilled spirits, wines, and malt liquors during the years 1881 and 1887. Report of the Treasury Department of the United States.

COUNTRIES.	DISTILLED SPIRITS.		WINES.		MALT LIQUORS.	
	1881. Gal.	1887. Gal.	1881. Gal.	1887. Gal.	1881. Gal.	1887. Gal.
United States.....	1.37	1.18	.47	.54	8.63	11.96
United Kingdom..	1.00	.98	.43	.38	33.90	32.88
France	1.22	....	30.75	1886. 26.74	....	....
Germany.........	1.14	1.09	....	... ...	22.35	24.99
Canada.........	.91	.84	.11	.10	2.33	3.50

APPENDIX II.

A table from the United States Census of 1880, showing the number of persons, and males, engaged in useful occupations, in the United States, above the distinctively daily-wage workers ; the number of farmers ; and the percentage of the total of each class to the population, to the total population over sixteen years old, and to the male population over sixteen years old.

	Males.	All.
Farm and Plantation Owners . . .	2,912	3,106
Florists	4,248	4,545
Stock Raisers	16,406	16,528
Actors	2,974	4,812
Architects	3,358	3,375
Artists and Teachers of Art . . .	7,014	9,104
Auctioneers	2,328	2,331
Authors and Literary Persons . .	811	1,131
Boarding and Lodging-House Keepers .	6,745	19,058
Chemists and Metallurgists	1,919	1,969
Civil Engineers	8,259	8,261
Clergymen	64,533	64,698

	Males.	All.
Clerks	48,493	53,232
Collectors and Agents	4,163	4,213
Dentists	12,253	12,314
Designers and Draughtsmen . . .	2,757	2,820
Employés of Government	28,254	31,612
Hotel Keepers	30,317	32,453
Journalists	12,020	12,308
Lawyers	64,062	64,137
Musicians	17,184	30,477
Officials of Government	64,909	67,081
Physicians and Surgeons	83,239	85,671
Restaurant Keepers	12,228	13,074
Teachers and Scientific Persons . . .	73,243	227,710
Veterinary Surgeons	2,130	2,130
Agricultural Implement Makers . . .	4,776	4,891
Bridge Builders and Contractors . . .	2,582	2,587
Builders and Contractors	10,787	10,804
Clerks and Brokers in Manufacturing . .	9,801	10,114
Gold and Silver Workers and Jewellers .	25,975	28,404
Manufacturers	43,612	44,019
Millers	53,069	53,440
Officials of Manfg. and Mining Companies .	8,179	8,198
Photographers	9,481	9,990
Publishers	2,742	2,781
Railroad Builders and Contractors . .	1,206	1,206
Others in Manfg., Min., and Mech. Industries	10,243	13,542
Others in Professional Services . . .	3,822	4,570
Agents	18,073	18,523
Bankers and Brokers	15,112	15,180
Book-keepers	57,278	59,790
Brokers		4,193
Clerks in Stores.	315,126	353,444
Clerks and Commercial Travellers . .	54,767	55,442
Officials of Telegraph Companies . .	20,228	22,810
Officials of Banks and Insurance Companies	16,811	
Officials of Railroad Companies . . .	2,069	2,069
Salesmen	24,402	32,279
Traders	475,372	491,045
Total	1,762,272	2,033,671
Farmers and Planters	4,169,136	4,225,945
The Total Population was		50,155,783
The Total Population over 16 Years old was		30,112,124
The Total of Males over 16 Years old was .		15,359,866

The 2,033,671 Persons Engaged in Useful Occupations
above Daily-Wage Workers were therefore of Total
Population . . . . . .   4 per cent.

Of the Population over 16 Years old .   .   6.75 per cent.

The Farmers and Planters were of the Total
   Population .   .   .   .   .   .   8.4 per cent.
Of the Population over 16 Years old .   .   14 per cent.

The 1,762,272 Males Engaged in Useful Occupations
   Specified above was of the Male Population over
   16 Years of age' .   .   .   .   .   11.4 per cent.

Male Farmers and Planters were of Males over 16
   Years old .   .   .   .   .   .   27.7 per cent.

APPENDIX III.

Table showing occupation previous to arrest of convicts received into or serving in several penitentiaries specified, and the percentage of the total admissions or inmates which they constitute.   From the published reports of the several penitentiaries.

	Admissions, 1889. Western Penitentiary, Pa.	Admissions, 1890. Eastern Penitentiary, Pa.	Admissions, 1891. Ohio Penitentiary.	Admissions, 1890. Illinois State Penitentiary.	Convicts—Sing Sing Prison, N. Y. Sept. 30, 1891.	Convicts—Auburn Prison, N. Y. Sept. 30, 1891.	Convicts—Clinton Prison, N. Y. Sept. 30, 1891.	Admissions, 1891. State Asylum for Insane Prisoners, N. Y.	Totals.
Accountants .					1				1
Actors . . .				2	1	1			4
Advertisers . .					1				1
Agents . . .		2			2	8			12
Alderman . .	1								1
Artists . . .					1				1
Astrologers . .					1				1
Auctioneers . .			1						1
Baking Powder (Clerk)		1							1
Bankers . .	1					3			4
Base-Ball Players .			1						1
Book-keepers .		5	9	19	37	26	9	1	106
Boot and Shoe Dealers			2						2
Brewers . .				2		1			3

	Admissions, 1889. Western Penitentiary, Pa.	Admissions, 1890. Eastern Penitentiary, Pa.	Admissions, 1891. Ohio Penitentiary.	Admissions, 1890. Illinois State Penitentiary.	Convicts—Sing Sing Prison, N.Y. Sept. 30, 1891.	Convicts—Auburn Prison, N.Y. Sept. 30, 1891.	Convicts—Clinton Prison, N.Y. Sept. 30, 1891.	Admissions, 1891. State Asylum for Insane Prisoners, N.Y.	Totals.
Brokers			2		3				5
Bridge and Boat-builders	2								2
Candy Merchants					1				1
Canvassers		1			3				4
Cashiers		1							1
Clergymen					1				1
Clerks	7	3	20	31	64	32	26	2	185
Collectors			1		1				2
Commercial Travellers			8		1				9
Confectioners				1		2			3
Contractors			2		1				3
Contractors and Builder				1					1
Copyists					2				2
Civil Engineers		1				2			3
Dairymen			1	1					2
Dentists					3			1	4
Deputy Sheriffs					1				1
Designers					1				1
Detectives					1	1			2
Dock Builders					1				1
Draughtsmen					1	2			3
Druggists	2		1		4	3			10
Drug Clerks					1				1
Drummers					1				1
Editors					1				1
Electricians					1	3		1	5
Engineers		2							2
Engravers				2			1		3
Express Agents			1						1
Expressmen					1	1	1		3
Florists			1	1	3	1			6
Gold Beaters					1				1
Grocers					2				2
Horse Dealers					2				2
Hotel Keepers					1	2			3
House-Keepers		2	15						17

	Admissions, 1889, Western Penitentiary, Pa.	Admissions, 1890, Eastern Penitentiary, Pa.	Admissions, 1891, Ohio Penitentiary.	Admissions, 1890, Illinois State Penitentiary.	Convicts—Sing Sing Prison, N. Y. Sept. 30, 1891.	Convicts—Auburn Prison, N. Y. Sept. 30, 1891.	Convicts—Clinton Prison, N. Y. Sept. 30, 1891.	Admission, 1891, State Asylum for Insane Prisoners, N. Y.	Totals.
Hucksters . .	2	4	1						7
Ice Dealers . .				1					1
Idle bef. Arrest, well Educated . .		6							6
Inspectors . .					1				1
Insurance Broker .					1				1
Interpreters . .					1				1
Jewellers . .	2	1	1	2	4	2			12
Journalists . .				2	3				5
Laborer (Clerk) .		1							1
Lawyers . .		1	7	1	6	1	1		17
Letter Carriers .	1	3			1				5
Lightning-Rod Agents			1						1
Liverymen . .			7						7
Mail Carriers .			2						2
Manufacturers .					1				1
Merchants . .		2	5	2	5	8	4		26
Messengers . .	1				2				3
Millers . . .	1		2					1	4
Ministers . .			1						1
Minstrels . .					1				1
Musicians . .				3	1		1		5
Music Teachers .	1					3			4
News Agents .			1						1
News Dealers .					2				2
Nurses . . .	1		1		7				9
Operators . .					3	1			4
Organists . .					1				1
Paper Makers .				1					1
Pawnbrokers . .					1				1
Peddlers . .	1	3	4	1	21	16	7	1	54
Phila. C. P. (Florist)		1							1
Photographers .	1	1	1	1	3	3		1	11
Physicians . .			2	2	3	3	2	1	13
Piano Tuners .			1						1
Policemen . .					10		2		12

	Admissions, 1889. Western Penitentiary, Pa.	Admissions, 1890. Eastern Penitentiary, Pa.	Admissions, 1891. Ohio Penitentiary.	Admissions, 1890. Illinois State Penitentiary.	Convicts—Sing Sing Prison, N. Y. Sept. 30, 1891.	Convicts—Auburn Prison, N. Y. Sept. 30, 1891.	Convicts—Clinton Prison, N. Y. Sept. 30, 1891.	Admissions, 1891. State Asylum for Insane Prisoners, N. Y.	Totals.
Police Officers			2	1					3
Police Sergeants					1				1
Preachers							1		1
Prefect		1							1
Press Office		1							1
Railroad Agents			1						1
Railroad Conductors		1		2		2			5
Railroad Presidents					1				1
Real-Estate Agents	1	1			1				3
Real-Estate Brokers					2				2
Real-Estate Dealers			2						2
Reporters				2			2		4
Restaurant Keepers					1				1
Salesmen		1		12	16	10		1	40
Saloon Keepers	3		2		6				11
School		1							1
School Teachers			3				1	1	5
Sea Captains					1				1
Seamstresses		1	2						3
Sewing-Machine Agents			2						2
Sextons					1				1
Shoe Dealers		1							1
Shoemaker (Druggist)		1							1
Showmen	2								2
Show Operators					3				3
Song and Dance Artists					1				1
Speculators									1
Stenographers					1	1			2
Stock Dealers			1	1					2
Storekeepers					1				1
Street Car Conductors		1			1				2
Supt. Paper Box Factory					1				1
Surveyors				1		1			2
Teachers				1	2	1	1		5
Telegraphers				2				3	5
Telegraph Operators		1	6		2				9

	Admissions, 1889. Western Penitentiary, Pa.	Admissions, 1890. Eastern Penitentiary, Pa.	Admissions, 1891. Ohio Penitentiary.	Admissions, 1890. Illinois State Penitentiary.	Convicts—Sing Sing Prison, N. Y. Sept. 30, 1891.	Convicts—Auburn Prison, N. Y. Sept. 30, 1891.	Convicts—Clinton Prison, N. Y. Sept. 30, 1891.	Admissions, 1891. State Asylum for Insane Prisoners, N. Y.	Totals.
Theatrical Managers					1				1
Thief (Gentleman)		1							1
Ticket Agents .	1								1
Timekeepers . .					1				1
Travelling Agents				1					1
Type Setters . .		1							1
Typewriters . .					1				1
Undertakers . .				1		1			2
Venders . .					5	5			10
Veterinary Surgeons			1			1			2
Writers . . .					1				1
Totals	31	56	126	99	275	144	58	13	802
Total Admissions, or Inmates . .	274	526	918	791	1592	1263	759	69	6192
Percentage of Totals	10.5	10.6	13.7	12.5	17.5	11.4	7.6	13.	12.9
Total of Farmers .	8	8	151	85	17	67	41	4.	
Percentage of Admissions . .	2.9	1.5	16.4	10.7	1.	5.3	5.4	5.6	

APPENDIX IV.

A Suitable Dietary for County Jails.

Days.	Breakfast.	Dinner.	Supper.
Monday,	Bread, coffee.	Beef-soup, with vegetables, rice, or barley; 1 pound boiled beef, potatoes, bread.	Bread, tea.
Tuesday,	Bread, coffee.	½ pound Bologna sausage, short-cake.	Baked potatoes, tea, bread.
Wednesday,	Bread, coffee.	Bean-soup, roast-beef, potatoes, bread.	Stewed dried fruit, bread, tea.
Thursday,	Bread, coffee.	½ pound pork, sauer-kraut, bread.	Bread, tea.
Friday,	Bread, coffee.	Fish-chowder, with potatoes, onions, and crackers.	Bread, tea.
Saturday,	Bread, coffee.	Mutton-soup, with vegetables, bread.	Bread, tea.
Sunday,	Fried potatoes, bread, coffee.	Meat-pie, made with vegetables.	Stewed dried fruit, bread, tea.

These dinners may be varied by substituting baked pork and beans, corned beef and cabbage, or corned-beef hash, on occasion, or salted fish and baked potatoes for fish chowder.

APPENDIX V.

WHITECHAPEL UNION, LONDON, ENGLAND.[1]

DIETARY FOR ABLE-BODIED PAUPERS—No. 1.

DAYS.	Adults.	BREAK-FAST.		DINNER						SUPPER.		
		Bread.	Oatmeal Porridge.	Bread.	Cooked Meat.	Potatoes or other Vegetables.	Pea Soup.	Suet Pudding	Irish Stew.	Bread.	Meat Broth.	Oatmeal Porridge.
		ozs.	pints	ozs.	ozs.	ozs.	pints.	ozs.	ozs.	ozs.	pints.	pints.
Sunday.........	Men.......	5	1½	..	5	12	..	..	..	5	1½	..
	Women.....	5	1	..	4	12	..	..	..	5	1½	..
Monday.........	Men.......	5	1½	4	..	..	1½	..	..	5	..	1½
	Women	5	1	4	..	..	1½	..	..	5	..	1
Tuesday.........	Men.......	5	1½	..	..	..	..	..	24	5	..	1½
	Women	5	1	..	..	..	..	..	20	5	..	1
Wednesday......	Men.......	5	1½	..	..	..	..	16	..	5	..	1½
	Women	5	1	..	..	..	..	16	..	5	..	1
Thursday.......	Men.......	5	1½	..	5	12	..	..	..	5	1½	..
	Women	5	1	..	4	12	..	..	..	5	1½	..
Friday..........	Men.......	5	1½	4	..	..	1½	..	..	5	..	1½
	Women	5	1	4	..	..	1½	..	..	5	..	1
Saturday	Men.......	5	1½	..	..	..	..	16	..	5	..	1½
	Women	5	1	..	..	..	..	16	..	5	..	1

Children between 9 and 16 years of age to be allowed the same diet as women.

Approved by the Local Government Board, January 21, 1882.

[1] By permission from Prof. Jno. J. McCook's report on out-door alms of the town of Hartford, 1891.

DIETARY FOR AGED AND INFIRM AND IMBECILE PAUPERS—NO. 2.

Days.	Adults.	Breakfast. Bread.	Breakfast. Tea.	Breakfast. Butter.	Dinner. Bread.	Dinner. Cooked Meat.	Dinner. Potatoes or other Vegetables.	Dinner. Pea Soup.	Dinner. Suet Pudding.	Dinner. Irish Stew.	Supper. Bread.	Supper. Tea.	Supper. Butter.
		ozs.	pints	ozs.	ozs.	ozs.	ozs.	pint	ozs.	ozs.	ozs.	pint	oz.
Sunday.........	Men.........	5	1	½	3	4	8	..	..	..	5	1	½
	Women......	4	2	½	2	4	8	..	..	..	4	1	½
Monday.........	Men.........	5	1	½	3	..	.	1	..	..	5	1	½
	Women......	4	1	½	3	..	..	1	..	..	4	1	½
Tuesday........	Men.........	5	1	½	3	..	..	..	..	24	5	1	½
	Women......	4	1	½	2	..	..	..	..	20	4	1	½
Wednesday......	Men.........	5	1	½	..	..	..	..	14	..	5	1	½
	Women......	4	1	½	..	..	..	..	14	..	4	1	½
Thursday........	Men.........	5	1	½	3	4	8	..	..	..	5	1	½
	Women......	4	1	½	3	4	8	..	..	..	4	1	½
Friday..........	Men.........	5	1	½	3	..	..	1	..	..	5	1	½
	Women. ...	4	1	½	3	..	..	1	..	..	4	1	½
Saturday...	Men.........	5	1	½	3	4	8	..	..	..	5	1	½
	Women......	4	1	½	2	4	8	..	..	..	4	1	½

The foods in the foregoing Table are to be prepared in accordance with the forms hereunto annexed. The sick and infants under two years of age to be dieted under the direction of the medical officer.

(Signed) JOHN OUTHWAITE, *Presiding Chairman.*

I consider the allowances in the above Dietary Table to be sufficient.

(Signed) HERBERT LARDER, *Medical Officer.*

The Local Government Board sanction the above Dietary Table.

(Signed) EDMOND H. WODEHOUSE, *Assistant Secretary,*
Acting under the authority of the General Order of May 26, 1877.
Local Government Board, December 3, 1888.

This Dietary came into force December 30, 1888.

FORMS FOR THE PREPARATION OF FOODS.

PEA SOUP.			SUET PUDDING. (*Baked or Boiled.*)			IRISH STEW.		
Name and Description of Ingredient.	Quantity of each Ingredient to a Gallon.		Name and Description of Ingredient.	Quantity of each Ingredient to a Pound		Name and Description of Ingredient.	Quantity of each Ingredient to 24 ozs.	
	ozs.	pints.		ozs.	lbs.	To make 24ozs	ozs.	pints
Raw Meat.	24		Flour......	8		Raw Meat.	3	
Bones.......	8		Suet.......	2		Potatoes (peeled)...	10	
[or Australian Meat]..	32					Carrots.. Onions.. Turnips.. etc.... }	2	
Split Peas or Scotch Barley...		1⅛						
Fresh Vegetables.	6					(To be slightly thickened with Barley or Flour.)		

APPENDIX VI.

Showing cost of pauperism to the tax-payer. Copied by permission from Prof. Jno. J. McCook's report on out-door alms of the town of Hartford, 1891.

HARTFORD COMPARED WITH THIRTY-EIGHT AMERICAN CITIES.[1]

A.D. 1885.

City.	Population.	Gross Expense for out-door Relief.	Net Expense for all Relief.	Tax per Capita for all Relief.	Tax per Capita for out-door Relief.
Hartford .	45,000	$40,372.84	$93,344.73	$2.07	$0.90
New Hav'n	76,000	38,906.75	98,935.64	1.30	.51
Bridgeport	36,000	26,362.62	37,278.04	1.03	.73
Waterbury	28,000	12,919.58	22,664.30	.81	.46
Norwich .	25,000	23,593.75	38,694.68	1.54	.94
Meriden .	25,000	12,094.53	18,680.24	.74	.48
New Brit'in	17,000	15,072.09	23,651.64	1.39	.89
Norwalk .	16,000	3,723.81	9,939.20	.62	.23
Danbury .	15,000	4,807.51	10,977.35	.73	.32
Derby . .	15,000	6,959.16	12,262.63	.82	.46
New L'nd'n	12,000	5,750.77	13,384.39	1.11	.48
Stamford .	14,000	8,398.08	[2]......	......	.60
Conn't, 12 cities. Total,	324,000	$198,961.49	$379,812.84	Av.$1.22	Av. $ .61
Boston . .	390,406	$95,804.06	$547,595.35	$1.40	$0.25
Worcester .	68,383	16,578.96	40,285.40	.59	.24
Lowell . .	64,051	17,981.00	66,311.96	1.03	.28
Springfield	37,577	5,268.08	25,103.74	.66	.14
Fall River	56,863	......	53,000.00	.93	....
Mass'tts, 5 cities. Total,	617,280	$135,632.10	$732,296.45	Av.$1.16	Av. $ .24

[1] Condensed from Henry C. White's *Report to the Executive Committee of the Taxpayers' Association*, New Haven, 1886, with one column added.

[2] Not ascertained.

City.	Population.	Gross Expense for out-door Relief.	Net Expense for all Relief.	Tax per Capita for all Relief.	Tax per Capita for out-door Relief.
Providence	120,000	$6,022.70	$18,606.51	$0.16	$ .05
Bangor .	18,000	4,945.00	11,836.03	.66	.27
Rutland .	12,500	6,319.52	9,935.59	.79	.51
Pawtucket	22,000	¹......	9,997.26	.45	....
Concord .	14,000	......	10,894.75	.77	....
Other N. E. cities, 5 cities. Total,	186,500	$17,287.22	$61,270.14	Av.$ .33	Av. $ .12
New York Kings Co., N. Y., of which Brooklyn constitutes 1¾	1,325,000	$32,051.52	$981,356.20	$0.74	$0.24
	700,000	......	286,760.11	.41	....
Buffalo .	225,000	52,452.85	162,148.92	.72	.23
Albany .	100,000	17,092.94	53,957.49	.54	.17
N. York, 4 cities. Total,	2,350,000	$101,597.31	$1,484,222.72	Av.$ .63	Av. $ .43
Philadel'ia	928,000	$20,000.00	$336,346.20	$0.36	$0.022
Pittsburgh	200,000	32,528.23	88,066.86	.44	.16
Allegheny	90,000	10,377.74	35,028.59	.39	.12
Scranton and distr.	77,000	8,942.14	36,346.74	.47	.12
Baltimore .	425,000	......	154,400.00	.36	....
1890, Scr'nton ² . .	83,450	9,149.14	74,738.47	8.95	10.9
Penn. and Maryl'd, 5 cities. Total,	1,720,000	$71,848.11	$650,188.39	Av.$ .38	Av. $ .04

¹ Not ascertained.
² Scranton added by the author.

City.	Population.	Gross Expense for out-door Relief.	Net Expense for all Relief.	Tax per Capita for all Relief.	Tax per Capita for out-door Relief.
Chicago .	700,000	$117,376.49	$554,397.26	$0.79	$ 0.17
Cleveland .	185,000	23,491.56	54,204.64	.29	.13
Detroit .	160,000	37,495.55	90,513.42	.56	.23
Milwaukee	158,500	28,172.40	59,076.69	.37	.18
Toledo. .	75,000	[1]	21,767.46	.29	....
Charleston (figures for 1882) . .	49,984	......	36,248.34	.72	....
Norfolk .	26,188	......	16,822.50	.64	....
West. and South'rn, 7 cities. Total,	1,354,672	$206,536.00	$833,030.31	Av. $ .62	Av. $ .17

SUMMARY.

State.	Population of the cities included.	Gross expense for out-door relief.	Number of cities.	Average tax for out-door relief.	Net expense for all relief.	Number of cities.	Average tax for all relief.
Connecticut cities	324,000	$198,961.49	12	$ .61	$379,812.84	11	$1.22
Massa'tts cities .	617,280	$135,632.10	4	.24	732,296.45	5	1.16
Other N. E. cities	186,500	17,287.22	3	.09	61,270.14	5	.33
N'w York cities .	2,350,000	101,597.31	3	.04	1,484.222.72	4	.63
Penn. and Maryl'd cities .	1,720,000	71,848.11	4	.05	650,188.39	5	.38
West. and South'rn cities .	1,354,672	206,536.00	4	.17	833,030.31	7	.62
Totals	6,228,452	$532,900.74	18	$ .11	$3,761,008.01	26	$ .60

[1] Not ascertained.

APPENDIX VII.—POLICE.

Statement showing the police statistics for each of fifty-one of the largest cities in the United States that have made complete returns, including the number of each force divided as to grade, number of arrests annually, average annual cost of force, with percentages and ratios.—From *Census Bulletin* No. 100, *Eleventh United States Census*, with Scranton added.

CITIES.	Population.	Miles of Streets.	Force. Total.	Force. Officers, Detectives, etc.	Force. Patrolmen.	Average Annual Cost of force.	Number of Miles of Street to each Patrolman.	Number of Patrolmen to each sq. Mile of Territory.	Number of Arrests Annually to each Patrolman.	Percentage of Arrests to each Head of Population.	Percentage of Force to each Head of Population.	Cost of Force to each Head of Population.
New York, N. Y........	1,515,301	575	3,421	499	2,922	$4,391,766	0.20	72.65	25.53	4.92	0.23	$2.90
Chicago, Ill..........	1,099,850	2,048	1,625	167	1,458	979,894	1.40	9.08	27.37	3.63	0.15	0.89
Philadelphia, Pa.......	1,046,964	1,151	1,717	292	1,425	1,000,000	0.81	11.01	35.09	4.78	0.16	0 96
Brooklyn, N. Y........	806,343	653	1,157	257	930	859,184	0.73	34.01	31.52	3.52	0.14	1.07
St. Louis, Missouri.....	451,770	1,061	613	78	535	475,408	1.98	8.72	32.98	3.91	0.14	1 05
Boston, Mass..........	448,477	408	916	237	679	963,355	0.60	19.25	48 41	7.33	0.20	2 15
Baltimore, Md.........	434,439	780	782	163	619	677,914	1.26	21.81	42.96	6.12	0.18	1.56
San Francisco, Cal.....	298,997	342	406	70	336	545,500	1.02	21.73	69.68	7.83	0.14	1 82
Cincinnati, Ohio.......	296,908	486	433	33	400	330,000	1.22	16.00	35.00	4.72	0.15	1.11
Cleveland, Ohio.......	261,353	462	319	67	252	250,000	1.83	10.13	29.76	2.87	0.12	0.96
Buffalo, N. Y.........	255,664	372	342	70	272	297,994	1.37	6.97	41.00	4.36	0.13	1.17
New Orleans, La.......	242,039	625	266	93	173	170,000	3.61	4.66	86 71	6.20	0.11	0 70
Milwaukee, Wis........	204,468	419	196	24	172	122,488	2.44	10.12	20.82	1.75	0.10	0.60
Detroit, Mich.........	205,876	400	368	63	305	222,509	1.31	14.81	23.27	3.45	0.18	1.08
Washington, D. C.....	202,998	235	408	43	365	399,060	0.64	35.64	48.71	8.76	0.20	1.97
Newark, N. J.........	181,830	186	214	33	181	170,000	1.03	10.19	31.91	3.18	0.12	0 93
Minneapolis, Minn....	164,738	800	199	33	166	151,337	4.82	3.21	28.14	2.84	0.12	0.92
Omaha, Neb..........	140,452	508	95	15	80	65,000	6.35	3.27	13.75	0.78	0.07	0 46
Rochester, N. Y.......	133,896	240	123	25	98	99,307	2.45	6.28	40.82	2.99	0.09	0 74
St. Paul, Minn........	133,156	970	170	45	125	98,708	7.76	2.43	25.60	2.40	0.13	0 74
Denver, Col..........	106,713	756	100	25	75	50,000	10.08	4.84	66.67	4.69	0.09	0.47
Indianapolis, Ind......	105,436	400	101	22	79	55,079	5.06	7.85	45.35	3 40	0.10	0.53
Worcester, Mass.......	84,655	195	94	10	84	73,332	2.32	2.47	38.99	3.87	0.11	0.87
Toledo, Ohio..........	81,434	438	85	15	70	73,000	6.26	3.55	53.19	4.57	0.10	0.90
New Haven, Conn......	81,298	140	112	27	85	102,481	1.65	11.24	65.33	6.83	0.14	1.26
Lowell, Mass..........	77,696	105	76	10	66	70,552	1.59	5.92	49.56	4.21	0.10	0.91
Nashville, Tenn........	76,168	251	76	11	65	46,000	3.86	7.70	69.23	5.91	0.10	0.60
Scranton, Pa..........	75,620	80.75	37	3	34	38,195	2.4	3.52	53.11	2.37	0.049	0.505
Fall River, Mass.......	74,308	106	95	18	77	70,407	1.38	7.03	29.69	3.07	0.13	0.95
Cambridge, Mass.......	70,028	79	79	14	65	71,756	1.22	11.15	23.82	2.21	0.11	1.02
Camden, N. J.........	58,313	100	43	1	42	30,000	2.38	9.68	59.52	4.29	0.07	0.51
Trenton, N. J.........	57,458	100	64	14	50	55,000	2.00	12.66	50.00	4.35	0.11	0.96
Lynn, Mass...........	55,727	125	47	3	44	40,000	2.84	4.14	37.73	2.98	0.08	0.72
Hartford, Conn........	53,230	130	53	3	50	55,000	2.60	3.41	68.00	6.39	0.10	1.03
Evansville, Ind........	50,756	136	52	9	43	28,098	3 16	9.73	46.51	3.94	0.10	0.55
Los Angeles, Cal.......	50,395	800	78	5	73	28,800	10.96	2.64	31.60	4.58	0.15	0.57
Lawrence, Mass........	44,654	82	43	8	35	32,717	2.34	5.25	56.43	4.42	0.10	0.73
Hoboken, N. J.........	43,648	30	60	10	50	42,000	0.60	34.01	36.00	4.12	0.14	0 96
Dallas, Texas.........	38,067	529	47	15	32	40,000	16.53	4.17	92.69	7.79	0.12	1.05
Sioux City, Iowa.......	37,806	340	15	1	14	12,000	24.29	0.45	9 71	0 36	0.04	0.32
Portland, Me..........	36,425	56	40	3	37	33,906	1.51	14.74	58.84	5.98	0.11	0.93
Holyoke, Mass.........	35,637	50	29	2	27	20,000	1 85	6.78	37.04	2.81	0.08	0.56
Binghamton, N. Y......	35,000	80	17	3	14	8,340	5 71	1.39	71.43	2.86	0.05	0.24
Duluth, Minn.........	33,115	224	38	7	31	40 000	7.23	9.60	67.74	6 34	0.11	1.21
Elmira, N. Y..........	29,708	90	32	12	20	17,838	4.50	4 49	73.25	4.93	0.11	0.60
Davenport, Iowa.......	26,872	140	19	8	11	11,958	12.73	2.49	72.18	2.95	0.07	0.44
Canton, Ohio..........	26,189	150	19	2	17	8,400	8.82	2.50	55 88	3.63	0.07	0.32
Taunton, Mass.........	25,448	200	22	3	19	18,863	10.53	0.40	41.89	3 13	0.09	0.74
Lacrosse, Wis..........	25,090	125	19	6	13	10,000	9.62	1.59	142.31	7.37	0.08	0.40
Newport, Ky..........	24,918	30	16	3	13	10,000	2 31	10.83	53.85	2.81	0.06	0.40
Rookford, Ill..........	23,584	120	11	3	9	7,500	13.33	1.41	33.89	1.29	0.05	0.32

INDEX.

A

Abnormality of criminals and paupers, 171, 265

Abnormals carefully maintained by modern civilization, 269

Adaptation, the panacea of the present, 131

Alcohol, a cause of criminality, 139; to be made to pay as it goes, 155; proper taxation of, 156; trial of, by Common Sense, 139; annual damage to the people, 141, 151, 165; percentage of, contained in beverages, 143

Alexander of Russia, 131

Alien population of Pennsylvania, 12; of Lacka. Co., 22; instruction of, 54

Allegheny County, of Pennsylvania, 22, 30, 91; Jail, 24; Workhouse, 147, 174

Almshouses, in Lackawanna County, 20; support of paupers in, 222; location and construction of, 224; administration of, 225; discrimination as to admissions, 228; motives of management, 229; Dietaries for, Appendix IV., 304; grading of responsibilities, 233; duties of directors, 234; religious privileges, 234; misuse of the poor fund, 235

Americanization of immigrants, necessity of, 60; how to accomplish, 53

American, Institute of Civics, 58; Institutions, National Leagues for Protection of, 58; table of mortality, 143; institutions, beneficence of, 44; immigration, statistics of, 46; citizenship, value of, 50; price of, 51; rights of Congress to prescribe, 52; qualifications required, 52

America, the land of the Bible and the Sabbath, 55

Anarchists of Paris, escaping to America, 239

Andrews, W. P., paper quoted, 174

Appropriations of public funds non-sectarian, 56

Army ration of several articles of diet, 202

Arrests for trivial offences, proportion of, 185; use of patrol wagon in, 254

Atkinson, Hon. Edward, quoted, 148

Auburn Prison, 298

Autonomic government of cities, 115

B

Babylon, proportion of upper class in, 275

Beaver, Gov. James A., 40

Beer drinking, increase of, 151

Ben Ishmael, tribe of, 176

Bible, the, America, the land of, 55

Biddle University, 84

Binghamton, Inebriate Asylum, 162 ; police of, 252
Biological law of reproduction, 267
Board of Public Charities of Pennsylvania, 9, 18, 19, 26, 41
Booth, General of Salvation Army, 101, 179
"Breeding in," 267 ; faulty, of humanity, 279
Brush, Warden, 16
Bryce, Professor James, 113

C

Cable, G. W., on the negro, 75, 85 ; education, 75
Campbell, Mr., of Ohio, quoted, 120
Cassidy, M. J., Warden, of Eastern Pennsylvania, 192 ; dietary recommended by, 201
Chain gangs in the South, 70
Charitable institutions should be Christian, if public, 56
Charity, indiscriminate, in cities, 110 ; organization of, 110, 220 ; institutional, criticised, 110 ; true in spirit, a public duty, 222
Chicago, foreign population of, 59
Children, illegitimate, 211 ; homeless, 214 ; police supervision of, 242 ; in cities, 99, 242 ; laws of punishment, 187 ; of immature parentage, 284 ; of the senile, 284
Children's Home, Washington County, Ohio, 176
Child-saving institutions, 188
Christian, Home for Inebriates, The, 162 ; Sabbath, 55 ; Bible, 55 ; land, America, 55
Church, and State, 58 ; its duty to immigrants, 60 ; Roman Catholic, appeal to, 61
Cities, density in tenements, 101 ; lower classes in, 101 ; clubs in, 107 ; ancient, 113 ; government of, in United States, 114 ; autonomy necessary, 115 ; suffrage in, 122 ; immigration to, 123 ; value

of police to, 123, 253 ; local politics distinct, 125 ; statistics of churches in, 126 ; growth of, 5, 93 ; contributions to crime, 90 ; population of, in Pennsylvania, 12, 115 ; density of population, 101
Citizenship, American, value of, 50 ; essential qualifications of, 52
City life, reformation of, 94 ; three classes of population in, 96 ; children of, 99 ; political phases, 112
Clinton Prison, 298
Club life in cities, evils of, 107 ; growth of, 107
Coffee- and tea-houses recommended, 167
"Collegiate prisons," 190
Color prejudice absurd, 78, 83
Compensation for slavery, 83
Confinements to be avoided when possible, 185
Congregate system of imprisonment, 192
Constabulary to be exchanged for police, 243
Consumption of intoxicants in United States, 152
Convict lease system of the South, 71
Convicts from rural and urban districts, 90
Cooking, good, a preventive of intemperance, 168 ; should be taught in public schools, 168
Cooper, Peter, 133
Costs of criminal arrests in U. S., 8 ; of crime and pauperism in Pennsylvania, 10, 11 ; in Lackawanna County, 21
Country-roads, 118
County House, the, 39 ; prison of Allegheny County, 22 ; visitors recommended, 223 ; duties of, 224 ; workhouses needed, 229 ; jails, 193, 194 ; Dietary for, 303 ; Eugene Smith on, 194 ; number of, in United States,

INDEX. 317

organization, 250 ; waste of present system, 252 ; interchange of information, 255 ; Commissioners of Milwaukee, rules of, 246 ; discipline of, 256
Policeman, qualifications of a good, 245 ; appointment of, 245 ; dismissal, 245 ; must be independent of politics, 246 ; instruction and drill of, 249 ; life insurance and pension fund, 249 ; arrests discouraged, 250 ; duties, 251 ; number, 252
Political position of the Negro, 76 ; phases of city life, 112
Polytechnics of Quintin Hogg, 133
Poor laws scheme suggested, 39, 40
Population, foreign, in United States, 43 ; contributions to criminality, 43
Porter, Hon. R. P., number of paupers and criminals in United States, 148
Potter, Isaac B , quoted, 120
Preparation of Foods, forms for, 306
Preventive measures, and remedial, 267
" Probation " system in Boston, 186 ; to be promoted by proper police regulations, 256
Prohibition unsound in principle, 154
Prohibitions existing in many States, 164
Public opinion concerning Negroes, 76 ; schools, 134
Pughe, Hon. Lewis, 40
Punishment of criminals, absurd, 36

R

Real estate, values in cities, 117
Reformation, of city life, 94 ; of penal legislation, 189 ; to begin with the laws, 35
Reformatories, State, 188 ; of Great Britain, 191 ; number of, in United States, 193

Reform schools, 188 ; reclamations in, 189
Registrar-General, the English, report on marriages in 1889, 285
Regulations for jails, 196
Religious privileges for paupers, 234
Reproduction of criminals and paupers to be limited, 180, 270
Republics, decay of, due to physical degeneracy, 286
Restrictions upon immigration, 52, 53
Ries, Col. F. J., Chief of Police, report, 247, 250
Roman Catholic Church, 212
Rural contribution to criminality, 90 ; and urban population of Pennsylvania, 90

S

Sabbath in cities, 98, 102, 104
Saloon, substitutes for, suggested, 166
Salvation Army, 127
Saving in taxation, 33
Schools, public, should teach cooking, 168
Schuylkill County prisoners, 24
Scranton, 22 ; police of, 252
Sectarian appropriations, 56, 235
Senile parentage, evils of, 284
Sentences indeterminate, 190 ; of penitentiary convicts, white and black compared, 70 ; average length in various States, 70
Separate system of imprisonment, 192
Separation of prisoners, 197
Shaw, Albert, 133
Sheriff management of jails, 194
Sichart, Herr, quoted, 172
Sing Sing Prison, 298
Smith, Eugene, on county jails, 194, 195
Southern, neglect of penological principles, 72 ; sentiment concerning the Negro, 74

www.ingramcontent.com/pod-product-compliance
Lightning Source LLC
Chambersburg PA
CBHW021106270326
41929CB00009B/751